SOUL TALK

POWERFUL, POSITIVE COMMUNICATION FOR A LOVING PARTNERSHIP

Nina Atwood

SOURCEBOOKS CASABLANCA™
AN IMPRINT OF SOURCEBOOKS, INC.®
NAPERVILLE, ILLINOIS

This publication is designed to provide accurate and authoritative information in regard to the subject matter covered. It is sold with the understanding that the publisher is not engaged in rendering legal, accounting, or other professional service. If legal advice or other expert assistance is required, the services of a competent professional person should be sought.—*From a Declaration of Principles Jointly Adopted by a Committee of the American Bar Association and a Committee of Publishers and Associations*

Published by Sourcebooks, Inc.
P.O. Box 4410, Naperville, Illinois 60567-4410
(630) 961-3900
FAX: (630) 961-2168
www.sourcebooks.com

Library of Congress Cataloging-in-Publication Data

Atwood, Nina.
 Soul talk : powerful, positive communication for a loving partnership / by Nina Atwood.
 p. cm.
 ISBN 1-4022-0051-X (pbk. : alk. paper)
 1. Interpersonal communication. 2. Man-woman relationships. 3. Interpersonal relations. 4. Love. I. Title.
BF637.C45 A89 2003
306.7—dc21   2002153536

Printed and bound in the United States of America
BG   10   9   8   7   6   5   4   3   2   1

To Kristin, Carl, and Anna—the angels in my life.

By Nina Atwood

Be Your Own Dating Service:
A Step-by-Step Guide to Finding and
Maintaining Healthy Relationships

Date Lines: Communication from Hello
to I Do and Everything in Between

Contents

Acknowledgments

A huge "thank you" to my agent, Denise Marcil, for standing by me and for supporting my vision for so long. Thanks and appreciation to Deb Werksman and all the folks at Sourcebooks for "getting it." Thank you to my "family of choice" for encouraging me and for reminding me of "who I really am" when I need it the most. Most of all, gratitude and love to my Soul Partner, Mark, for showing me what is really possible.

Introduction

In my research for *Soul Talk*, I came across two very interesting statistics. One, that divorce rates increased by 300 percent between 1970 and 1997, was no surprise. Everyone knows that divorce in recent decades is much more prevalent than it once was. The other, that marriage rates (number of marriages per capita) have remained about the same over the past seventy years, I found to be quite fascinating when placed alongside the first.

These two indicators together tell me a story; despite the overwhelming evidence that relationships are harder to sustain than ever before, we keep trying! In fact, as a whole, our hope for good, sustainable love connections remains constant, no matter our experiences.

This, to me, is evidence of the power of the human spirit. When it comes to love, we persist no matter what, and this I see over and over again in the lives of the people whom I coach and train, as well as in my own.

Reflecting deeper, it occurs me that with regard to love, it is not just a matter of hope. If we merely "hope for better things to come," we do not necessarily take the steps to change, grow, and make better things happen. It is our *intention* for better things that supplies the energy to make a real difference.

My intention with this book is, in a nutshell, to make a real and sustainable positive difference in the direction that love relationships are moving.

That intention is simply an extension of the intention that I hold every day for my own relationship—to be the most loving partner I can be—in thought, word, heart, and deed.

In everything I have learned and discovered, one truth remains constant. As it turns out, real love is not passive but quite active. It is energy in its most powerful form and a force to be reckoned with—recognized, honored, cherished, respected, and consciously brought forth in all of our relationships.

This book carries a message of hope and belief—that good, loving, sustainable lifetime relationships are possible, even in today's world. The power of love is immense! I encourage you to make it your intention to embrace that power and infuse your life with the limitless positive energy to which it gives us access. May this book be an asset in that endeavor—to you and to all those whose lives you touch.

Nina Atwood
April 2003

Chapter One
The New Love Relationship

There is a new love relationship on the horizon. This is not a new person or opportunity for romance. Rather, it is a new way of relating that is changing how men and women view the nature of love and how they express themselves to one another.

What we are expressing as men and women today is the yearning for more depth and satisfaction in our relationships. We are unsure that this level of closeness can be achieved; yet the craving for more pushes us forward in the search. We are seeking physical and emotional intimacy; quality time together; passion; growth, both individually and in the relationship; a deeper sense of love and commitment; and the ability to express oneself fully to a partner and to have him do the same. Couples and singles alike agree—great communication is a *must* for all of their relationships.

Growth and Discovery

Many of us today are in a process of personal growth and discovery. At first, we have an increasing sense that something is missing. We make painful realizations about our partners, our lives together, and ourselves. Sometimes, we lose a love in the process. Gradually, however, each of us learns to understand and validate what we need.

Sometimes, the truth is that we simply need to find someone else, someone who shares our values, who wants what we want. Most often, however, it is an issue of *how we relate to one another*.

We need new ways of looking at love. We need a deeper understanding about what real love is and how to bring that into focus. We are seeking a deeper, more satisfying connection with the person whom we love.

What we want is something new, something beyond the ordinary, *a whole new way of relating*. We are beginning to become aware that there is more available in a love relationship than we have experienced in the past. What we are beginning to visualize is a new model, or new paradigm, of romantic love and man/woman relationships.

The New Model: Soul Partnership

We, the men and women of today, are redefining romantic love, lifetime partnership, and marriage. From this process of redefinition, a new model is emerging, which I call Soul Partnership.

In a nutshell, *Soul Partnership is a connection between equals in which the primary purpose of the relationship is for personal and spiritual growth*. For an increasing number of people, Soul Partnership is replacing the old model of love relationships that has been handed down for generations. As we will see, this is not happening quickly, nor is it an easy process.

We are demanding more than ever before from our relationships. Meanwhile, as this new model of love is evolving, we are struggling to understand how to relate to our romantic partners *now*.

Soul Partnership is an innovative way of relating, and it requires a brand new view of love relationships, their purpose, and the structure for maintaining them.

Soul Partnering is the process of creating and maintaining this dynamic and active new approach to love, encompassing the new model of man/woman relationships, as well as the tools for making it happen.

Soul Partnering is a process that calls us into focused action on a day-to-day basis. To make this transition to Soul Partnership and to maintain that over a lifetime requires powerful, positive, open-hearted communication. I call this way of communicating Soul Talk.

The New Tools: Soul Talk

The key to Soul Partnership is *communication*—the ability to speak from the heart and soul. In essence, Soul Talk is the language of Soul Partnership, designed for creating and sustaining a relationship in this new model of love. For couples, Soul Talk is intended to assist you in opening your hearts and deepening the love connection that you share or to revive the connection that you may have once felt and have now lost. For anyone, Soul Talk is necessary as you incorporate the concepts of Soul Partnership into your life and your love relationships.

Soul Talk is about speaking and listening in some unique ways to one another. It allows two very different individuals to understand one another, resolve conflict, and deepen and enrich the love they share.

Soul Talk combines tried-and-true communication concepts with innovative new distinctions and techniques. With conscientious use, Soul Talk alters the way that we speak and listen to all of our loved ones, especially the one with whom we are most intimate. The learning and practice of Soul Talk changes the course of our lives and our relationships in a much more positive and loving direction. This happens through *understanding certain distinctions* and *utilizing certain ways of interacting*, such as:

The Power of Intentions

Often, the ways we as men and women talk to one another lead to power struggles. Selfish intentions ("I want what I want"), both conscious and unconscious, inhibit the flow of the conversation. This distinction helps shift the focus away from self-centeredness toward the good of the relationship, allowing a much deeper understanding between us.

Creative Communication

Typically, when emotions run high, we communicate as a reaction to our negative feelings. This leads to escalating conflict and painful issues that come up repeatedly with no resolution. Learning to communicate from the most creative and loving part of ourselves allows us to avoid most conflicts before they happen.

Listening Empty

Most of us put our efforts into talking, with each person trying desperately to get across our own point of view. With practice, we can learn how to listen to one another in a unique new way, allowing both points of view to be heard and respected. Listening empty helps us heal our hurts together and resolve our own conflicts. This technique is so powerful that its use can bypass the need for couples' therapy.

Compassionate Listening

When we struggle, we often listen to one another with judgment, causing each to feel invalidated and wounded, and eventually to avoid sharing thoughts and feelings. Using this tool as partners, we learn to break the cycle of communication-avoidance so that we draw closer together, even during difficult times.

Intuitive Listening

Often, we listen to each other to "get the facts," missing the subtle unspoken language of the heart and soul. This technique helps us understand and utilize our intuition when listening to our partner, opening up the relationship to a richer, more loving level of connection.

Speaking to Empower

Most of the time we are unconscious of the power our words hold over one another. Thus, we often speak in ways that leave the other person feeling "one-upped" and emotionally drained. Developing this skill shows us how to esteem one another in every conversation, reinforcing an uplifting connection in all our interactions.

The Healing Apology

An important step in healing the hurts that are a normal part of every relationship, but that usually go unfinished, is apology. As partners, we can learn to make sure they are lovingly resolved and put in the past.

Heart-and-Soul Forgiveness

Not just an intellectual exercise, this skill builds forgiveness that truly dissolves resentment.

Gratitude, Acknowledgment, and Appreciation

Probably the most powerful tool, this one fills the emotional bank account of our relationship to overflowing.

Life Enhancement

I believe these tools offer rewards that go beyond our relationships. The mastery of these skills and the others that follow can take a lifetime. Yet, with them, the journey is one of insight, discovery, and personal enrichment. To become proficient with these tools requires increasing mastery over both mind and emotions. Thus, to learn and practice them enhances both personal and spiritual development for any individual who chooses to follow that path.

In a relationship, the opportunity is to deepen our understanding of one another and manage our conflicts with grace and compassion. The relationship itself naturally becomes clearer as we get better and better at Soul Talk. We gain greater insight into our attraction to one another, the challenges we face to continue our connection, and the healing steps that we must take on our journey through life as Soul Partners.

Soul Talk helps couples determine the appropriate direction for their relationship. Through using these processes, couples take the steps to a conscious Soul Partnership if that is what they choose. The skills help to revive a weakened connection or deepen a strong one.

Soul Talk can help separating couples maintain the threads of what brought them together in the first place. Thus, these tools enable you t͡   ͡e. apart gracefully and lovingly, if that is the appropriate step.

Soul Talk paves the way to the new model of love. To going, we need to revisit where our culture has been ˙ ships. Let us look first at the old model of love tha͡ why we are doing so.

Romantic Love: Past and Present

People in prior generations typically chose someone who would help take care of business: raising children, running the farm or family enterprise, providing protection from the dangers of being alone in the world. A loving and growing relationship based on the presumption of equality would never have entered their minds. Love, when it happened, was a bonus.

Couples of earlier generations took a huge risk with their happiness when they chose a life partner. If it worked out, they found a measure of love and companionship, and for many, that was the case. For many more, it was not. Regardless of what they found in their marriages, they accepted it. There were few other options available.

Staying together, regardless of the quality of the connection, became the top priority. Being happy together was a much lower priority.

Transition into New Values

Our view of relationships and their purpose has changed. It is no longer enough just to get along, to function as a family unit, or to handle the business of survival. If that is all there is, we eventually become restless and dissatisfied.

Some say that the frequency of broken romances and split marriages is a sign of disaster, that it is evidence of the loss of the family values that have built our culture. Perhaps there is some truth in that idea, but I firmly believe there is a higher truth at work in all of this heartache.

As *human beings, we are in transition, and thus, so are our relationships.* Our focus is shifting away from the basics of survival and toward one of enlightenment. We are centering our lives today on new values, such as the realization of our potential as human beings and spiritual and personal growth. These are concepts that would have bewildered previous generations. Indeed, they are concepts with which we are just beginning to grapple and about which we have an incomplete understanding.

The majority of us today are searching for a special kind of partnership that because it *should*, but because we want it to. We do not *need* our least in the sense that previous generations did. We *want* romantic love with a special partner, but we can survive very well without it. Thus, our priorities are shifting from love relationships as necessity to *love relationships by choice*. We are moving toward something much better, toward relationships for the right reasons that serve a higher purpose.

An Evolution of Love

Love relationships today barely resemble the ones of yesterday. What many of us saw in our parents' marriages contrasts strikingly with our own ideal vision of love. Our parents were "role bound" in their relationship. They fulfilled certain functions together and they followed certain unwritten rules. Mom kept the house in order, cared for the children, and cooked the meals, while Dad worked outside the home. They rarely displayed affection for one another and they conversed mainly about the necessities.

Neither spoke about wanting more from their relationship, nor did they model open, honest communication. They seemed content to live with what they had created together. We, however, want very different things out of marriage.

One recent article revealed that 75 percent of college women surveyed in 1965 said that they would marry a man they did not love if he met other criteria. Not anymore. A recent Rutgers University study found 94 percent of people between the ages of twenty and twenty-nine agreed with the statement: "When you marry, you want your spouse to be your soul mate, first and foremost."[1]

This is a huge shift in a new direction for love relationships, and it is not just by happenstance. It is a reflection of our changing needs as human beings. More importantly, it is a representation of the power of the human potential movement over the last fifty years.

Self-Help and Love Relationships

The human potential movement is, in a nutshell, the study of what it means to be a self-actualizing human being. In the past few decades, this study has moved outside of the exclusive inner circle of scholars, theologians, scientists, and philosophers—once an inaccessible domain for most people—and into the mainstream of society. Today, most of us read self-help books, attend workshops, and even watch television shows that explore human nature and help us understand ourselves.

Because of this "mainstreaming" of the human potential movement, our growing knowledge of human psychology and emotional make-up is now accessible to the average person. Most of us have made some degree of informal study of romantic love and the dynamics between men and women. Terms such as *intimacy, commitment, codependency,* and *significant other* are now part of the everyday lexicon.

Psychotherapy is no longer exclusively for the mentally ill or hopelessly neurotic; it is almost a necessity of modern life. It is also the place where many have discovered the world of self-help and personal growth. This is a very recent phenomenon in our history as human beings. The relationship concepts and terminology that we casually converse about today would have been considered a foreign language just two generations ago.

What have we learned so far? About love, we have learned a great deal. We now know that *equality within a relationship is imperative.* Healthy love is only available once we acknowledge the other person as a peer and equal. We also recognize that *there are differences between us that need to be honored.* Though we are equal, we are not alike—a distinction that allows us to accept one another as unique beings of differing genders.

The awareness of these basic realities between men and women has given us a better foundation upon which to build our love relationships. Certainly, the opportunity to love and accept one another has been enhanced through this self-help and study. Yet, despite all of the knowledge gained, our ability to actually relate well to one another has far to go.

Ironically, in the age of global communication, we seem unable to talk meaningfully in our personal relationships. We exchange voice mail and email, but stumble through face-to-face conversations. With our romantic partners, we are struggling to learn new ways to connect that will take us to the next level in our quest for fulfilling relationships.

The next level of understanding needed is to examine the deeper purposes served by our attraction to one another and our presence in each other's lives. This new level of study will lead us directly to the concept and the practice of Soul Partnering. We need to then take these new concepts into our daily behaviors and methods of communication so that love is deepened, fulfilling, even uplifting, and then lifetime relationships become a possibility.

Our world has changed, and with those changes come new choices. We rarely take time to realize how much freedom modern conveniences give us; yet once we do, we then must make a choice about what to do with the time and energy we are afforded. Do we utilize the extra time and energy to zoom forward into a fast-paced day to pursue more goals that drive us to an even faster pace so that we can accumulate even more money and possessions? Do we fall into bed exhausted and depleted at the end of the day, only to rise the next and do it all over again? This cycle, we realize, brings us no closer to inner peace and satisfaction.

Instead, we can choose to gratefully acknowledge the gift of those extra minutes and energy, stopping each day to focus inward, perhaps to meditate, pray, read, or practice some sort of spiritual exercise, with the intention to forward the growth of our spirit.

Increasing numbers of people are making these practices a part of everyday life. We are experiencing the desire for, indeed the necessity of, that which promotes inner peace, personal growth, and spiritual direction. We are choosing the path of spiritual enlightenment in addition to participating in the world in much the same way that others do. Yes, we have cell phones and email, but we also endeavor to balance a progressive lifestyle with the quest for personal growth and inner fulfillment.

Most of all, we want to know that our lives have meaning, that we are growing emotionally and spiritually. Our development is therefore directing itself to the exploration of what it means to be a human being on a spiritual journey. We are seeking out the next, and perhaps last, great frontier—the evolution of the human spirit.

Spiritual Evolution and Romantic Love

The quest for self-actualization and spiritual enlightenment is affecting our relationships. We are departing from the patterns of previous generations that married for life, regardless of the degree of happiness and fulfillment. We are no longer willing to remain in abusive, draining, stale, or unloving relationships just because it seems like the right thing to do.

As we seek greater inner peace and as we engage in a process of personal growth, we naturally expand that energy to our closest relationships. Thus, the desire for a better, more loving relationship is a direct and natural outgrowth of the quest for spiritual and personal enlightenment.

Our quest is worthwhile, yet not easy. We must honor our search for personal and spiritual growth while also learning how to honor our relationships. The challenge before us is to explore fresh relationship concepts, create new ways of speaking about them, and adopt more empowering ways of communicating with one another.

Because the old relationship rules and roles are being abandoned, everything is tossed up into the air; *nothing can be assumed.* Virtually everything must be discussed and sorted out between us. Thus, our need for better ways to communicate and relate has grown tremendously as a result of the shift away from the old model of love.

Embracing the Challenge

Exploring these new concepts is potentially stressful for a relationship. The temptation is to look at your partner and offer advice, rather than to look inward. It works best, however, to use these ideas for your own growth and then bring that to the relationship to support and uplift one another.

As you read, focus primarily on your own learning, on the way that you communicate and interact with your partner. Endeavor to open your heart to your partner, communicate your loving intentions, and trust that process to reveal to you both over time the true direction of your relationship. In this way, you set the stage for the possibility of Soul Partnering. Keep in mind that, for most of us, Soul Partnership is a *possibility*, something toward which we are aiming.

This framework is intended to provide enlightenment about the general direction in which we are all moving in love relationships, conscious of it or not. By focusing mainly on learning and practicing Soul Talk in your relationship, the rest will naturally unfold.

Chapter Two
Soul Partnering

All communication occurs in a context. Context refers to everything that was present before we began interacting, as well as everything that affects our interaction. Money issues, health concerns, stress, family or relationship conflict; the weather, the stock market, the seasons; grief and loss, joy and ecstasy, depression—all affect how we speak and listen to others.

I remember a time in my life when I was going through a divorce and was also suffering from a back injury. I probably felt more helpless and hopeless during that six-month period than at any time I can recall. I am quite sure that the conversations I had with my closest friends were not filled with expressions of joy and optimism! I am also sure that I had little energy or focus on my friends' life concerns and issues. In fact, I understand very well my divorcing clients who often say that they are going through a "selfish period."

During this time, my niece came to visit and help me out. I was in a lot of pain that day, both physically and emotionally. My niece at that time was happily married and pregnant with her first child. At one point, she began telling me about something I had done recently that had hurt her feelings. In the context of my own life struggles and pain, her concerns seemed so small and petty that I failed to feel the compassion I would normally feel about her issues.

Resentment welled up inside of me. How dare she confront me with such pettiness at a time like this? How could she focus on my small failings as an aunt when I was in so much pain? To my point of view that day, she had everything that I had lost. Her life was great, mine was in the toilet, and now I was supposed to deal with her petty grievances. Something in me rose up and said, "No!" The wounded, hurting part of me threw up a barrier of self-protection.

Therefore, instead of listening to my beloved niece, honoring her feelings, and working out our differences—processes that I value very highly and endeavor to practice every day—I snapped at her in anger. "Why don't you just let it go?" I said to her. I then pointed out how small and insignificant her complaint was when compared to all that I had given her in the past. "Just get over it," was the gist of my response. Wisely, she chose not to challenge me further at that time, but I heard about this again later in another conversation. Our interaction that day left her feeling hurt and us with a mess to clean up in our relationship. Fortunately, the bond that we share gets us through times like this!

The context of my life at that time being what it was, my ability to respond to my niece in an empowering way was severely limited. That does not make me a victim of my circumstances, nor does it absolve me of responsibility for my part of the transaction. Stepping back and taking a look at what happened does help me raise my awareness. Taking into account the context helps me understand and accept my limitations and therefore myself.

Understanding context allows for acceptance of my own and others' humanity. Thus, I am more prepared to handle my interactions with grace in the future. Looking at the context of our communication provides a point of intervention, a point of reference, and more room to make other choices. I call that "stepping into the gap," a phenomenon that we will discuss at greater length in chapter 4.

There are other, more subtle and unconscious forces that affect how we communicate: gender differences, race, religion, all aspects of the society and culture in which we live, education, level of awareness, values, perceptions, beliefs, and point of view, just to name a few. Historically, one of the most powerful influences on man/woman relationships, and therefore the way that we communicate, is gender roles.

The Origin of Soul Partnering

A tremendous social shift took place in the last century, and because of it, Soul Partnership as a new paradigm became a possibility. That shift was the alteration of men and women's roles in Western society. In a nutshell, women gained economic freedom as well as the ability to choose their time of childbirth (through the introduction of the birth control pill).

Prior to this enormous change in our social structure, Soul Partnership was not viable. The inherent inequality of men and women in society, as well as the unfeasibility of divorce, did not permit truly open communication. For instance, if a couple strongly disagreed about something fundamental to their happiness in the old paradigm, there was only one possible resolution: someone had to give in, often to the detriment of that person and the relationship. Out of necessity, any attempt at an even exchange of ideas was prohibited.

Soul Partnership requires open, honest communication between equal partners. Therefore, our societal structures had to shift in order for that possibility to emerge. We had to change our fundamental view of men and women so that true equality could be explored in our society, a process that continues to unfold today.

I stress the word "possibility" here. Old paradigms take a very long time to cycle out, and the archetype of men and women as unequal is by no means gone from our culture. All of the old patterns have not changed, and they will take a very long time to do so. What has changed is that we have introduced a new set of ideas into our culture, one in which it is possible for a man and woman to be equals. These new ideas lead to more discussion, more exploration, and more growth. What we are aiming toward is encouraging this possibility to become more and more real, or grounded, in our culture.

Equality Today

True equality is understood between partners, as they each possess sufficient intellectual, emotional, economic, and other resources to establish them as such within their society. Additionally, their society contains certain structures that support that equality, such as the right of women to own property and to vote.

Gradually, women have gained economic power and thus a greater measure of equality. For the first time in history, in any society with which we are familiar, a woman can live independently of a man or her family of origin if she chooses, without the social stigma that once marked her if she did not marry. This is an astonishing phenomenon! It is an unparalleled accomplishment for women, and one that we, as Western women, take entirely for granted.

Because of the efforts of women before me, I wake every day into a world of supreme independence. I own my own home, and I make my own decisions about my body, my health, my life, and my development as a person. I have the ability to travel alone to most parts of the developed world if I choose to do so. I make hundreds of decisions, from the smallest to the largest, without feeling the need to defer to someone else's choices just because of that person's gender.

In my relationship with my Soul Partner, it is understood that decisions affecting us both are made jointly. This makes for lively and spirited discussions that are not limited by gender roles and rules. We may disagree and we may struggle at times, but we never force our individual needs upon the other based on the presumption of one person's superiority. What a wonderful way to live life! What a liberating experience it is to be connected to a man in love, by choice, and without fear. This is the gift that I am able to receive as a result of the blood, sweat, and tears of so many women before me.

Of course, the idea of woman-as-less-than-man has not totally evaporated. Women have not yet attained complete equality in our society. It will take several more generations of enlightenment for this relatively new concept to fully develop. Globally, it may take much longer, as there are still a number of large societies on our planet in which women are disempowered, considered inferior, persecuted, and even tortured because of their gender.

Likewise, the old model for marriage has not disappeared. Consciously or unconsciously, we still may choose many of the elements of the "traditional" man/woman relationship. Is that bad? Certainly not. The point is that *we now have the ability to choose*. We are no longer so tightly bound by the rules and roles of previous generations. Today's men and women have inherited a birthright of choice in love. Our privilege is that we may examine the ways that men and women have interacted in the past, and we may consider new ways of partnering.

A New Model and a New Structure

Soul Partnering is both a new model and a new *process* for love. It is a way of looking at relationships and *a way of managing them*. As the old model of love began to disappear in our society, along with it we lost a great deal of the structure that once held our relationships intact through difficult times. Now, we need new structures that hold our relationships together and that also support our growth and expansion.

Today, a woman is in a position to challenge her partner if she feels that he is not supporting her empowerment as a woman and as an equal partner. Because women have struggled so much to attain a position as equals, they are more sensitive to the issues that arise as we attempt to form these new kinds of partnerships. For example, without the traditional role definitions from the past, we must sort out who does what without automatically resorting to stereotypes (i.e., the woman cooks and cleans, and the man mows the lawn). When I counsel couples, I find that women are more likely to point out the presumption of these stereotypical roles and to object to them than are men.

Women today who are aware of the possibilities seek relationships that honor them as equals *and* as feminine beings with unique desires and needs. Such women want emotional support as well as support for reaching their full potential, and they let their partners know it if their needs are not being met. Thus, women tend to be the ones to express dissatisfaction in relationships and to push for change.

Today, men are being challenged as well. Because relationships are changing, with women wanting equal partnership, many men are feeling confused. Their mothers nurtured their fathers and asked mainly for economic security in return. Today's woman asks for a great deal more. She asks for communication, love, partnership, romance, and the willingness to work through issues together. She gives nurturing *and* she expects it in full measure in return. These are emotionally based skills that are vastly different than the kinds of skills men were expected to display in the past.

The new relationship parameters require a great deal more emotional development in men than was previously the case. This pushes many men well outside their emotional "comfort zones," sometimes so far that they will not continue the relationship, especially if deep love is not present. *Today's man sometimes exits because the relationship has become more challenging than his love will hold.* This means that, in order for him to be willing to stretch beyond his old comfort zone, a man must feel that he is with a woman whom he loves very deeply and to whom he is very committed.

Recently I shared a conversation at a dinner party with a woman, Mary, who had just divorced her husband of fifteen years. Mary shared with me that, though her ex was a loving and devoted father and a wonderful provider, he did not demonstrate a heart and soul devotion toward her. "He wanted to stay home with the children, which was wonderful. But he never wanted to be alone with me, to go out on a date, to share special time just for us."

The lack of romantic intention in their relationship made it unfeasible for both Mary and her ex-husband. They were, and remain, great parenting partners and good friends. As romantic Soul Partners, whatever connection they originally shared had died long ago. There was no struggle about divorce because it made sense that they simply declare it over and get on with their lives.

In the old model of love, this couple would be deemed crazy for divorcing. What was the problem? The fact that there was absolutely no romantic connection in their relationship did not mean that they could not have a good family life.

In the new model of love, there was no reason for Mary and her ex to stay together. Totally devoted to their children, they have created the least stressful divorce possible. Both are actively involved in their children's lives on a day-to-day basis. The children are happy, healthy, and assured of their parents' love and constant attention. Mary and her ex are free to pursue their individual growth and expansion, no longer limited by a marital tie that did not serve them.

In Mary's case, her husband's love for her was not large enough or deep enough to move him in the direction of emotional growth for their relationship. She recognized this and, rather than pushing him for growth that he did not want, released him from the obligation. In so doing, she released herself as well. She recognizes full well that as a single woman, she is open and available to attracting someone who will bond more deeply with her and be far more devoted to her than was her ex.

The more emotionally aware man of today wants more from a relationship and leaves for the same reasons that women with comparable expectations do: lack of fulfillment, absence of a deep connection, and therefore lack of opportunity for personal growth and fulfillment. The more emotionally developed he is, the more a man seeks a partner with whom he feels intellectually, emotionally, sexually, and spiritually connected, someone with whom he feels safe enough to grow into his full potential and whom he can support in achieving hers. When he does not find that within the relationship, he moves on.

The new model of Soul Partnering is challenging for both men and women. Soul Partners today are beginning to realize that they must evolve at a higher level so that they move beyond the old models that suppressed each of them. They are gradually coming to understand that their challenges are the challenges of all men and women, and that their choices profoundly affect the evolution of love for all humans. Soul Partners are discovering that a large part of their journey through life involves learning lessons together and, by their example, forwarding the ongoing evolution of the human spirit and of romantic love.

Soul Partnering: The Challenge

Soul Partners have lessons to learn together. They are attracted to one another very powerfully in various ways. On the positive end of the spectrum, they see in one another the embodiment of everything they have been seeking in a partner: someone to love, admire, respect, care for, and walk with through life.

On the other end of the spectrum, they present to one another certain challenges. Because they are so strongly attracted and so deeply connected, they evoke powerful emotions in one another. When love is flowing, those emotions include passion, desire, intimacy, fulfillment, attachment, and joy. When love is blocked, those emotions may include intense anger, sadness, fear, and detachment.

These darker emotions bring out the parts of us that have the most difficulty with loving and being loved, those parts of our souls that are wounded and in need of healing. When our emotional wounds emerge, we often act out the pain that we carry, creating damage in the relationship. At that precise moment, we are presented with tremendous challenges to keeping our love strong. Sometimes, the challenges persist for days, weeks, months, and even years before we gain enough wisdom and insight to move through them to a more positive place.

Given these dynamics, Soul Partners have many questions for which they are seeking answers.

1. When challenged, how do we manage the inevitable conflicts, the thwarted expectations, the letdowns and frustrations?
2. How do we grow our love together and be the best we can be?
3. Where do we find the energy to persist in a relationship until it turns around in a more positive direction?
4. How do we navigate the troubled waters of this transition from the old model of relationships to the new model that stands before us?

The Purpose of Soul Partnering

Ironically, the point of the most distress in a Soul Partnership is also the point of maximum growth potential. We cannot heal that which we cannot feel, and as Soul Partners, we serve an unconscious purpose in helping one another get in touch with those parts of ourselves that are wounded and in need of recovery.

This is our true purpose in coming together as Soul Partners, whether we are conscious of it or not: to uncover those parts of ourselves that are in need of healing and to support one another in that healing process. It is a profound mission in life—the healing and growth of our souls. It is why we are here. Everything in our lives, from the parents who raised us and the people who influenced us to the choices we make and the love that we share, is purposeful toward this end. We are here to heal and to grow on a spiritual level.

When we choose our intimate love partners, whether conscious of it or not, we are intentional and diligent in finding the exact right person to bring out both the dark and the light in our soul. The very nature of romantic love in all its intensity sets this process in motion and calls this phenomenon into being. It cannot help but happen.

Who but the person I love most can more effectively shake up my emotions and my life? Each time I open my heart to my Soul Partner, I take the risk that I will be hurt. In taking that risk, I must confront my deepest fear: that I will be abandoned just at the point that I become most comfortable. As I come face-to-face with my fear, I also confront the darkest moments of my life: the day my father left, the lonely years spent just trying to survive growing up in a broken family.

Each relationship with a man has given me the opportunity to confront those issues, and with each came the opportunity to heal. For years, I ran away from those opportunities. I avoided loving men, I clung to unloving ones, and I avoided real intimacy in favor of chemistry alone, hoping it would magically turn into real love.

I ran from myself as well. I unconsciously used my bad relationships with men and all of the inherent drama and consumption of energy to distract myself from the real issue: my spiritual growth. I blamed men for my distress with myself, rather than taking responsibility for creating my own happiness from within.

I am quite clear that all of this was necessary for my growth. All of this pain and drama brought me to the point of maximum suffering, and thus, to the point of choice. In the dark night of the soul, there is always a choice: to continue suffering, or to dedicate myself to healing and growth. It takes a certain level of awareness and consciousness to choose the latter. I had been cultivating this awareness for years, through my own therapy and through a number of personal growth facilitated experiences.[2] The choice that I was confronted with was to be *more dedicated to my own self and to my own healing than to my attachment to any man.* Making that choice truly turned my life around and led me into maximum healing and growth.

Later, as my awareness grew, I made choices that were more conscious. One of my relationships, with a man who was very special to me, I chose knowing that our compatibility for the long-term was questionable. Initially, things were good between us. We shared genuine respect, love, and attraction. Over time, we provoked one another, activating deep levels of wounding in each of us, causing our connection to become painful. At one point, I chose to stay connected to this man even though it was painful because I was aware enough to know that the issues he was provoking in me were the very ones that were stopping me from having the life I wanted.

Instead of running away from the relationship as I had in the past, I stayed with the conscious intention of continuing my own healing process. My hope was that if I could work through my own issues, either our relationship would become viable for the future, or I would release some very old patterns and be available for a better relationship with someone else. It turned out to be the latter, though I did not know that at the time.

Now I have a Soul Partnership that is conscious, dynamic, loving, flowing, and full of growth. Our love is not in question and our commitment is not frivolous. We are in it for the long run. We both consider ourselves to be extremely blessed to have found one another, and we express our gratitude for what we have every single day.

I am very aware that I was not emotionally available for this kind of connection in the past. I needed every experience that happened in my life prior to this in order to raise my consciousness to the level that it takes to have this kind of relationship. I also needed the communication strategies that I practice, teach, and continue to develop—tools that enabled me to be honest with myself and to open up to the men in my life. My growth as a person and as a relationship partner is a direct result of being dedicated to empowering communication in all areas of my life.

New Tools for the New Relationship

Soul Partners, whether unconscious or conscious, whether together for a lifetime or for only a short time, are together to help one another grow. This healing, however, does not happen automatically. *It happens when we have the awareness that we are in a healing process and because we possess the tools for doing so*. It also happens when both partners are willing to grow and are open to the process of change.

The core skills necessary to Soul Partnering are all centered on communication. How we speak and listen to one another on a day-to-day basis is critical to this process. In order to nurture a relationship and to assist one another to be the best that we can be, we must learn and practice ways of communicating that empower one another. It is not enough to discuss news, weather, and sports at the end of the day. We must be able to open our hearts and souls to one another, to express emotions and listen to them respectfully, and to create a deep level of understanding that sustains us during difficult times. We must be able to resolve conflict in a way that respects our position as equals, not simply one partner acquiescing to the other. We must be able to reveal the essence of our inner selves (who we are) to one another. With this kind of communication, there is nurturing, healing, respect, love, and freedom for the heart to dance. That kind of communion is true Soul Talk.

The Soul Talk tools are powerful! Therefore, they must be handled with the utmost consciousness and respect. These are not tools for manipulating one another or for getting what you want in a relationship (selfish needs). In fact, through the use of these tools you may discover that you are not right for each other and decide to move on with your lives separately. As you use them in other areas of your life, you may find that some of your friendships and other relationships change form or even draw to a close. That is one of the natural consequences of coming to know your own truth and then expressing that honestly and compassionately to others.

These tools are to be used to create understanding, to empower each other in being the best that you can be, to reach for your true potential, and to assist one another in a journey of personal and spiritual growth. They are a powerful and potent part of the process of self-actualization.

The tools offered in this book are useful in other relationships as well. The principles and practices address the essence of what it takes to have positive connections in general. They apply to all relationships in life, as the key is the same in every single one of them: *communication that empowers, that deepens understanding, and that fosters healing and growth.*

Soul Talk: Gender Differences

As we discovered earlier, all interactions between men and women are influenced by the context of their gender. In our culture, we are struggling to find a position of equality. There has been a long history of inequality, and transitional times are always challenging. Additionally, the reality is that men and women are different in physiology and in the way that we think, feel, experience, and express ourselves.

The way we view our differences makes a huge impact on the way we relate. If my view is that my Soul Partner is male and I am female and that because of that we are defined a certain way like the color of our eyes or that of our hair, then a limitation is imposed. It goes something like this: "He's a man, and because he's a man, he can't possibly understand the depth of my emotions or how I feel them. Therefore, why bother trying to share how I feel? He can't hear it, can't understand it, and we will get nowhere with that conversation."

If I take that view, I close off a part of myself from my partner without ever consulting or including him in the discussion! What we lose from that is the opportunity to challenge our presumptions about what it means to be a man and a woman, and to create a new possibility in the relationship.

What if I took a very different approach? I might say to myself, "I want to have a conversation with my partner, and I want to express how I am feeling about some things. I know that handling difficult emotions, in fact any emotions and their expression, is not the easiest thing in the world for him. Logic is easy for him, emotions are not—*for whatever reason.* Therefore, I will choose my timing and set the stage for this conversation so that there is the maximum opportunity for him to listen and to be there for me. I trust that by engaging in that process, we will both learn and grow even if it is difficult."

With this approach, one that is not limited by preconceived ideas about gender differences, I am open to having this conversation with my partner. Also, because I can honor the ways that he is different without carving those differences in stone, there is the opportunity for learning and growth in our relationship.

We are all born with a mixture of both masculine and feminine energy. Through the influence of genetics and social forces, we tilt more in one direction than in the other. Boys tend to grow up to be primarily masculine, while girls tend to be primarily feminine in their self-expression.

The degree of masculine and feminine energy, that is to say, the percentage of each in a person's energy, creates differences from one male to the other and from one female to the other. Some men are highly masculine and exhibit almost no feminine energy, while others are less masculine and more comfortable with feminine expression. The same is true of women. This is part of what make us unique as human beings. Not only are we different *between* genders, but we are also different *across* genders. Therefore, our attempts to categorize men and women as being a certain way due solely to gender do not generally work.

If we say, "A man is like this. He thinks, feels, and expresses himself like this, and only like this," then we limit the range of expression that is available. If we say, "A woman is like this. She thinks, feels, and expresses herself in this way," then we limit her, as well. In this view that men and women are a certain way, we have no new choices in the way we relate to one another. We are stuck with our gender roles and the rules that have been handed down.

As Soul Partners striving to be more conscious and loving and to evolve to a higher level as spiritual beings, our task is to look beyond the biological and sociological limitations that have held us back in the past. We can look at our differences as a matter of masculine and feminine energy, both energies shared by both people to different degrees. *Within this view, new possibilities emerge.*

Feminine energy is receptive, nurturing, emotional, and caretaking. Can a man have and display this kind of energy? Of course! One only has to observe a loving father with his newborn infant to see an otherwise masculine person's feminine energy. Feminine energy is also intuitive, creative, and visionary. Can a man have that kind of energy? Absolutely! Many of the world's greatest artists and visionaries are men.

Masculine energy is assertive, moving outward, doing, thinking, and accomplishing. Are there women with this kind of energy? Take a look at corporate America today. Some of our most successful and high-powered executives are women who display this kind of energy every day.

The more broadly we define what it means to be masculine and feminine, the more we begin to see the individual qualities that comprise those energies, and the more it is revealed that they are not limited to one gender or the other. A man can be nurturing and emotional. A woman can be assertive and logical. We may be strongly influenced by our biological and social predisposition, but it does not have to limit us.

We have the capacity to *choose the balance of these energies* we wish to incorporate into our behaviors and self-expression. Is that always easy? No. Often there is stress when we move out of our more natural energies into energy that is less so. A woman who is primarily a giver and nurturer and who wishes to be successful in the corporate world may find that as she is required to exercise her more masculine qualities, her stress level increases. A woman in this position may have a double-whammy. During the day, she is stressed because she is exercising parts of her energy that do not come naturally. At night, she is stressed because her natural feminine energy does not automatically return. Often women who work in corporate America report that their relationships suffer because they find it difficult to "turn off" the masculine parts of themselves at the end of the day.

Likewise, a man whose work requires him to be aggressive and unemotional all day may find that his stress level goes up when he is asked that evening to nurture his partner and connect with her emotionally. Men also report that their relationships suffer due to their inability to turn off the masculine (aggressive, demanding) and turn on the feminine (supportive, nurturing) parts of themselves at the end of the day.

In our relationships, *our challenge is to incorporate, accept, and express all parts of ourselves*, both masculine and feminine. In fact, as we explore those aspects of energy that fall outside of the typical gender roles, we find that whole new possibilities for life are revealed. This is perfectly aligned with our quest for Soul Partnering, as we need those energies to bring our relationships into full expression.

It is a new world for man/woman relationships. Many men today are no longer comfortable being the sole providers of all financial resources. They, too, long for a sense of partnership and support in this part of life. Many women are not comfortable being wholly dependent upon a man for financial survival. They, too, desire the sense of freedom, power, and autonomy that self-generated wealth can bring.

Today's woman wants and demands nurturing behavior from her masculine partner, and he wants the same. Both will have to expand their limiting ideas of how men should behave in order to bring that aspect into their connection.

In these areas, and many others, our relationships have been out of balance. As Soul Partners seeking greater balance, we can choose to develop in ourselves the traits that are not dominant. Thus, we take on the path of maximum growth, both personally and spiritually. In so doing, we expand our sense of self, we expand our sense of possibilities for self-expression in life, and we enrich our connection. How do we do that?

Quite simply, we aim for balance. *We honor the primary energy of our souls, we honor the secondary energy that is latent and less developed, and we honor our desire to have both.* We honor that in ourselves, and we honor it in our partners.

As a woman, I do not have to be ashamed of wanting more power in the form of financial resources. My partner need not hide the fact that he enjoys caring for me emotionally and also wanting someone to share the bills. We can find humor in the situations in which he seems to be more feminine that myself and I seem to be more masculine than he is, and vice versa. We strive for acceptance of all of the expressions of who and what we are, male and female, masculine and feminine.

At those times that we are not comfortable, we have the opportunity to stretch ourselves. Rather than falling lock-step into the patterned male-female responses of the past, we can stop, listen with compassion, and choose new responses. Choosing new definitions of ourselves as a man and a woman, and viewing one another through that open lens, we are more loving and supportive Soul Partners.

Consciously Choosing Soul Partnership

Two people who come together, not to fill in the empty spaces but to contribute to one another the gifts they possess, create the new love relationship. They offer one another emotional and spiritual wisdom, love, respect, caring, their material resources, and support for being the best they can be as individuals. They form a true partnership, one that is based on the love in their hearts and the desire for self-actualization in their souls; in essence, they become Soul Partners. When done consciously, this choice elevates the relationship to a new level of joy, fulfillment, and satisfaction. With that comes a higher level of commitment as well.

For Soul Partners, commitment is a vehicle for even deeper, more loving self-expression and connection. It is not a burden to be avoided or a game to be played. It is something that is carefully considered, discussed at great length, and arrived at jointly because it is the right time and the right path for both members of the relationship.

Soul Partners recognize that though their commitment is deep and they have every intention for it to last a lifetime, they do not have the power to promise forever. Conscious and aware of the unpredictable nature of life, they are too smart to swear that they will never part. Instead, they promise to put every bit of their intention and energy toward maintaining a loving, ever-growing connection.

This kind of commitment calls us forth into action. To promise that I will do everything that I can to honor and cherish my Soul Partner, to be supportive of him, to be open and honest with him, and to be there in action and deed every day, is a huge commitment. It is easy to say, "I will never leave you," especially in the first bloom of honeymoon love. It is far more difficult to say, "Even if things get tough, I will continue to open my heart to you, give to you, work through issues with you, and be a loving partner to you."

The most challenging commitment of all is the one that says, "I will honor our connection through ups and downs, highs and lows, good feelings and bad ones. I will communicate fully with you no matter how much I want to run away, hide, or jump ship."

This kind of commitment requires rigorous tools for communication. It means that we dedicate ourselves to open, honest dialogue at all times, no matter how difficult. That dedication is the essence of conscious Soul Partnership, and Soul Talk is a way to achieve it.

Chapter Three
Context and Intention

Verbal communication is made up of two basic parts: speaking and listening. In every interaction with another person, we are either speaking or listening at any given moment. Sometimes we attempt to do both at the same time. This is commonly referred to as an *argument*, also defined as *two people trying to win at the same time that both are losing.*

Speaking and listening are not discreet behaviors we arbitrarily choose. Speaking is not just the words we speak. Listening is not simply having the ability to hear and having a language in common with the speaker. Those things provide a great start, but there is a great deal more to the story. In fact, there are many things occurring with regard to communication *prior to* the actual process of speaking and listening.

Speaking and listening are intricate, complex processes that are guided by other intricate, complex processes. If it were not so, then we would all easily and automatically say what we mean, mean what we say, say it in a clear, concise way that others can understand, and hear what others say with perfect understanding. What a different world it would be if we could do that in all of our relationships!

The ways we speak and listen are a direct result of the imperfect processes that make us human. To strive for communication mastery, therefore, is not to strive for perfection, but rather to *aim for greater wisdom and a higher level of skill.* Our lessons in this critical area are an ongoing part of life development.

I am not a perfect communicator. I am a (mostly) conscious, aware person fascinated with the processes of how human beings interact. I have studied communication a great deal, leading to many discoveries and "ah-hahs" that I am committed to implementing in my own life and passing along to my clients. It is a deeply fulfilling though not a perfect journey.

In my personal life, I do not practice perfectly every skill with each and every family member, friend, and loved one at all times. I am sure that anyone who is close to me will verify that—and the closer they are, the more so. Hopefully, I am able to convey a sincere intention to be more compassionate and loving in the way that I communicate as I learn and grow on my own path.

I encourage you not to aim for perfection, but rather to aim for greater understanding and compassion, first for yourself, and then for others, cultivating the following qualities that will make the journey easier and more rewarding:

1. Aiming for a greater level of awareness;
2. Having curiosity about what it means to be human and to communicate with and relate to others;
3. Being open to new thoughts, perceptions, and ideas:
   • Open-minded is good;
   • Open-hearted will allow miracles to occur;
4. Being open to the role of communication in the development of our souls both individually and in our relationships;
5. Having the intention to practice, learn, and grow.

Guiding Processes

There are numerous complex processes that guide everything we say and hear. These include our level of awareness, the context in which the communication takes place, our perceptions, and our intentions.

My *level of awareness* is how much I am attuned to the inner and outer forces that shape my world, our relationship, and our conversation.

The *context* is everything that is present *prior to opening my mouth to speak to you,* or attempting to listen to you, which includes:

1. cultural and gender issues (as we touched on in chapter 2);
2. personal history: my experiences in life thus far;
3. emotional and physical state: how I feel overall at a certain period of my life, and how I feel in any given moment;
4. power or the perception thereof: how much I feel I have the ability to control the outcomes of my life or of a particular situation;
5. wants, needs, desires, and expectations: for my life, for my relationships, and for a given situation.

My *perception* is what I think and what I believe about you, me, and whatever we are discussing;

My *intentions* are the conscious and unconscious outcomes that I am driven to produce in my life, in my relationships, and in our conversation.

Awareness

Our level of emotional and psychological awareness is subject to change. As we experience more of life and as we deliberately "tune in" to the opportunities for learning that we encounter, we grow. Simultaneously, we become more aware about ourselves, about the nature of life and human beings, and about our spiritual selves. The more aware and conscious we are of the dynamics that drive us as human beings, the more wisdom we bring to our communications and to our relationships.

Context

As awareness increases, the context of our conversations becomes more noticeable. Context is the *background* of communication. It is like the air that we take for granted as we breathe. We do not have to be aware of the context of communication in order to interact. We are immersed in it. It simply exists as the backdrop to everything we do, hear, and say. However, in order to learn to communicate more powerfully and lovingly, it is important to notice context and to understand how it works. This next section contains some examples of the varying aspects of communication context and how they influence us.

Context: Personal History

One of the purposes of psychotherapy is to help individuals achieve some sense of closure about the past: to resolve and come to terms with loss, regret, resentment, and emotional pain. When we do not effectively deal with the past, it spills over into the present, contaminating current relationships and connections. Thus, it is vital that we know and understand our past history in a way that provides the freedom and energy to create a desirable life in the present.

In relationships, we can bring the awareness of our past history into the present so we are mindful of emotional reactions that are out of proportion to the current event. (Later, we will look at this process and the tools for dealing effectively with emotions more closely.) As we come to terms with our personal history and as we understand it in one another, it becomes a powerful tool for healing and growth. The Soul Talk tools can greatly aid this process.

Context: Emotional State

My Soul Partner and I were working on a home-remodeling project together. We do not always agree on ideas about color, style, and furniture placement, so when we discuss those things, we are generally a bit stressed. One evening, we were having one of those discussions, but we neglected to take into account the context of our conversation. It happened to be a day that was highly stressful for each of us, and I was particularly drained and emotionally sensitive. Therefore, we found that we simply could not get through the conversation in a productive manner. Finally, we stopped and acknowledged our *emotional states* and agreed that now was not the time for this discussion. We tabled it and focused instead on destressing and relaxing activities.

Context: Power

In one sense, there are very real issues of power, or the perception thereof, that can tilt a relationship off-balance, and it is important to be aware of them. A client of mine, Tim, could not understand why the woman he was dating had gone into a rage one night when he suggested a different restaurant than the one she had selected. We looked at the situation more closely, at the *context* of the conversation (the woman's personal history and current emotional state). She was at that time battling a debilitating illness and was losing. Prior to that, she had gone through a bitter divorce and was essentially alone in the world. Nothing that she had intended for her life had worked out, and her *sense of personal power* at the moment of that conversation must have been almost zero.

Given those issues, her rage was much more understandable. She was attempting to exert control over the only aspect of her life that was within her immediate influence: where to go for dinner. This man had nothing but good intentions—he truly wanted to help her through this horrible time of life. Good intentions, poor outcome. Why? Because he was unconscious of the underlying issues of power and vulnerability that were out of balance in this woman's life. He could not have changed those issues, nor was he responsible for them, but with greater awareness, he might have chosen a different, more supportive response to her that night.

On another level, the issues of power in a relationship can be traced back to each individual's overall sense of intrinsic empowerment. Self-care; self-esteem; integrity; personal goals and the pursuit thereof; sense of "directing my life" as opposed to "it happens to me"; spiritual connection and growth: *all are vital to personal empowerment.*

When we experience both an inner and outer sense of fulfillment in life, we feel empowered to express ourselves fully in our relationships. We do not need power *over* anyone else, nor do we surrender our personal power in order to be taken care of.

As a self-actualizing person, I realize that it is my responsibility, and mine alone, to create my experience of life each and every day. Thus, I am not a burden to my partner, but a gift. As another self-actualizing person, he is a gift to me as well.

Those issues in our lives that stand in the way of an overall sense of fulfillment are the same issues that tilt our relationships out of balance. If I long for creative expression but deny that to myself, then I will, on some level, feel out of balance and resentful. That resentment, sooner or later, spills over into my interactions with my partner, especially if I see him exercising his creative expression. I feel less powerful, he seems more powerful, and our interactions reflect that out-of-balance dynamic. This leads to repetitive arguing over other issues in nonproductive ways. Alternatively, it leads to my acting out my resentment in passive ways, such as "forgetting" what time we were supposed to meet for dinner. In couple relationships, we call this dynamic a "power struggle."

The Soul Talk tools help eliminate power struggles through the promotion of a deeper understanding of the real issues. Rather than arguing about what to have for dinner, we can talk about what is really bothering us. With the standard blocks to understanding removed, we are able to hear one another as if for the first time. New awareness emerges, new creative responses are possible, and there is no longer the need for struggle. We then become one another's supportive partners in achieving all that we can be as individuals and as a couple.

Context: Wants, Needs, and Desires

At any given moment, we are all being driven by our deepest wants, needs, and desires. To be conscious of what those are is essential to productive living. Knowing what I want out of life is the first step to achieving my goals. On a deeper level, I must also know and realize what those things represent.

For instance, many people want and desire financial wealth. Yet, they often do not stop and ask themselves, "What will I have if I achieve my financial goals—what will that afford me?" Sometimes the answer to that question reveals something that is achievable today, not in the future with a larger balance sheet. Freedom, the ability to travel, a sense of security; these are things that you can have today, given a particular set of intentions and a change in perception. In this way, knowing what my goals represent opens up new possibilities.

In relationships, it is critical that we understand our wants, needs, and desires and their true purpose that we are holding in our hearts. When we look at these, we often find that we are projecting them onto our partners, expecting the other person to fulfill all of our wants and needs. These expectations create a block in the relationship because the reality of this situation is that *no one has anything to give another person except love.*

My Soul Partner does not possess all of the things that would fulfill me and give my life purpose. So my efforts to get him to give me what I want wind up in power struggles with both of us ending up frustrated and resentful—I am still unfulfilled and he feels blamed for that lack in my soul. Over time, these struggles become huge obstacles to loving partnership. Therefore, *anything we think our partners can give us that we do not feel we currently possess has the potential to be a block in the relationship.*

For instance, my clients often tell me that they want a relationship for purposes of emotional security. Wanting emotional security is human—we all long for it to some degree or another. Feeling that you *do not have it* and *expecting a partner to deliver it* is a potential relationship block.

To the degree that you do not feel emotionally secure when you meet your partner, he or she will be operating from that degree of deficit in trying to fulfill your need. Are you slightly insecure? Perhaps your partner can fulfill some of that need, as long as you are aware that it is your deficit and you are working to correct it.

Are you deeply and profoundly insecure? Has your experience of life and relationships been that no matter how hard you try, you always end up alone/used/abused and that you can count on nothing and no one? It is unlikely that your partner can even come close to fulfilling the need inherent in that dynamic, especially if you are not aware that it is your responsibility to take care of it.

Sometimes, stopping to assess where we are in our lives individually versus where we want to be helps us realize how we may be expecting too much from our partners and our relationships. Wanting what we cannot have is a formula for dissatisfaction and frustration. Therefore, it is helpful to periodically stop and make an assessment.

EXERCISE: RAISE YOUR LEVEL OF AWARENESS

What are your wants, needs, and desires for your life? What are they in a relationship? Begin a list of these things for the purpose of raising your level of awareness. I have put some examples in the following chart.

Wants, Needs, and Desires

For my life	For my relationship
Personal and spiritual growth	Sharing personal and spiritual growth; spiritual connection
Abundance of love and intimacy	Emotional and sexual intimacy that is fulfilling to both of us
Financial abundance and planning	Agreement on financial matters; financial goals and a plan for our future
Education	An intellectual connection: we can talk about the things we are each learning
Travel and adventure	Planning trips together; openness to new experiences; common interests and activities that we share
Health, energy, and fitness	Supporting one another in eating healthily and exercising
Fulfillment and growth in my work	Clarity with regard to what has to be accomplished in our life together: who does what and why
Connection with friends and family	Activities that we share in our community of family and friends

Now, go to a deeper level and look back over your list. Put a check mark next to the things in the left column that you *want* but feel that you *currently do not have*. Ask yourself: how important is it that I have these things? What is standing in the way of my achieving them? If your answer is "my partner," you may be projecting your unmet needs upon your relationship.

Perhaps some of your wants, needs, and desires have acted as blocks in your relationship. Have you expected too much from your partner? Have you wanted him or her to provide you with happiness and fulfillment? Have you let *yourself* down and then blamed your partner for not fixing the situation or you? Make a fearless inventory of your life, looking at what you wanted and needed, what you have accomplished, and what you intend for the future.

This exercise may not be easy. There may be buried hopes, dreams, and desires that are very painful to face. It takes courage to pull those things out of the recesses of your mind and heart and face them for what they are. Be sure and obtain support for this part of your process—a friend, family member, a good therapist, or a coach.

Do this exercise anytime you are frustrated with your relationship, especially if it seems as though your partner can *never do enough* for you or if you are walking around with a constant sense of uneasiness. Use this process to begin separating your own issues of life fulfillment from the issues of the relationship itself.[3] Later, there will be some exercises to help you and your partner co-create a Relationship Mission and Purpose Statement and establish intentions and goals together.

Context: Expectations

When our expectations slip to the unconscious level, we call those "hidden expectations": hidden from ourselves and from our partners. The following are typical hidden expectations in relationships, usually experienced as "If you loved me, then you would…":

- always know what my needs are and automatically fulfill them without my having to tell you;
- be nice to me (however I define that) every day, all the time; give me my way at all times;
- do things my way around the house (let me be sloppy/keep it as clean as I like it); be affectionate when and how I want;
- connect with me when I want/give me the freedom to disconnect when I want; speak and listen to me in the ways that most nourish me at all times without my having to guide you in what that is;
- have sex my way, when I am in the mood, and be understanding when I don't want to;

- handle finances my way at all times without my having to tell you what that is or be responsible for our financial outcomes;
- never be angry, rejecting, grumpy, selfish, emotionally distant, needy, or anything that detracts from my happiness at every moment;
- be OK when I am angry, rejecting, grumpy, selfish, emotionally distant, needy, or with anything that I may be, do, or feel when I am not at my best; give me unconditional love at all times;
- expect nothing from me—view it as a gift and be grateful when I give my love to you.

And the biggest and most damaging hidden expectation of all is:

If you truly loved me, you would *make me happy*, all the time!

What else needs to be added to this list? What other unspoken expectations might you be bringing to your relationship? Again, do a fearless inventory and tell yourself the truth. Be willing to look "stinky" in this exercise. We all are! You will not be alone.

Just in case you are wondering if perhaps this expectations list is not so unreasonable, try the following exercise. Take each statement and rewrite it (do this with every one) so that it reads like this:

If I truly loved my partner, then I would always know what her needs are and automatically fulfill them without her having to tell me.

If I truly loved my partner, then I would give him his way at all times.

If I truly loved my partner, then I would speak and listen to her in the ways that most nourish her at all times without her having to guide me in what that is.

If I truly loved my partner, then I would handle finances his way at all times without his having to talk about what that is or be responsible for our financial outcomes.

If I truly loved my partner, then I would make him happy all the time.

And so on, for the rest of the list.

What is your experience when you reverse the list? What are the thoughts and feelings this exercise evokes? What you probably are finding is that the feelings you get from these expectations are roughly equivalent to those that your partner feels from having to deal with your expectations.

When we operate with one another from hidden expectations, we set one another up to fail. This is because one human being simply cannot know and be attentive to another person's expectations at all times and fulfill them perfectly. It is, in fact, a waste of time and energy even to try.

Does this mean that you adopt an attitude of uncaring for your partner's needs? Does it mean that you focus exclusively on yourself and your needs, aiming only to satisfy yourself and leaving the other person to satisfy herself? This approach has actually been tried by some couples, but the end result is often not what they were hoping to accomplish. With no attention to your partner's needs, it is too easy to "disconnect" from the other person and to therefore lose touch with the very thing that brought you together: love.

Love requires a certain amount of focused attention on the other person. When balanced with self-caring and personal responsibility, attention to another's needs is actually fulfilling. This morning my partner was rushing around preparing to fly out of town on business. I saw that he had very little time to accomplish everything he had to do prior to leaving, so I offered to do some of his tasks for him. Bringing him that cup of coffee and his breakfast and helping him pack was immensely satisfying for my heart as well as his.

It is natural and loving in a relationship to pay attention to one another's day-to-day needs and to fulfill them whenever and wherever possible. It is not natural nor is it especially loving to wear yourself out trying to meet another's unspoken expectations. This makes for one exhausted human and one irritated human! Your relationship suffers, you suffer, and ultimately, so does your partner.

If my partner had *expected* me to take care of his needs this morning, without communicating them, this might have become a block in our relationship. Perhaps I would have felt that he had certain expectations, and maybe I would have taken on the job of fulfilling them without his input. This would have put me in the role of having to read his mind. What if I got it wrong? What if he did not want the coffee? What if his real need was for me to iron his shirts? Or, simply stay out of his way? Potentially, I could have spent the morning rushing around doing the wrong things for him and being of no real help.

The other scenario is that I might have resented his expectations. After all, I am frequently quite rushed in the mornings and have no one to do those chores for me—he is usually gone earlier than I am. What right does he have to demand these things from me? By *expecting* me to take care of him, without communicating his needs, he likely would have raised my internal resistance.

Harboring hidden expectations usually accomplishes the reverse of what we want. Rather than opening the other person's heart and motivating him to be more giving, expectations often create the effect of provoking the other person's resistance, stubbornness, and resentment.

Trying to satisfy another person's expectations, particularly trying to make the unhappy person happy, is exhausting to both parties. The unhappy person will still be unhappy—doing things for a person in this state makes no real difference in the long run. Depression, lack of fulfillment or joy, self-loathing, and a negative outlook on life are changeable, but *only if the person seeks appropriate care and help*. The person in this state is not truly helped by an overly attentive partner who has taken on the job of making his life OK. *Hidden expectations impede the natural process of movement through issues and resolution from within and damage our connection in relationships.*

Life is change. Because life is full of change, the context of our communication changes over time. To understand context requires flexibility in the way we hear others. My friend Peggy, for example, tells me one day that she is no longer in love with her boyfriend, Christopher, and they are breaking up. A month later when I see her again, she tells me that she is totally in love with Christopher and can't imagine being with anyone else but with him. One of Peggy's statements is not false and the other true. *Both are her truth* in the context of the day they were spoken.

Another example is that of David and Michelle, who struggled over understanding one another. David listened to Michelle as if every word she spoke was written in stone. If she said it, it must be true, and it would always be true exactly the way she spoke it the first time. If it were ever not true in the future, she obviously lied when she expressed it another way previously. David did not understand *context* in communication and the way it changes over time.

Michelle said, "Yes, I have charged some things to my credit card, but not much, and I am assuming responsibility for paying it off."

Michelle said, "I don't have any debt that is current and I have almost paid off my old debt."

Michelle said, "I have a lot of new debt and I am behind on my payments."

David could not understand why she had all these different stories about the same thing. He began to believe that Michelle was a chronic liar who he could not trust. Even when she behaved in a very loving way toward him, he kept his distance, not believing that anything she said or did was sincere.

Later, when Michelle got into D.A. (Debtor's Anonymous) and began working a recovery program, her story changed yet again. Now, she said, "I have a problem with spending and debting. I use it to make myself feel better about myself. When I told you things about money in the past, I was being so dishonest with myself that I could not possibly tell you the truth."

Gradually, David came to understand that in the *context* of addiction, Michelle's ability to tell him the truth was severely diminished. Yes, it made her untrustworthy, but not for the reasons he assumed. It had nothing to do with a desire on her part to "take him to the cleaners." Rather, it had to do with a damaged relationship with herself that was erupting through overspending.

Given how complicated context is in communication, how do we ever find a way to understand one another? What is the solution to these relationship blocks? In a nutshell: open and honest communication. What makes that possible is to understand our soul's true intentions both on our life path and in our relationships.

Intentions

There are two communication drivers that have the potential to either block the flow of love between partners or to promote powerful healing and growth. Primarily, these are the processes of perception and intention. *Perception* refers to the emotional, psychological, and belief-system filters through which we listen to others. *Intention* refers to the desired outcome of the interaction, situation, or relationship. In the next chapter, we will look at the dynamic of perception. Here, we will look at the dynamic of intention.

Intentions may be conscious or unconscious, higher or lower order. *Intentions are not the same as goals.* Goals are measurable and definable in concrete terms. Goals are statements of end results: "Lose ten pounds, stop smoking."

If we were talking about a ship, a goal would be the destination. There is no mistaking that—you either arrive in New York or San Diego. Intentions are like the rudder of a ship. They steer you on your course of life, and they act as a guide for thoughts, feelings, and behavior: "Be open and honest in my relationships, be self-caring, take personal responsibility for my life." Intentions are also like the gasoline in a car. They provide energy, power, and motivation in order to move us forward.

Relationship goals define the end results that we want with a partner, such as:

- get married
- stay married for the rest of our lives
- have children together
- have sex three times per week
- have one date per week

There is nothing wrong with having relationship goals, as long as we realize that most of them are outside of our direct control. I may have a goal to marry my partner and be married for the rest of our lives, but the end result of that goal depends just as much on the other person as it does on me.

What we do have is *influence* over the course of our relationships, and we may exert that influence in pursuit of a relationship goal. For instance, if a man has the goal of marrying the woman he is dating and staying married to her for the rest of his life, he may *influence* that process by being a loving partner and by showing her that he is devoted to her. He may buy a diamond ring and arrange a romantic setting in which to propose to her. If she loves him and is also intentional about spending her life with him, he will succeed in influencing the course of the relationship into the commitment of marriage. His influence in this case moves the process forward. He does not *make* it happen, he *influences* the course of events, but *the goal of the man will not be achieved unless his partner has the same goal.*

Thus, relationship goals may be set, but unless both partners are in agreement on the goals, they are unlikely to be fulfilled in the long run. Far more powerful is to set relationship intentions with agreement and alignment from both partners.

Individual goals that *affect* our relationships may be set, and over those, we have complete control. For instance, we may have goals such as:

- kiss and hug my partner every day
- ask my partner out for a date once a week
- bring flowers to my partner at least once a month
- give my partner a handwritten card or love letter at least twice a month
- prepare my partner's favorite meal once every two weeks

Goals such as these, though within our control to fulfill, are not effective if the *intentions behind them* are not aligned with our partner's. For instance, a couple may be going through a very difficult and strained period in their relationship. Perhaps the man sees a marriage counselor who advises him to bring back into focus his romantic behavior toward his wife. Armed with this information, he goes home and begins implementing his list of relationship goals. He brings his wife flowers, he takes her out, he buys her gifts, he tells her he loves her, he spends more time with her, and so on.

If the man's lack of devoted behavior was the true problem, then these goals will be effective. She will see that he is focusing on her and their relationship once again, and if he maintains the behavior over time (without reverting to his old pattern of neglect), she will eventually relax, and her loving feelings toward him will return. Their marriage will improve, and they will both feel more satisfied together.

If, however, the real problem is that the woman no longer loves her husband or intends to share her life with him, all the loving behavior goals in the world will not repair their relationship. This is why couples often fail to heal their marriages by addressing the details of who does what and how to do it without looking at the underlying intentions. Sometimes, this happens in marital therapy.

Intention: Relationship Completion

The primary reason that most couples seek marital therapy is not marriage repair or enrichment. It is *relationship completion* for one or both partners. What does that mean?

One possibility is that the primary intentions of their souls in being drawn together have been fulfilled (i.e., to have our children; to re-experience our childhood pain by duplicating old family dynamics; to gain emotional and financial security for a period of time so that we could grow). Having fulfilled those purposes, there is a new choice to be made.

Do we recreate our intentions to share life together based on new purposes, or do we complete the marriage part of our relationship and go forward separately? Most couples do not realize that they have this choice. Once they have the sense that they have completed a primary purpose in choosing one another, they automatically decide to break up.

With the decision to break up often comes suffering over when and how to separate. There is also suffering over the fear of speaking the truth and the consequences that it brings: *I no longer wish to be your marriage partner*. Thus, the main job that falls on most marital therapists is assisting couples to either divorce with as little animosity as possible or to "settle" in some way, perhaps to complete their job as parents or because there are so many painful consequences for divorcing.

Sometimes one partner is clearer than the other that their time together as a couple is coming to an end. That partner may initiate marital therapy under the guise of healing and enrichment, but the true *intention* of the person is to complete the relationship and move on.

Happy, content couples do not seek marital therapy. Individuals who are aligned from their hearts and souls on staying together and being fulfilled do not suffer in their relationships. Couples who practice loving behavior and openhearted communication are usually quite content.

Happy, content couples willingly express the choice to be together. At some time in the history of their relationship, they *consciously chose* to travel through life together, and they made a commitment to one another based on that choice.

The truth of relationships is that people *choose* to be together, or they do not. They choose to be together for a while (weeks, months, years, or decades), or they choose to be together until one of them dies. This choice (from desire, not obligation) springs straight out of their souls' intentions for healing and growth and the recognition that this partner is a truly right person for that process.

The choice of partners from our souls cannot be forced. It cannot be rationalized *into* being (i.e., this person is so wonderful and has so many great qualities, so perhaps I should be with him), nor can it be rationalized *out* of being (i.e., this person is not perfect, so maybe I should leave her). If your souls choose one another, that is it! You are together, for however long you *choose to be*, from your souls' intentions.

Thus, marital therapy often provides little result in the long run, or it provides a "quick fix" that fades almost as soon as the couple exits the therapist's office. *The real issue is the lack of alignment in souls' intentions, and until that is addressed, real love is blocked and the relationship is at risk.*

Sometimes, the painful reality is that one person's soul chooses to be together while the other person's soul does not, or does so for a period of time, but not for a lifetime. When your partner's soul *chooses out* of the relationship, there is nothing you can do to stop that process. You may bring every ounce of your influence to bear upon the situation in an effort to encourage the person to stay, but that will not give you a satisfying relationship.

This is why when one partner has a genuine desire to leave and the other exerts pressure for that person to stay (i.e., "If you leave, I will make sure that you don't see your children," or, "Our friends/family/therapist/minister say it is wrong for you to divorce me,"), it never works. Even if the person stays, it will be in name only, but not in heart and soul. Therefore, if a partner expresses the desire to leave, it is vital to determine what is the *true intention behind it*. Only then do we have the power to intervene and potentially change the course of the relationship.

Intention: Completion and New Possibilities

There is another possibility at play when couples separate. Sometimes, the desire to leave carries the *true intention of changing the path of the relationship in a new direction*. By separating for a time, old patterns are broken and space is created for new ones to emerge, provided there is some process for learning them. These couples often reunite later in life (days, weeks, months, or even years later) and have a totally different way of connecting that is much more satisfying. One couple actually divorced for several years, then reconnected later with an entirely different and far more loving focus. Because their deepest intentions are for relationship change, couples such as this can and often do seek marital therapy or enrichment with positive results.

When the moment of choice is brought to full consciousness in an empowering way, couples may realize that there is a choice to move forward in a brand new way. Breakup and divorce are not inevitable when a relationship no longer works. With the intention to end old patterns and create new ones, the past can be "completed" in a way that opens up new possibilities for a better future. Later, we will look at processes for doing exactly that.

Intention: Avoiding Pain

Sometimes, a person's true intention in leaving is to avoid pain. There is nothing wrong with wanting to get away from that which is perceived to be causing you pain, and when relationships are going through difficult times, it is painful. However, the intention to avoid pain in the short-run does not often yield relief in the long-run.

Often, we leave the current partner in an attempt to end uncomfortable or painful feelings without doing the inner work to determine the cause of those feelings. If the cause of those feelings is our own thoughts, perceptions, reactions, and other dynamics, then changing partners will not solve the problem.

The soul's true intention is always for healing and growth. However, we often read that intention as a reason to switch partners and "jump" out of the relationship. In truth, the partner we originally chose may be a truly right person for fulfilling our soul's intention.

Discovering Intentions: Due Process

How do you know the difference between leaving because it is truly your soul's intention to move on and leaving in order to accomplish another intention? I often give couples the assignment to move toward divorce only after "due process." That means that they make a commitment to remain connected until they have given one another the opportunity to process their emotions, get closure with the past, uncover their true feelings and intentions, and communicate them responsibly and respectfully. Only then can they understand one another's true desires, intentions, and motivations, and choose the appropriate course of action.

In the same way that we must understand intentions in the choice to stay or leave, so also we must strive to get to the heart of our intentions as we interact with one another. Often, the true message, and therefore the energy that brings forth the end result, lies squarely in our intentions. Therein lies one of our most powerful resources for positive change and growth.

The Power of Intentions

Intentions may be of a higher order or of a lower order. *Higher-order intentions aim at bringing forth that which is in our greatest and highest good*: "Practice open, honest, empowering communication in all of my relationships, especially with my partner." *Lower-order intentions aim at having immediate gratification or emotional relief*, often to the detriment of ourselves and others in the larger picture: "Say whatever it takes to keep myself and others from getting upset so that I can feel comfortable at all times."

Both higher- and lower-order intentions are ultimately directed toward healing and growth. *Higher-order intentions get faster results than do lower-order ones*. For instance, if the intention to feel emotionally comfortable at all times with others is ruling your life, and if your relationships are empty and unsatisfying, this is actually working toward your healing. Each time you interact with someone in your life and walk away feeling empty, thwarted, or unfulfilled, you are presented with an opportunity. That opportunity is to re-examine your intentions, shift them to ones that are directed toward your highest and greatest good, and thereby speed up the healing process.

Intentions may be in conflict, especially if they are unconscious. For instance, I may have the conscious intention to have loving, satisfying relationships. Unconsciously, I may have the intention to avoid conflict at all times. If the unconscious intention is stronger than the conscious one (and it usually is), then I will be silent when I know I need to speak up, even though the issue I need to address with the other person is critical. Avoiding dealing with issues in relationships is an emotionally comforting behavior; expressing upset feelings or dissatisfaction to someone else is not. Until I allow myself to get in touch with the emotionally driven, lower-order intentions that are directing my behavior and deal with them, I am bound to fall short and feel thwarted in my conscious, higher-order intentions.

When intentions and goals are fully aligned on both the conscious and unconscious levels, results happen naturally and easily. We create powerful intentions when we step back from the unwanted result (unfulfilling relationships) and consider the larger picture of our lives (being fully alive and self-expressed). Wanting better relationships *represents* something else. It represents a higher-order intention that is aligned with our physical, mental, emotional, and spiritual growth.

If the goal is not aligned with our highest good, we cannot sustain it. That is why we sometimes work so hard for goals that seem to slip away. What we truly need is *change that is healing* and that comes from our highest level of growth. This kind of change yields lasting results. How do we accomplish that? We must begin with our unconscious, lower-order intentions—those that interfere with having what we want.

How do you know what your unconscious intentions are? Look at your life and your relationships and see what you have. *What you manifest* (create, do, are, have, be, tolerate, etc.) *is a direct result of your strongest intentions.* If you do not like what you see in your life or your relationships, the first place to look is at your unconscious intentions: find out what those are, change them, and you will be empowered to make new choices. The results that you desire will follow naturally. The following exercise is designed to assist you in that endeavor.

EXERCISE: UNCONSCIOUS INTENTIONS

Have paper and pen with you. Sit quietly and relax with your favorite soothing music in the background. Light candles if that helps. Close your eyes and take several slow, deep breaths. Do your favorite meditation or prayer if that is supportive to you. When you are ready, open your eyes, take the pen and paper, and begin listing your current life situations (results, what you have, and condition of your relationships) that are not what you want. Do one unwanted result per page, leaving the rest of the page blank for now.

Now, go back to the beginning of the list and, for each unwanted life result, ask yourself, "What is it that I really want?" and write those things down. Again, go back to the beginning of the list and ask for each item, "What thoughts, feelings, patterns, and behaviors have stood in the way of my having that?" Do a fearless inventory, listing all of your current limitations. It is crucial that you do this without self-blame, judgment, or guilt. Blaming yourself for your limitations lets you off the hook from doing something about it.

There is always a psychological gain for what we choose, even with the most limiting and negative patterns. (For example, the psychological gain for not speaking up in a relationship is temporary emotional comfort, which we may seek even though we realize there is damage in the long run.) To address that, go back to the beginning and, for each item, ask yourself, "What have these limiting patterns done for me or given to me?" Dig deep—this information is often not easy to get in touch with. Last, go back to the beginning and ask yourself, "What is the intention that has supported this limiting pattern?" Again, be fearless in your self-inventory. This is for you and you alone.

This is an example of what your exercise might look like:
unwanted result in my life: unfulfilling relationships
what I really want (desired result): to create and maintain loving, fulfilling relationships both with friends and with a special partner (be specific)

Thoughts, feelings, and behaviors that have stood in the way of my having that:
thoughts—I can't do it. I've tried everything and it's just not possible. I'm not comfortable opening up to people or trusting them. I always seem to make bad choices when I fall in love or make friends.
feelings—hopelessness, helplessness, despair
behaviors—avoiding new social situations; trying too hard to "make" people like me; avoiding conflict at all costs; complaining about my lack of close friendships and blaming others

What I have gained from having these limiting patterns:
I feel safe not being very close to others—that way I won't get hurt;

I get to avoid responsibility for choosing new behaviors;

I feel temporarily emotionally comforted when I avoid saying what I really feel;

I don't have to reach out to others for connection—something that scares me;

I get to keep the "status quo"—change is scary!

The intention that has supported these limiting patterns:

to be psychologically and emotionally comfortable by maintaining things as they are; to avoid the pain of facing my fears and overcoming them; to feel safe

This intention is a lower-order intention. It is designed to give you immediate gratification at the cost of something that is important to you over the long run. Lower-order intentions are a result of fear. Now you know what you are dealing with. You have come face-to-face with your fears and you are empowered to make a new choice. It is your choice—to succumb to fear or to step into it and overcome it.

You can choose, today, to face your fears and deal with them. Or you can choose to sidestep this moment, maintain the status quo, and continue to have unfulfilling relationships. It is entirely up to you. There is power in *choosing your current situation,* and there is power in *choosing something new.* Either way, you are no longer a victim of your circumstances; you are no longer frustrated and thwarted. It is clear: *you have exactly what you have intended and chosen.* No one is to blame—not you, and certainly not anyone else. Now, how does all of this apply to our love relationships?

Relationship Intentions

Relationship intentions are often both *unconscious* and *lower order.* One very common lower-order intention in love relationships is to *get unconditional love.*

There is nothing wrong with wanting to be loved. We are born into very small bodies having no ability to care for ourselves. We literally must have someone to love and care for us in order to survive.

Parents and other caretakers are human beings who are flawed and lacking in sufficient resources to satisfy every need of an infant or child. This is a reality of life. Thus, even though most of us get our needs met at a sufficient level to survive and grow up, very few of us get our emotional needs met to our *fullest satisfaction*. Thus, almost all human beings enter adult life with an emotional deficit of love to one degree or another.

In our love relationships, we carry that need to our partners, sometimes consciously, but usually unconsciously. Without realizing it, we may secretly believe that this person who loves us today will be the person who will *always love us unconditionally and perfectly forever and ever*. Thus, one of our primary intentions in choosing a romantic partner is to *get the love* we have always wanted and never quite gotten. Paradoxically, the other primary intention in a romantic relationship is to *protect myself from hurt*. How does this happen?

Being human our partners are never able to give us the perfect, unconditional love we are seeking. They always fall short of our wants, needs, desires, and expectations. We then feel emotions along a continuum from disappointed to wounded to devastated to angry to enraged. These painful emotions are then associated with our partners' failings and shortcomings. The way we see it, this person, because he is the way he is, has *let me down, hurt me, and failed to love me*.

Sometimes, we leave the person at that point. If we stay, however, we may experience a certain amount of healing from the hurt with the passage of time and by shifting our point of view about the situation. However, if the wound is not addressed in a way that truly resolves it, then some measure of the pain is carried forward. This leads to a bit of self-protection or "emotional armoring." The idea is that "since you hurt me, I will not be quite so vulnerable with you in the future." Now the intention to be self-protective kicks in.

Conflicting Intentions

The intentions to *get love* and *protect myself* are conflicting intentions. In order to *be loved*, we must *attract love* by being loving, openhearted, trusting, and emotionally vulnerable. When our hearts are open and we are vulnerable, the possibility exists that we may get hurt. This means that in order to be loved, we must behave in ways that go against the intention to protect ourselves.

Likewise, in order to protect ourselves from hurt, we must behave in ways that go against the intention to be loved.

If we are unconscious of these conflicting intentions, our relationships can be somewhat schizophrenic. One minute we are loving, trusting, and openhearted with our loved one. The next minute, when he or she does something that "pushes an emotional button," we are angry, defensive, guarded, and untrusting. Pushed to the extreme, these diametrically opposing intentions and the resulting reactions lead to high drama. Acted out, this is the couple that makes passionate love one day, then fights ferociously and breaks up the next.

High drama in a love relationship is interesting to observe on the movie or television screen. In fact, human beings have been writing and portraying these kinds of "love stories" for ages. In real life, it blocks our connection and slows down our access to personal and spiritual growth.

When our hearts are wide open and trusting with another person, it is like a big balloon inflating with all kinds of positive feelings and sensations. Imagine that while the balloon is inflated, you begin to argue. As you express your differences calmly and gently, the air is slowly leaking out of the balloon—not much, just a little. Just enough air (heightened positive emotion) leaves the balloon so that your energy can shift to a more rational perspective to solve the issue that is on the table. When the issue is solved, you reconnect, and the balloon slowly inflates with positive emotions once again.

Now imagine the same scenario, only this time your argument escalates rapidly into shouting, name-calling, expletives, and crying. Your differences are not being sorted out; instead, you are holding firm to your positions with guns blazing. Now, look at the balloon. POP! All the positive emotions are exploded into the air and are replaced by toxic feelings of outrage, pain, and despair. Your rational self has fled the battlefield, your heart has taken cover, and there is nowhere to hide.

This kind of scenario is shocking to the system, like having a car crash. Even if your body is not seriously wounded, you still suffer from a degree of shock. Your system needs recovery time before it is fully functioning once again. Perhaps you need a few hours, or perhaps you need a few days, depending on the degree of emotional damage.

If you have sufficient recovery time, by behaving in very gentle ways with one another over the next few hours, days, and weeks, there is a good possibility that you will be able to move past this damaging episode. You have the possibility of reconnecting, reviewing what took place with compassion, and forgiving one another for the mistakes that were made. Your love, trust, and openhearted connection can be restored. You can actually grow from the experience and enrich your partnership. This is only possible, however, if you and your partner are able to shift away from the lower-order intentions of *getting love* and *being self-protective* and into the higher-order intentions of *giving love* and *being openhearted.*

If the lower-order intentions run the show, you are likely to continue to behave in a knee-jerk fashion. You pull apart and remain wounded. The emotional wounds fester, you keep up your guard, and the intention to protect yourself remains locked in. Your heart aches with the desire for your partner to come to you and make it all OK. You want his/her love, but are unable to reach out in love, leaving you in a very painful emotional state.

Soon, you react from your pain, and another argument or fight ensues. Since the old wounds were not healed and your connection was not restored, you have even less to draw upon in the wake of this second "crash." If this becomes a repetitive cycle, the relationship deteriorates into a series of battles with periods of calm. The original sense of deep love and connection, of trust and positive emotions, is lost. Because you are so emotionally guarded, you are unable to deeply connect. Growth is inhibited, slowed to a crawl as you find yourselves suffering, coping, and getting by.

Higher-order relationship intentions go straight to the heart of love and focus on the quality of our connection. Examples of these are:

be affectionate with my partner on a daily basis
be emotionally open and available to my partner as much as I am able
notice my partner's needs and address them whenever and wherever possible

Love in its most powerful form is much more than a feeling. It is a strong and true intention, containing heartfelt emotions, and manifesting as behavior.

Love is an action verb, not merely a psychological or emotional state. Loving behavior demonstrates love far more powerfully than the words, "I love you," although it is powerful to say those words when they are sincere.

Setting Powerful Relationship Intentions

Language is a huge part of the behavior of love. How we speak and listen to one another in our day-to-day interactions conveys potent messages of our deepest thoughts, feelings, and intentions. Likewise, the intentions we consciously set for our relationships enable us to have communication (both language and behavior) that nurtures and empowers us in our Soul Partnering. This is done through a conscious process of *noticing* (by looking at what we are currently manifesting), *redeciding* (choosing another way to take care of our needs), and then *recreating* (a higher order and thus more empowering intention).

In conscious communication, we attend closely to our intentions, striving to set positive ones that encourage honesty and openness in the process. If I notice that I am intending to "protect myself" from pain and I realize that that is a very low level of intention, I can choose to correct my intention. I may remind myself that there is nothing to protect myself against (letting go of the illusion of control), and I may decide to trust the process. I can set an intention that we both have an empowering outcome from our conversation.

In conscious communication, we examine the possibility that we may have a personal agenda standing in the way of a fulfilling relationship. A personal agenda that takes care of one person without fully honoring the other (as a separate person with other thoughts, feelings, needs, etc.) creates a block in the relationship. For instance, goals/agendas such as the following work against an open, loving, honest Soul Partnership:

get someone to change;
make someone love me;
get someone to commit to me;
prevent loneliness;
get over someone else;
get someone to marry me so that I can "get on with my life"; i.e., have children, create a family, be secure, etc.;

avoid dealing with my fears;

make up for past disappointments and pain;

get someone to "rescue" me from my life;

sidestep emotional pain or issues in my life.

In order to set empowering intentions in your relationship, you must truly understand one another, what is in your hearts and souls, your individual and joint paths of life, and your wants, needs, desires, and expectations. In short, *you must truly listen to one another and honor all that you hear.* This takes an extraordinary depth of communication! Later, once the Soul Talk listening and speaking tools have been utilized and practiced, you will be ready to co-create and set powerful, loving intentions for your relationship, intentions that are for the greatest good of both partners and all those whose lives you touch.

R E L A T I O N S H I P   E X E R C I S E

Reflect on your last interaction that seemed difficult. Now, ask yourself, "What was the *context* of that conversation?" List the things that were going on in your lives, your emotional state, your partner's emotional state, etc. Be sure to acknowledge anything that may have had an effect on how the conversation went. Next, ask yourself, "What was my *true intention* in that conversation?" Dig deep, and be willing to acknowledge any personal agenda (expectations, wants, desires, etc.) that you may have brought to the conversation. Now, take turns sharing what you discovered about yourself in a compassionate and gentle way. Do not try to "fix" your partner's issues. Simply listen respectfully. Keep reading—in chapter 11 there will be specific exercises for setting powerful relationship intentions that maximize love and growth together.

Chapter Four
Perception, Stories, and Projection

All of communication is energy—words that are spoken, a look in the eye, body posturing, behavior, and facial expression. *All of these things and so much more make up the energy that flows between us.* Someone once said that there is no such thing as *not communicating* in a relationship. Even the act of refusing to talk is a communication, as anyone who has ever been given "the silent treatment" knows.

Energy is discernible between partners who are closely connected. When it feels "off," the intuitive part of us "knows" and cannot feel quite right until we find out what our partner is feeling.

When we communicate, in whatever way we choose, we pass energy to our listener. If we feel loving, then the ways we speak to one another, look at one another, or touch one another convey that energy. Our loving energy is circular, passing from each of us to the other, enriching our experience together.

Last night was one of those experiences for us. It was a beautiful, rare, quiet night in the city. We held hands, strolled along, and talked softly. Suddenly, in the sky, we witnessed a huge, bright streak falling slowly to Earth (asteroid or comet—we did not know). We dubbed it our "shooting star" and talked about how it might be symbolic of our hopes and dreams for our lives together. We ate dinner sitting on the terrace of a quaint neighborhood restaurant, gazing into each other's eyes, talking and laughing together. We both commented over and over that it was a "magical" evening. Love was flowing. We both felt a heightened sense of well-being that spilled over into the next several days.

Not all of our evenings are like that. Like all couples, we occasionally have tension between us. When that happens, we comment that we feel drained and tired afterward. There is a definite correlation between our emotional state together and our mental and physical well-being in general.

It is well documented that loving, positive energy from one person to another is beneficial emotionally, spiritually, and physically. One of the largest studies on aging concluded that a good, loving, long-term relationship is an essential ingredient to growing old well. Of the four key factors to successful aging, three had a direct bearing on relationships:

1) gratitude, forgiveness, and optimism
2) empathy
3) the ability to reach out[4]

Negative relationship energy is strongly correlated with mental and physical ill health. When I work with clients who have spent years in draining, unloving, or toxic relationships, a large part of our work is focused on the process of recovery—of physical, mental, emotional, and spiritual well-being. *Therefore, it is important to look at communication, not just as words or even body language, but as the essence of the energy we give to one another.*

In distressed relationships, couples often "act out" that which they do not feel comfortable saying. Instead of saying, "I feel threatened when you go out. I am afraid that you will meet someone new and that you will leave me for someone else," Steve becomes resentful and childish when his partner spends the evening out with her girlfriends. He is short with her, he gives her the silent treatment, and he rolls over away from her in bed when she comes home that night. Instead of saying, "I feel controlled by your actions and angry with you because of that," Cheryl withholds affection and love for several days after.

Even though they are not speaking their true feelings, this couple is nevertheless conveying energy—he is sending fear and anger to her, and she is responding with resentment and disconnection.

Remaining unconscious to the feelings that are generating the behavior/communication/energy, we feel something, do not like the feeling, react, and give a knee-jerk (not thought out) response to our partner. *Knee-jerk reactions and the resulting behavior are the source of most relationship distress.* This is the opposite of well-intentioned, creative communication.

Stories: Fact or Fiction

What causes knee-jerk reactions? In a nutshell, it is the *stories* that we make up in our minds and hearts *based on our perceptions* about a person and a situation.

Human beings love to create and tell stories. Our incredibly complex minds give rise to language with its infinite variety of expressions. Language enables us to represent our world. With it, we create stories enabling us to relate to the world and to other people, to attempt to make sense of our lives.

Stories happen in a constant stream throughout our day, whether we are conscious of them or not. "It's Friday…now I have to go home and face Lisa…she's probably ticked off that I'm running late…it won't make any difference that I stopped off and bought flowers for her…she only remembers what I do wrong…I'm tired of her critical attitude…I really don't know if I want to be in this relationship anymore…but it's really not that bad…anyway, I doubt if there's anyone better out there…" and so on and so on, infinitely. About everything and everyone.

Stories may be critical or they may be loving, based on facts or fiction. We may keep our stories internal (self-talk) or we may externalize them (communication).

Stories are actually *mostly fiction*. This is a difficult concept for most humans to grasp—that our treasured stories are mostly created.

For instance, in the internal monologue above, what are the actual facts in this story? If the person's watch is accurate and if he has an agreement to be home at a certain time, then he is, in fact, late. All the rest is made up. The remainder of that monologue is fiction.

But, wait, you say. What if he is right about his partner? What if it is true that she won't like him being late again? And what if the rest of it is true as well? What if he is right that she never notices when he does things right and she is critical?

It is still fiction *until there is validation for it*. When he walks in the door and he asks her, "Are you upset I am late?" and she says yes, then that part of his story becomes fact. When he asks, "Does it help that I brought flowers and that I am normally on time?" and she says, "No," then that part becomes fact.

The problem is that we rarely take the time to confirm the validity of the stories we have about the other people in our lives. We do not check out our perceptions about others with the source—the other person. It is so much easier to carry on the internal dialogue and self-validate it. The problem is that we then go one step further. We *decide* or *conclude* that our story is fact, and then we become righteous about it.

If someone challenges us about the correctness of our story, particularly if it is the other person involved, we may become inflamed and indignant and begin to argue. It is easy at that point to get into the position of, "I'm right and you're wrong!" Once we get into right/wrong dynamics, we are on the way to creating damage in the relationship. It can happen so fast that unless we consciously step back to examine the process, we are unaware of what has just transpired, and any possibility of understanding one another is lost.

Stories to Keep Us Safe

In the absence of information or clear communication, the mind will make up a story about what is happening. I call this "filling in the gap." One of my clients, whom I will call Tony, had a painful story to tell. He and his partner had broken up abruptly (initiated by her) and with virtually no communication. Almost from one day to the next, they were a couple and then they were not. Tony tried in vain to get her to talk to him about what was wrong, but she refused to do so.

Without knowing his partner's true heart and mind about the situation, Tony was left to his imagination. He ruminated and obsessed about the relationship, examined everything that had taken place from the moment they met until the day they parted. Why, he wondered, did she leave?

Then one day, Tony reported that his ex, Sharon, had called and invited him to dinner. They spent over an hour together, yet he did not ask one question about why she broke up with him. I was astonished! He went to dinner with her three times, and each time, he participated in keeping the conversation entirely superficial despite my coaching that he invite her to share about what went wrong.

Tony was reluctant to get the truth on the table. In fact, he was afraid of hearing the truth *because it might not be what he wanted.* It was easier to go on with the internal dialogue, the constant speculation and assumptions about what she was thinking and feeling, and the self-created stories. That way, he could maintain the hope that she might magically return to him.

Our stories are comforting to us. They represent our world view to which we are firmly attached. We cling to them and wrap them around us like worn security blankets because we do not want to be disturbed by unpleasant truths from the outside.

Maintaining our story helps us feel safe, but it does not foster growth. In relationships, the stories we create can act as tremendous blocks to intimacy.

Intimacy, personal growth, and spiritual expansion require truth, *especially when it hurts.* Only by looking at how things truly are can we make well-informed and therefore wise choices.

The Nature of Our Love Stories

I do not think we have a choice about creating, thinking about, and talking in stories. It is simply human nature to do so. What we have a choice about is the *nature* of the stories that we make up about our lives and our relationships.

Our stories may be slanted in a particular direction. They may be told in a way and from a point of view that is negative, withholding, judgmental, harsh, critical, and disempowering. They may be told in a way that obscures the truth and maintains illusions. On the other hand, they may be told in a way that *embraces the truth without being emotionally crippling.*

Have you ever listened to a friend who has recently been through a bitter divorce? It is difficult to imagine how your friend could have ever married such a demon. Yet, prior to and on the wedding day, you heard such glowing stories about your friend's beloved. This is such a contradiction that it is hard to fathom.

The typical way we reconcile these two opposing stories about our relationships is to make up yet another piece of fiction. "My ex sure had me fooled!" While there are certainly true-life cases of con-artists who set out to trick someone into marriage, that is not what the vast majority of people do. However, during courtship we all put our best foot forward, then naively believe that our partner's most wonderful and charming qualities are all of who they are.

The reality is that because we are human, we inevitably get around to showing the parts of ourselves that are not so cool. In good relationships, we forgive those qualities and avoid making up negative stories about them. In distressed relationships, we latch onto them and make up long, dramatic stories about our partners.

In our love relationships, we make up the greatest number of stories. These are the stories that are at the center of our lives—how we relate to those we love and they to us. The *nature* of these intimate love stories has everything to do with how happy and fulfilled we are with our partners. Therefore, *the nature of our love stories has everything to do with the nature of the energy that flows between us.* When our stories about our partners are negative, the love that is normally present in our hearts is blocked, damaging our connection and our ability to address the issues. Later in the chapter, we will look at how to create what I call "useful fiction" that empowers the flow of love.

Misperceptions

Why would we make up negative stories about our partner? We do so because our *perceptions* and *beliefs* about what is happening in the relationship are often inaccurate. They are misperceptions, "missed perceptions," quite literally.

Misperceptions are the results of analyzing, judging, assuming, and drawing conclusions about others' thoughts, feelings, and behavior. They are also the result of knee-jerk emotional reactions that are based in the past and often have little to do with the present. Misperceptions feed into disempowering stories that tear apart our connection. Negative stories feed into more misperceptions. Over time, this can become a vicious cycle that is difficult to break.

These negative perceptions and the resulting emotions can, and often do, escalate over time if they are not interrupted. Painful emotions in a relationship lead to ineffectual and even toxic behavior, and those can eventually become habitual. I call these "Communication Habits That Do Not Work."

EXERCISE: COMMUNICATION HABITS THAT DO NOT WORK

As you read the items on the list, simply *put a check beside the ones that you have ever done at some time in the past.* (If you are like most humans, including myself, you will have a lot of check marks!) When I do this in workshops, I usually hear a lot of moans and groans. It is not easy to admit the less than wonderful behavior that we have displayed in our relationships! Uncomfortable as it is, I encourage you to be fearlessly honest with yourself. This is for no one but you and is for the purpose of your growth. At the same time, I caution you to not indulge in self-blame either.

____Putting words in someone else's mouth: i.e., "You don't love me…" or, "You don't really want to go out with me tonight, that's why you have to work late."

____"You" statements (which are usually combined with some sort of negative judgment): "You forgot to call me because you are so inconsiderate…"

____Disguised "you" statements: "I *feel* that you don't really want to go out with me…"

____Listening judgmentally: (thinking) "What a bunch of bologna! You're just saying that because you don't want to take responsibility for your own behavior."

____Listening with no attempt to understand the other person: instead, planning your own rebuttal points, having an emotional reaction, or waiting for them to stop talking so that you can have your say.

____Second-guessing: (thinking) "You don't really mean that. You're just saying that to get to me. I refuse to believe that the thoughts and feelings that you are expressing are true."

____Sentences that begin with, "You always" or, "You never."

____Teasing, ridicule, sarcasm, or jokes at someone else's expense.

____Put-downs, insults, berating.

____Rather than addressing the issue at hand, putting the entire relationship on the line: "This just isn't going to work; it's too hard; we're too different; I don't trust you, etc."

____Deflecting the issue at hand by bringing up another: "Oh yeah? Well, how about the time you…"

____Being right or being righteous: "I don't care what you say about it, this is how it *really* is." Alternatively, "No matter how my actions affect you, I was right to do what I did."

____Shoring up your position of being right by telling your friends or associates what the person did (from your point of view only).

____Talking over, talking louder, yelling.

____Using expletives.

____Withholding important communications by having both sides of the conversation internally, drawing conclusions, and deciding not to share.

____Cutting off communication because you are angry, hurt, or scared.

____Ending a relationship (friendship, romantic, or family) by distancing yourself because you are hurt, angry, or scared, without communicating to the other person what hurt, scared, or angered you.

____Making negative interpretations about someone else's character based on something he/she did: i.e., "I asked you to bring me a glass of water while I was doing the yard work, and you refused. Therefore, you are mean, selfish, and incapable of giving."

____Speaking for another without permission.

____Withholding attention with no notice: e.g., the other person is talking and you think about something else, watch television, or read the paper, pretending you are listening. Even worse, getting defensive when they point it out. (The truth is, you *cannot* truly listen to someone or, more importantly, give that person the experience of being listened to, without giving that person your undivided attention.)

____When someone comes to you with a genuine apology, instead of being compassionate and forgiving, using that opportunity to blame the other person for your own reaction to what he/she did.

____Dumping your emotions with no commitment to resolving the issue.

____Analyzing and labeling the other person without his/her permission: "You did that because you are commitment-phobic, because you are codependent, because you were adopted, etc." Even worse, drawing conclusions and projecting a negative future based on your analysis and conclusions: "Therefore, you are not a good risk as a relationship partner."

____Not keeping a promise. "I'll call you at 6:00," but you do not call until 6:30. Even worse, making an excuse rather than acknowledging your mistake and offering an apology. (When this becomes a habit in a relationship, trust and respect are seriously undermined.)

____Making demands that carry negative consequences, issuing ultimatums, or manipulating the other person to get your way.

____Asking questions in order to "corner" the other person into admitting something they do not wish to share that is personal, private, or potentially embarrassing.

____Asking questions in order to manipulate the other person into agreeing with your point of view or in order to get your way.

____Having expectations of the other person without communicating them.

____Keeping score against your partner.

____Debating and arguing without setting up the rules of debate or having a stated purpose in doing so. (A debate can be very useful, provided two or more people agree that that it is a debate, and they agree on the rules.)

____Being "the martyr." Blaming oneself for the whole issue, getting upset and crying in the middle of the discussion, and putting oneself down. (This one is insidious, as it looks like we are taking responsibility when, in fact, we are avoiding responsibility by being pitiful.)

Are there more? Without a doubt! This list could go on and on. Unfortunately, we are so creative as human beings that we can think of endless ways to interact that are hurtful in our relationships. Why would we choose such behaviors? Why would we not easily and naturally listen with open hearts and speak lovingly at all times?

Fear

In a nutshell, we do these things for the most part unconsciously and for one main reason: as a reaction to or as a result of something else. That something else is *painful emotion*. The most painful emotion of all in a relationship is fear. Fear (of being hurt) leads to defensiveness and that leads to a closed heart, a judgmental mind, disempowering stories, and any one or more of the behaviors in our list above.

Additionally, we add to the cycle of pain each and every time we interact in a negative way, particularly if we do not have a system for "clearing up" the past hurts. Unresolved hurt leads to more hurt and emotional sensitivity, all of which leads to more defensiveness, and thus, more bad behavior. You see the vicious cycle in which we may find ourselves trapped. How do we break this cycle?

First, we must examine the true source of painful emotions in a relationship, and that is the phenomenon of *psychological projection*. What that means is that we all have the very human tendency to project our own history, issues, and emotional baggage onto another person, particularly our romantic partners.

Projections
Hidden Obstacles

The most common misperception that we have in communication is that the other person *causes* us emotional pain. When something goes wrong in the interaction and it feels bad, the human tendency is blame the other person for those painful emotions. Of course, other people always manage to behave in ways that make it very easy to do this.

For example, imagine that you and your beloved have a date after work on Thursday night. You agree to meet at 7:00 at your favorite restaurant for drinks and dinner. You arrive promptly at 7:00 and take a seat in the bar. At

8:00, your partner breezes in the door with a huge smile, kisses you, and orders a martini. What do you do? How do you respond to this situation?

The answer is, "It depends." It depends on your past history together, your history prior to this relationship, the level of stress that day, how apologetic your partner is, how much alcohol you have consumed while you were waiting, and maybe half a dozen other factors. If your partner is almost never late, your response might be a huge sigh of relief and a question or two to find out why this happened. If your partner is frequently late, you may launch into a lecture about how inconsiderate it is of him to do this to you again.

If you have a past relationship in which someone stood you up at a restaurant and then broke up with you by telephone two days later, you might burst into tears. The emotions that you are feeling have a huge bearing on your reaction. Your past history and many other factors dictate your emotions. Thus, *each person's reaction to the same circumstance will be different.*

One person might simply enjoy the time sitting in the bar, perhaps watching a game on television and sipping a cool drink, grateful for the "down time" after a hard day at work. Another person might spend that time worrying and fantasizing about accidents and hospitals. Yet another person may think, "My partner is with someone else having an affair!" Yet another person will simply leave after twenty minutes and figure there was a miscommunication and you will see each other later.

The point is this: *the emotions, if any, that are triggered in this incident stem more from each person's past experiences and current context than they do from the incident itself.* Yet, we often fail to recognize this in our responses to our partners' behaviors.

Let us say that you are the one who has been stood up and dumped in the past. When your partner comes in the door, first you feel relief—there was no accident! Then you feel anger. You are shocked that your partner could be so inconsiderate—an hour late, no phone call, and no apology.

Your thoughts then go toward remembering other times your partner has not been considerate of you. The more you focus on these feelings and painful memories, the more your body quakes with the intensity. Deep down, your anger is covering the fear that you felt as you waited endlessly for your partner to show up. If you let yourself get in touch with it, you feel the sense of abandonment down to your core. Bouncing around in the depths of those emotions, you then encounter rage—the rage of wanting something so much that you cannot have, of being out of control of others and their behavior.

Being a human being and struggling with these kinds of emotions, especially in a crowded restaurant, is not easy. If you are like most human beings, the way you handle it is to attack your partner for what you are feeling. Being human, you are going to *blame your partner for causing your emotions by being late*. That is how projection works.

Projection is the basis of most relationship illusions. Relationship illusions are beliefs about our partner (or the relationship itself) that have gone unchallenged for so long that in our minds they are facts. Once illusion becomes fact, it is extremely hard to change.

Projections that are allowed to perpetuate can undermine the very basis of our relationship, erode our love, and destroy our connection. What can we do to avoid this trap? Let's begin by examining where they come from and what the true purpose is of projections.

Opportunities to Heal

At the moment of greatest upset with a partner, we are witnesses to the qualities we most dislike in another person. We see in other people anger, greed, lust, selfishness, laziness, and dishonesty. In our partners, we see rudeness, lack of consideration, lack of caring, self-centeredness, and stubbornness. We see in that person the traits that we do not wish to see in ourselves. We see these "negative" qualities over there, in that person, because *it is far easier to be a witness to someone else's failings than it is to acknowledge our own.*

The purpose of projection is to protect the ego, that vulnerable part of ourselves that seeks to be worthy in all ways. The ego is that part of the self that is the depository of every message that we have ever been given about ourselves. It contains our parents' voices, either building us up or tearing us down. It contains the voices of teachers, childhood peers, siblings, extended family members, and religious leaders, all of whom gave us feedback about how we were doing.

"You can do anything!"
"You're no good and you'll never amount to anything!"

"You're a wonderful artist!"
"Maybe math isn't your best subject."
"I'm so proud of you."
"I'm so ashamed of you."

The ego also contains the conclusions that we have drawn about ourselves and the decisions we have made based on the feedback we were given.

"I've got to try harder!"
"What a screw-up I am."
"I'll show them—I'll be somebody!"
"What do they know?"
"They were evil! I'll never let anyone hurt me that way again!"

The ego's purpose is to take all of this material and create a reason to live and a way to be. Its mission is to fashion a self-portrait that is viable and defendable. The ego has no outside perspective—it is focused on itself and its own survival.

There is nothing wrong with the ego and its purpose. However, the ego is limited in its usefulness when it comes to intimate relationships. The ego is often so busy protecting itself that it fails to be compassionate toward another.

The ego does accomplish one very valuable function in relationships. It can serve to remind us of our self-esteem when that is necessary. When presented with an abusive relationship, a healthy ego demands action. Either change it or leave it.

On a higher level, projections serve another, far more powerful purpose than simply protecting the ego. Let us look at how this works.

Continuing with the example above, as your partner defends himself, there is a process of judgment taking place within you. You look at him, you hear his words, and what you see is that he is, without a doubt:

uncaring
insensitive
rude
not loving
etc.

Because of the ego's function, your judgment tells you that these qualities you are witnessing in your partner belong exclusively to him. Yet, have you not ever acted in an insensitive way to another? Have you *never, ever* been rude? Have you not at times placed your needs above another's in an uncaring way?

Your ego says, "No!" However, your higher truth says, "Of course!" At this moment, you are presented with a choice: *to listen to your higher truth or to listen to your ego.* If you listen to your ego, you will quite naturally attack and blame your partner, accusing him of displaying the very characteristics of which you are yourself guilty. If you listen to your higher truth, you will step into a tremendous opportunity for learning and growth. This is a truly wonderful opportunity, believe it or not!

This is the opportunity for self-examination and exploration, for noticing those parts of the self that are wounded and in need of healing, and for intervening in a destructive cycle. Our partners, when they behave in ways that "push our emotional buttons," give us the chance to see those aspects of ourselves that we do not want to see. Yet, we need to see *all parts of ourselves* in order to experience unconditional self-love and self-care and be able to extend that to another.

I cannot accept only the good in myself and be whole. If I say that I am all-giving and never selfish, then I refuse acceptance of the selfish part of me. Because I do not accept the selfish part of me, I repress it—that is, I attempt to push it away, *not* to be selfish. If I am never selfish in my behavior, then I am likely also to deny myself the dynamic of self-care. There is, after all, an element of selfishness in being self-caring.

I cannot only see the negative in myself and be whole. If I constantly examine my "faults" and shortcomings, criticize myself, and fail to see my assets, I become a victim to myself and to my own way of thinking. I cut myself off at the emotional knees, disempowering myself and letting myself off the hook from taking action in my life. After all, what can a worthless, no-good person do to make things better?

All human beings are flawed. All humans have parts of themselves that are selfish, self-centered, egotistic, lazy, resentful, mean, bigoted, uncaring, unloving, and pathetic.

All human beings are perfect. All humans have parts of themselves that are wise, loving, insightful, generous, accomplished, capable, committed, and powerful.

I am all of these things and more, and you are all of those things and more. We are every quality that we admire and respect, and we are every quality that we loathe and disdain.

We are all of these things, but we do not always choose to act on these qualities. We may act on some of them and not on others. We may act on some of them a lot, on others not much. Thus, the universal human traits that we all possess exist within us as a *field of possibilities*. Like the genetic blueprint that is common to all humans, so is the blueprint of our emotional and behavioral characteristics and traits.

What creates our experiences in life and in our relationships is not so much the potential of all human qualities (the field of all possibilities) that we possess, but rather the degree to which we bring forth certain ones of those qualities in our attitudes, perceptions, choices, and behaviors.

I am at heart very selfish. I think about myself, my needs, my feelings, my wishes and desires, and my life from the time I wake up until the time I fall asleep. I could tell you a big long story about how I got that way, but the bottom line is that I am selfish!

I am at heart very giving. There are many hours each week that I spend listening to and supporting others, some as clients (that is my job for which I get paid) and some because they are friends and family.

I am both giving and selfish. I am also self-caring, though sometimes I forget to be. I endeavor to reach out to others and care for them, though at times I forget to do so.

The fact that I am giving at times does not justify the fact that at times I am overly selfish. When I neglect a relationship or hurt someone's feelings, I still have the job of stepping forward to make amends wherever possible.

The fact that I am self-centered at times does not take away from the times that I am caring toward others. When I reach out to someone else, take care of a friend who is sick or down, or give to a cause, it is in no way diminished by my careless deeds at other times. The two sides of me are simply that—the two sides of me. I have had two sides of my nature since the day I was born, and I will have two sides until I pass away from this lifetime.

All of this does not mean I have found total self-acceptance. Far from it! There are days that I am proud of my accomplishments. There are also days that I am deeply remorseful for my perceived failures. I do not know if I can reach total acceptance of all parts of me in this lifetime. I have an intention to do so. In choosing to develop self-acceptance, I open the door to more fulfilling relationships and a more rewarding life. I cannot give to others what I am blocked in giving to myself.

When we deny our negative nature, we wrap embarrassment, secrecy, and shame around those qualities. Then, we "pretend" that they do not exist so that we do not have to feel the embarrassment. This is like having a wound, putting the thickest bandage on it that we can find, and pretending it is not there. Without looking at it, we cannot know what kind of treatment is needed. Over time, it festers, becomes infected, and turns into an overall health issue.

When another person displays the very thing that we are denying, it creates a feeling of recognition. *We see in that person what we refuse to see in our self.* Not only do we feel recognition, we also feel the pain of the wound that is at the core of that characteristic (usually painful events and/or relationships in our past). All of this happens in a flash.

Knee-Jerk Reactions

When projections grip us and we are in the midst of intense emotions stemming from old issues, it is difficult to temper our responses. However, it is not impossible to do so. In fact, I have trained lots of people to do exactly that.

First, consider the process. Something happens and it reminds us of past hurts. In the brain, the connections between the present and the memories of past pain are activated. There are actual neural pathways that connect the present to the past, and our thoughts and feelings are activated by those connections almost instantaneously[5].

Once the connections are made, a response or reaction is inevitable. The first response is biological. If the situation evokes feelings of fear and pain, heart rate goes up, skin may begin to perspire, the stomach goes into a knot, breathing becomes shallow and rapid, and the eyes dilate. Adrenaline is dumped into the blood stream, putting us into "red alert." This is what is known as the "fight or flight" response, essential to human survival since the dawn of time, enabling us to have sudden bursts of energy in order to escape something threatening or to fight if needed.

When fear is activated, these biological responses are not a choice, at least initially. Our bodies are designed to respond in this way and *we do not have a choice about that*.

The next step, however, is something about which we have a great deal of choice, and that is action. What action follows these emotional and physical responses? In unconscious communication, it is the knee-jerk reaction. We react in ways that stem directly from intense, painful emotions—no good outcomes flow out of that. However, it does not have to be that way.

There are solutions that help us change our emotional state and choose new responses in our relationship. I call them "taking back the projections," "widening the gap," and "creating useful fiction."

Soul Partnering and Self-Acceptance

The gift of relationships is that they offer the opportunity for us to take off the emotional bandages, examine the wound, provide the appropriate care, and heal. In doing so, we find the miracle of self-acceptance. In the same way that we must learn self-acceptance, we must also develop acceptance of others in order to have a great relationship. Because Soul Partnerships are so intimate and often quite intense, they bring up our "core" issues, the ones that go to the heart of what our lives are about. These are our deepest issues, the ones that require the most healing.

Unconsciously, we choose people who have the ability to push those emotional buttons that go to our "core" issues. On the level of our soul's intentions to heal, this is how we choose who to love and by whom to be loved. On a conscious level, it rarely occurs to us when we are falling in love that this person will be an agent for our healing and growth.

This works in regard to both our positive and negative traits, both our light and dark sides. I have difficulty acknowledging the impatient side of me. Sure enough, my partner "shows up" as impatient, and I feel irritated, annoyed, and irrationally judgmental. Sometimes, I do not instantly realize what is happening, and I find myself snapping at him about his lack of patience. Often the very next minute, hour, or day, I am pushing him or someone else about something—impatient and wanting things on my timetable.

Sometimes I forget that I am good, loving, and generous. Then my partner "shows up" around me being incredibly generous and giving, and I see that as being *his* quality and not mine. I actually feel smaller in his presence because he is being so "big" with his heart. Then he gently reminds me that I am that way as well, and my heart swells so that it feels as if I cannot contain it. Sometimes, at the moment that I am being acknowledged by him, tears flow. These tears are healing those parts of me that are absolutely magnificent but that were denied and repressed earlier in life.

In this way, my Soul Partner helps me gradually reclaim all parts of myself. Not that he *does that* for me. He *presents the opportunity for that* by being in my life and by expressing himself. What an incredible gift!

Taking Back the Projections

When we communicate unconsciously, we believe that what we see in our partner belongs exclusively to the other person. Interacting from our projections, we have only two ways to respond: blame or guilt. Either way, we feel powerless and doomed. We cannot change our partner and we cannot instantly change ourselves.

If I recognize myself first, then you, I am in my healing path and my eyes are opened about the dynamics of our relationship. That is something I can influence. That is "taking back the projections"—the first step to conscious communication.

Conscious Communication

In conscious communication, we realize that there is *always some element of ourselves we are seeing in the other person when we are upset*. We acknowledge that whatever it is we are judging in the other is on this side of the fence as well.

In conscious communication, we begin with our perceptions, recognizing they are simply that and nothing more. What I believe about you may or may not be the truth, and it may be standing in the way of my knowing you. What my experience is in the past with relationships has little or no bearing on my current situation with you, and it may be preventing me from dealing with you in the present moment.

In conscious communication, we view the internal distress over our partner's "bad behavior" as an opportunity for self-healing. (The exercises at the end of this chapter will assist in that process.)

What creates a positive outcome that allows love to flow is *being responsible for our own emotions*. We take back the projections when we acknowledge that no one ever truly *makes* us feel what we feel. We open the door for our own growth and that of the relationship when we view our upsets as an opportunity to know and accept ourselves on a deeper level.

People do what they do! That is a fact of life. Sometimes people, including our beloved partners, do things that are not loving, considerate, or empowering. Sometimes they do things that are downright mean, nasty, selfish, careless, and ugly. Do we have feelings about that? Of course! We would not be human if we did not.

We do not, however, have to be a prisoner of our own reactions to others' behavior. We have a choice in the "moment of truth" about what we do. We can step back, take inventory of ourselves, and recognize the projections that are taking place. We can consciously choose self-discovery, recovery, healing, and growth.

Stepping into the Gap

In between the internal response mechanisms and the behavior lies *the gap*. The gap is *the split-second after the feelings and prior to the behavior*.

In unconscious communication, the gap is very small and very short. Something happens, feelings erupt, and like the old saying, "Bada bing, bada boom!" We react with angry, hurtful words, and often a raised voice.

In unconscious communication, we make no distinction between the event (other person's behavior), the internal responses (biological, chemical, emotional), and the reaction (our behavior). Thus, it feels as though they are all one and the same. The end result is the perception that "you made me do it!" or, "I have no control!"

The truth is that there is a distinction. My partner does what he does. I feel what I feel. I respond the way I respond. He feels the way he feels. He responds the way he responds. *Those are separate and distinct events.*

In conscious communication, we recognize the separation between those events. One person's actions do not automatically create a certain set of responses in the other person. We recognize that our unconscious, automatic responses are due to our own history, perceptions, and so on. Most important, we recognize that *we have a choice* over our behavioral responses. In this way, we *step into the gap.*

Widening the Gap

In conscious communication, the objective is to *widen the gap* for myself. This means that I become creative in finding ways to widen the gap between the event and my response. I may have no control over the biochemical reactions taking place in my body, but I have *complete control over what I do as a result of it.*

One of my most intense emotional triggers is the fear of abandonment. Though I have directed a great deal of intention and energy toward healing that part of myself, I am still susceptible to being triggered. In the past, I reacted to the fear of being abandoned by pursuing my partners in a needy way. I might call if I didn't hear from him, but not in the way of reaching out to him. My call was more in the way of trying to draw him to me. Of course, since I was sending "needy energy" to my partner, his reaction might be to pull away, thus increasing my anxiety and prompting more needy behavior. What a destructive cycle.

Eventually, what I learned was that it was my responsibility to address the neediness I felt. I learned that at those times it was a signal to me to be more self-caring. I learned to meditate, to do spiritual exercises, and to do other things that restored my sense of internal peace and balance. I learned to *delay my response to my partner* until I was in a more positive state. Gradually, I discovered that there is a core of strength and resilience inside of me that sustains me. Thus, I have widened the gap between events that evoke the fear of abandonment and my reactions and responses.

In relationships, we often get into cycles of reaction and response that do not support a loving connection. In conscious communication, we learn to develop habits that encourage a gradual "widening of the gap" and therefore, more creative communication. The next step is to examine our typical scenarios and then devise strategies to "widen the gap." In essence, *we become one another's partners in being more calm and resourceful together.*

In this way, over time, we discover resources we never imagined could have such a positive impact on our relationship and on our own well-being. We strengthen our confidence in the relationship, we open the door for more love to flow, and we deepen our connection.

In practice in our relationships, we widen the gap when we:

- recognize that we are responsible and in control of our reactions;
- make a commitment to react less;
- "turn down the volume" on our less desirable traits;
- reset our intentions in a positive direction;
- prepare separately for important conversations to have together;
- hit the "pause" button when an interaction gets too intense, giving ourselves and our partner time to decompress;
- co-create specific ways of signaling to one another that our feelings are escalating and it is time to "pause."

Here are examples of how some couples found creative ways to pause, get calmer, and "widen the gap."

Visual cues can interrupt old patterns and make way for new ones. When Patty and Jack became stressed with each other and their interaction was headed toward the "red alert" zone, she pulled a yellow handkerchief out of her purse and waved it, in essence communicating "caution!"

Exercise has a moderating affect on the nervous system. When Dave and Katherine found themselves getting too irate, the first to recognize it simply asked for time to take a brisk walk and decompress. The rule was that the exiting party had to promise a quick return and a negotiation of the best time to resume discussing the topic.

Gentle, safe touch stimulates the nervous system in a positive way, slowing heart rate and breathing, and creating a more relaxed state. Cindy and Steve found that if they were getting upset, simply reaching out to hold hands had a calming effect and allowed them to continue talking in a more productive fashion.

Being outdoors stabilizes the nervous system. Martin and Becky found that their best talks happened outdoors, walking in a park or around the neighborhood.

Individually, we improve our ability to "widen the gap" by utilizing practices such as:

Writing in a journal—it seems like a simple thing, but this is one of the most powerful tools for personal growth. There are specific neurological changes that occur when you journal—anxiety lowers, breathing slows down, and new insights emerge that enable new connections in the brain to take place.

Sharing with friends from the point of view of your own growth—it is essential that you break the habit of discussing your partner's flaws, and instead practice owning your own. This also creates new brain connections so that the processes of blame and projection gradually diminish.

Exercise, meditation, prayer, positive visualization, and whatever supports you in being more centered and calm.

Probably the most powerful step in widening the gap is when we let go of immediate results and focus on that which is in both of our highest and greatest good. This means that we learn to forfeit getting what we want right away in favor of letting the healing process unfold. Miracles often happen just by setting this intention and then allowing it to happen.

Creating Useful Fiction

We have the power to choose the nature of the stories that we tell, and therefore to create new emotional states, so I encourage my clients to practice *creating useful fiction*. What does that mean?

It means, in essence, that we slant the story in a direction that is empowering and useful. Instead of saying, "He is an hour late—that is so inconsiderate and thoughtless, and he is such a jerk for doing that!" I can say to myself, "He is an hour late—that concerns me and I feel upset and angry, but I know that he loves me and would not deliberately choose to hurt me."

Instead of, "She overreacts to anything that happens and she's far too oversensitive," he can say to himself, "She's emotional and sensitive and sometimes that is difficult for me to understand; however, she is very responsible in dealing with herself and her issues. I admire that, and I could probably learn a thing or two about that from her."

Useful fiction is not fantasy. To say, "My alcoholic husband who verbally abuses and hits me really means well and I know he loves me," is not useful. That kind of fiction can keep you locked in an abusive relationship and lead to great harm. Useful fiction is not a denial of reality. It is an *extension of reality in a direction that opens up new possibilities.*

One story (piece of useful fiction) that seems to apply to a lot of relationship distress is this:

"For whatever reason, my partner and I are not connecting, and love is not flowing between us the way it once was. We are both good people with good hearts and intentions, and we are capable of doing what is in both our best interests."

Another one is this:

"I love my partner, and I am confident that he/she loves me. We have this one issue that for whatever reason is difficult to discuss and resolve. We are both good people with good intentions, and I am confident that with compassion we can get to the bottom of it and create a win for us both."

Even when a relationship is dissolving, it is possible to have useful fiction to ease your separation. Instead of the usual drama and finger pointing, you might say:

"When my partner and I first began our relationship, we loved each other, and we did the best we could. For whatever reason, we are not able to continue at this time in a way that is a win for us both. We wish each other the best in life and will always care for one another." This, by the way, only works when you are ending a relationship with honesty, due process, and lots of integrity.

Again, useful fiction is an *extension of the truth,* not a fantasy. If you and your partner are fighting tooth and nail, it may be too soon to write an uplifting story. You might say, "We are having an incredibly painful time right now, and for whatever reason, do not see eye-to-eye on some important issues. I hope that we can resolve our differences very soon in a mutually beneficial way."

Creating useful fiction allows you to step back, take a deep breath, and direct all your resources toward reconnecting in a positive way. It minimizes drama and emotional escalation that can seriously impair your connection.

Putting It All Together

In conscious Soul Partnering, we bring together the power of understanding context, recreating intentions, rewriting our love stories, and taking back our projections. Think of these processes as "setting the stage" for the most important aspects of Soul Partnering. Now we are more prepared for the speaking and listening solutions that forge even deeper connection.

Chapter Five

Listening Empty and Mirroring

Being listened to is one of life's greatest gifts. Having another person hear us, really hear us, not just the words we say, but the true message underneath the words, is one of the most empowering experiences we can have. We experience it as *being understood*. Being truly and deeply listened to is also experienced as being *seen* and *known*, thus *validating our very existence.*

When one human being expresses thoughts, feelings, and ideas to another human being who listens, hears, understands, and responds with compassion, we experience the phenomenon of *connection*, a sense of almost melting together into one being.

Connection is the ultimate goal of all interaction and communication between human beings. Connection is what we seek because we literally need it to survive and to thrive.

We now know that human beings *require* interaction with other human beings in order to accomplish several vital functions in life:

Regulation of the nervous system. Being connected to other human beings in a positive way slows heart rate, lowers blood pressure, deepens the breath, and stimulates the release of certain healthy chemicals into the brain and bloodstream.

Without human interaction and connection, human beings not only lose these positive effects, they deteriorate from the lack of them. Socially isolated or neglected people tend toward physical ailments, loss of productivity, and mental and emotional problems.

Intellectual stimulation. We learn most powerfully, not from books, but by being around others who know what we seek to learn. This is why a really gifted teacher creates gifted students. It also explains why we seek stimulating conversation with other human beings and environments that encourage this. That is how we experience lifelong learning.

Personal and spiritual growth. Interaction with other human beings gives us feedback about ourselves, opening a window to the psychological "blind spots" that we all have. By hearing other's stories, we are inspired in our own path of personal development.

There are many ways to experience connection with other human beings, including touch, eye contact, walking together in nature, shared experiences such as attending a concert, and many, many more. Here, we will explore one of the most fundamental, core ways of connecting, and that is through the *art of listening*.

The Power of Listening

Listening is often absent in life. We are so busy rushing around trying to get things done and handling our endless lists of tasks and being self-focused that we fail to take time to listen to those who matter. Stress is epidemic in our culture, and one of the causes is our lack of connection. We simply do not take time to sit down with those we love to interact and connect.

Listening is so absent in our modern world that people pay lots of money to psychologists and therapists primarily to have someone listen. In fact, in my work I am well aware of *the healing power of listening*. Often, the gift of compassionate validation through listening is sufficient for healing and the discovery of one's own solutions.

I believe that a fair number of my clients would not be in my office if they had sufficient outlets to express their thoughts and feelings. If our lives were centered primarily on our relationships, on spending time with loved ones, connecting, sharing, and expressing ourselves, I believe that we would see a dramatic reduction in stress and stress-related diseases. We would also see a dramatic fall in virtually all of the societal ills that plague us: divorce, family violence, and crime.

Volumes to Express

Because listening is so critical in life, the lack of it is one of the greatest frustrations in human relationships. Few of us have lives that afford us the opportunity to be really listened to and understood on a daily basis. For most of us, this builds up unconsciously over time into a mountain of unspoken communication. Thus, the reality is that most of us are walking around with *volumes to express* and *aching to be heard*. This means that when you sit down to interact with another person, you are rarely facing an open and willing listener. Instead, you are most likely facing another *frustrated speaker*. Nowhere is this more apparent than it is in love relationships.

Listening and Love

In the beginning of the relationship, listening is easy. When we first connect and begin falling in love, our brains are flooded with a number of delightful chemicals that make us feel euphoric and that dramatically increase our capacity to bond.[6] This means that we see only the good in one another and that we are completely open to hearing one another.

We talk and talk for hours, and when one is talking the other listens rapturously. In this stage, we naturally take turns listening and speaking so that both people experience being seen, heard, and validated. We hang onto one another's every word, we exchange volumes of email, we talk on the telephone for hours, and we can hardly wait to see one another again so that we can, yes, talk and listen more!

Listening to one another is easy when we are in love. Listening is also distorted when we are in love, both with the beloved and with others. We have "selective listening," in that we hear only the good and we screen out anything that is potentially negative.

This explains why you can try to point out to your love-struck friend that her new love may have a few issues that could hurt her ("How is he supposed to make a commitment to you when he is still married?") but your words will fall on deaf ears. Literally, your friend cannot hear your words of warning due to the powerful pull toward being with her lover. This is what being in love does, the positive and the negative. It bonds us together powerfully—that is the good news. The bad news is that if we fall in love with the wrong person, it is difficult to see it or to break away before an attachment happens.

As a relationship develops and time goes on, the initial "love high" diminishes and we begin to see one another more realistically. "Well, maybe he's not perfect, but he's the one I want!" Making a commitment (marriage or however you define it) solidifies our path together and we settle into a more routine existence. Our attention naturally re-focuses once again on other things: work, friends, extended family, and children.

If we are like most couples, we soon begin to take for granted our connection, no longer making the time for heart-to-heart talks the way we once did. We fall into "patterned communication," meaning that we have certain conversations over and over again. Some of these are positive, such as, "Have a great day, sweetheart!" and, "I love you."

Some are not so positive, such as, "I can't believe you did that AGAIN!" or, "That is SO like you!" Negative patterned conversations are destructive to our connection and block the flow of love. We fall into them to the degree that we fall into the *absence of listening*.

How Listening Goes Away

Where does our openhearted listening go? It actually does not go away. The ability to listen is always here within each of us, but it becomes blocked. That occurs primarily through the *accumulation of joint personal history over time*. This is how it happens. As a relationship develops, we have certain interactions that leave an *emotional imprint*. In the beginning, these imprints are (fortunately) mostly positive. We have an imprint of the first time we met, our first kiss, the first time we made love, and the first time we heard our beloved mirror our feelings with "I love you." All of these initial imprints are very powerful and help us bond and create a sense of being a connected couple. These early imprints also provide a foundation of happy, loving memories that help us get through the inevitable difficulties ahead.

Many times, I have observed that happy couples tell these early stories over and over again, thus keeping the positive emotional imprints "alive." Likewise, happy couples do not tend to recount their negative imprints or stories, allowing them to fade and become less important.

These imprints of important emotional moments strung together form the "story of our relationship." Since we are so attuned to our ongoing stories, we are constantly writing them in our minds and in our hearts about the connection with our Soul Partner.

Every relationship eventually runs into rough water of one kind or another. At times like this, we may experience things that create a negative or painful imprint. If enough of these happen in a row, we create a story about it. If we repeat the story enough times to ourselves and to others, it becomes our reality. If the essence of the story is "My partner is doing me wrong!" or "I'm with the wrong partner," then our ability to listen to that person in an openhearted way is drastically limited, if not shut down altogether.

The interesting thing about how our brains work is that we are *selectively attuned* to the ideas we believe, focus on, and repeat. This means that if I say to myself and to my friends, "my partner is so logical all the time. He just doesn't hear or understand my feelings!" over time, that will become my reality. If I add emotion to the statement (feeling angry, hurt, and righteous about my assessment), then it becomes deeply imprinted for me. This is because strong emotions create powerful imprints and lasting memories. For some reason, negative emotions seem to do this even more so than do positive ones, which is why we tend to remember our painful life events so strongly. (Actually, we tend to remember the pain, the association with the person(s) involved, and the sensory data, but we rarely remember the facts of the events accurately.)

All of this imprinting severely limits my interactions in the present. One day, my partner asks me how I feel about something and really tries to listen to me and validate my feelings. At this point, however, I have so convinced myself that he is incapable of listening in this way that I do not take the time to speak in a way that makes it easier for him to hear. Instead, I become impatient, creating an emotional block between us, he becomes frustrated, and before we know it, I am saying, "See there, you just can't listen to my feelings!"

This is how real listening "collapses" over time in a relationship. We create stories about our partners based on emotionally imprinting incidents, we further imprint those stories by repeating them over and over to ourselves and to others, and they become our reality. If our partners "show up" in a way that goes against the "story," we dismiss it as a fluke, or we outright ignore or deny it.

This is why when couples divorce in anger, seeing only the worst in one another, they are surprised when the other party finds someone new. "Don't worry—as soon as she sees how he *really* is, that will be over!" It is shocking to see the person actually move on and have a lasting and loving relationship. Why? Because my story about my ex became so limiting and I became so convinced of it that I could no longer see his good qualities. In my eyes, *he is who I think he is based on my worst experiences with him!* Anything outside of that view of him must be false, including the viewpoint of his new lover.

In communication, the failure is in not separating the *person* from the person's *behavior*, and in not separating the *facts* of a given situation from the *stories* that we create about the facts.

The reality is that *we are not our behavior.* We are not our stories, nor are we other people's stories. *We are who we are.* We behave the way we behave and feel the way we feel. In the field of all human possibilities, we are capable of choosing new responses and new behaviors. That is what makes life so exciting—the fact that we are never stuck with one and only one way of relating to ourselves, to others, and to the world.

In relationships, we grow and expand to the degree that we see our partners without limitations. We learn as we interact creatively and spontaneously, giving up our negative patterned interactions and stories. We become better individually and as a couple through really listening to, seeing, knowing, and understanding one another on an ever-evolving basis. We are deeply enriched by connecting in a way that is *infinitely generative*—meaning that we constantly create new ways of loving and receiving the love that we want. We do this primarily through learning and developing powerful listening skills that open up our ways of seeing and knowing one another. I call this **listening empty,** and it is by far the most challenging yet the most potent skill that we can bring to bear in a Soul Partnership.

Listening Empty

Listening empty is remarkably similar to listening in the way that we did at the beginning of the relationship. The only difference is that we are not being bathed in mood-altering love chemicals! In a mature relationship, listening empty must be consciously chosen and practiced. In some respects, it does not come naturally. It is created through our intention to enrich our Soul Partnership with this skill.

A note of caution is needed before we go further. *Listening empty in a mature relationship is incredibly challenging!* It requires almost a reversal of numerous old patterns that may be deeply ingrained. Therefore, take your time with this chapter. Do not expect instant positive results.

Trying to explain how to listen empty is almost like trying to explain how to make love. It is part technique (knowing what goes where), part heart and soul (I want to be with you in this way), part intention (I want this to be wonderful for you), and part intuition (finding my way with no conscious thought). Listening empty gets better with practice and deteriorates with non-use. It works better from intention (I choose this) than it does from emotion alone (I will do it when I feel like it).

The technique part of listening empty provides a framework for practice, but it does not work with technique alone. In that sense, it is somewhat like learning music. We must learn the notes and practice the scales, but to make the music come alive we must *play from our soul.*

Intuitively, we all know we should listen more and speak less in a relationship. We forget to do it, except for those times when we remember. Then, we make a concentrated effort to listen to our mates, and that is better than making no effort. However, *the kind of listening that we normally do in a relationship is not the same as listening empty.* To effectively distinguish the difference, let us begin by looking at the typical ways we listen, or what listening empty is NOT:

It is *not* listening to words alone.

It is *not* planning a response while the other person is talking.

It is *not* having your own agenda ("I want what I want" or "How can I win this argument?").

It is *not* listening with interpretation, judgment, analysis, or pity.

It is *not* having an opinion about what the speaker is saying or trying to determine if I agree with it.

It is *not* listening while trying to figure out how to fix or change the speaker, the speaker's perceptions, or the situation.

It is *not* listening with one ear, while attending to or responding to other things or people.

It is *not* taking the speaker's words personally, getting hurt or angry, and feeling wounded.

Listening empty requires an entirely new focus in the communication process. It requires a spirit of contribution, the willingness to temporarily set aside my own needs, the decision to let go of my projections or my personal agenda, and the ability to love altruistically.

To love altruistically means to love as one human being to another; it means wanting the best for you, *even if what is best for you does not necessarily give me what I want.*

Romantic love is not the same as altruistic love, although it may include it. Romantic love has a selfish element, in that we tend to pay lots of attention to getting the "goodies" of love while falling in love.

To have a fully functioning Soul Partnership, we must learn to love bigger than romantic love. We must learn to love one another from the point of view of our humanity; that *who you are* as a human being is someone whom I immensely admire and respect. You are not just a "love object" or a person who "makes me feel good." You are a person whom I deeply love, *for who you are,* and wish to contribute to, regardless of what I receive in return.

Listening empty is an exercise in altruistic love. It is a gift from the heart and soul, and it fills the emotional bank account of our relationships to overflowing.

What listening empty IS:

Setting aside my own thoughts, feelings, opinions, and judgments.

Listening to and honoring the speaker's words as well as the underlying meaning of the words.

Listening to the essence of the speaker's message.

Listening with compassion.

Most important, listening empty is having the sole purpose of *understanding the speaker:* his thoughts, feelings, intentions, wants, needs, and desires.

Listening Empty in Practice

Now let us look at the actual exercise. In this section, I will describe the exercise, with lots of sidebars and anecdotes. *Use this part just for learning and understanding.* Later, there will be a summary from which you may practice.

Set the Stage. Carve out time for just you and your partner to focus on one another with no distractions. This means getting a baby-sitter if necessary or sending the kids over to someone else's house to play for a while. You may choose to wait until the kids are in bed asleep (although most couples are so exhausted at that point in the day that they have no energy for the exercise).

Sometimes, when I am introducing the parameters for practicing this exercise, couples will object by saying that they do not have the luxury of time alone with no distractions. My answer to that is this: *if you have no time to really listen to one another, then you have no time for your relationship.* If you have no time for that, you may as well begin saving up the money you will need for the divorce that you will be having sooner or later.

Relationships normally do not *call us into action* until they are in crisis. Once it reaches that stage, the lack of emotional connection often prevents couples from working toward healing. I suggest that you not wait for that, but take steps to avoid it.

Choose your path today. Healthy, loving, lasting relationships require a substantial investment of our time, effort, and energy. Setting aside time for heart-and-soul communication is a powerful way that you can support your commitment to intentionally nurture your connection.

Getting Started. Sit with open body language (no crossed legs or arms) and make full eye contact. Ideally, sit directly across from one another as close as possible.

Now, choose who will speak first and who will listen. One way that I encourage couples to choose is by reflecting on which role (speaker or listener) you feel you are not quite as comfortable with or as skilled with. If you are normally a great speaker but don't listen as well, then begin by being the listener and let your partner speak, and vice versa.

Now, while the listener is preparing for that job, the speaker chooses a topic about which to speak (see later in this chapter—Naming the Issues). For your first practice exercise, choose a topic, or issue, that is about mid-way on the emotional intensity scale. Do not begin with your "hottest" topic, the issue about which you constantly fight and that always ends in someone yelling, crying, or withdrawing.

Likewise, do not choose a topic that is so mundane it is hardly worth your time, like what's for dinner tonight. Choose something important, such as how you are going to carve out time for your next vacation alone together, but not critical, such as someone's affair or drinking problem.

Set an Intention. Take one another's hands, close your eyes, take several slow, deep breaths, and *focus inwardly on your intention to have this exercise empower your relationship, deepen your connection, and support your individual growth.* Choose your own words to set your intention, words that point you and your partner toward your greatest and highest good. Now, open your eyes and take turns speaking your loving intentions out loud to one another.

For one couple, this step looked like this:

Susan: "My intention is to find a way today for us to be more connected and more loving than we have been. I intend to listen with an open mind and heart to you so that I can understand how to love you better."

Ben: "My intention is to rediscover the best part of our love. I intend to support you in expressing whatever feelings you have for me to hear today, so that I can be a better partner to you."

Declare Your Honesty. Next, speak out your vows out loud to be absolutely honest with one another. This step is vital if you are to have a trusting relationship. If for some reason you do not feel that you can be honest at this point with your partner, then I suggest that you continue reading. *Do not practice these exercises until you are ready to be fully honest with one another.* It is better to put off the practice than it is to contaminate your relationship with additional dishonesty or withholding.

For one couple, this step looked like this:

> Becky: "I promise to be fully honest and open with you today and always. I promise to do my best to know my own truth and then to share that with you so that you can understand my wants, my needs, and me."
>
> Bill: "I vow to be totally honest with you today and every day. As much as I know my own heart and mind, I will share that with you. I will diligently search for the truth in all of our interactions."

Prepare to listen empty. This next section is for the listener. In order to listen empty, you must first become aware of any thoughts, feelings, perceptions, analyses, judgments, or anything else that you have in your mind right now about your partner. Picture these things as liquid filling up a cup or container (you) so that you are not an empty receptacle. You are full of your own thoughts, feelings, and point of view. Now, imagine what would happen if your partner attempted at this point to pour her thoughts, feelings, etc., into you (the container). In your mind's eye, picture the cup running over, its contents spilling onto the ground.

When I do this exercise with couples, I often ask them, "How do you feel at this point?" Both speaker and listener answer, "Frustrated," or something very similar. This is because the speaker feels *not listened to* and the listener feels *the same way*. With both trying to get their needs met (for being listened to and/or validated) at the same time, it is impossible for either one to feel satisfied.

Your job as the designated listener is to empty the cup (yourself) so that your partner has a place to put her communication. To help you do this, begin by realizing: these are your thoughts, feelings, perceptions, etc., and nothing more. Your way of seeing things is not necessarily *the* truth. It is neither right nor wrong. It is simply *your truth*.

- These thoughts that you are having now and that you will have when your partner begins speaking are not necessarily facts, although they may include facts.
- Your thoughts, feelings, etc., are valid from your point of view only. They may or may not be valid from your partner's point of view or from the point of view of the highest good for your relationship.
- Likewise, whatever your partner is about to say is valid from his point of view. You do not have to agree on your points of view about something in order to validate them.
- Even if your partner says something that you believe to be totally off-base, you can still validate it as being his point of view. You can still hear it, understand it, and respect it.

Set Aside Your Point of View. The next step is to *consciously choose* to *set aside your own point of view* about whatever the topic is. All you are doing is setting to the side your thoughts, feelings, etc. You are not saying that they are not valid. You are simply making room to hear your partner's point of view.

Now, visualize yourself taking the container that represents you and slowly pouring its contents out on the ground. Sometimes couples like to have cups that they tilt over as if pouring something out. This helps them create an image that they can use in the future.

Set the Intention to Understand. Last of all, and most important, *consciously choose* to make it your job only to *hear and understand your partner's point of view*. While your partner is speaking, continue to silently choose this over and over. "I want to understand you and how you see things." This is your *sole intention* as the listener.

Mirroring

There are actually two parts of listening empty. One part is *listening to understand*. The other is a skill called ***mirroring***. Like listening empty, mirroring is part technique, and largely heart, soul, intention, and intuition.

Mirroring is NOT parroting. Simply repeating back the words by rote is not the same as mirroring. When I do workshops, everyone expresses the sentiment that it is highly annoying to have a person parrot their words. It may be good technique but it has a poor outcome. This is because the most important part of mirroring is the *intention behind it*. What does that mean?

If my intention is to truly listen to you, to understand you, and to connect with you, then the actual words I mirror back are insignificant compared to the way my heart is reaching out to you. What you sense is my intention, and you connect with that. Even if I get parts of what you are saying wrong, we will move through that quickly because you feel the energy of my intention to understand you. Often when I am listening to my clients, I do not "get" what they are communicating right away. I am willing to mirror what I hear and I am not attached to whether I am right about it or not. Rather, it is a way to keep the conversation going until a full understanding is reached.

On the other hand, if I am not reaching out to you in compassion and loving intention with my listening, and if I simply parrot back to you the words that you say, you will feel the absence of genuine caring energy. In the absence of that energy, you will be highly focused on whether or not I got the words right. You may feel annoyed even when I get them right, because *something is missing in our transaction*. That something is connection.

Mirroring works when it comes from the *intention to understand and to connect, with no other agenda*. Mirroring is a way of saying, "I hear you so far, please tell me more." You know you are truly hearing someone when the response to your mirroring is a resounding "Yes! That's it."

I have observed actual physiological changes in people when they experience being heard. Facial muscles relax, breathing becomes slower and deeper, and posture becomes straighter. With couples, when one finally hears the other, there are often tears of relief. There is an outpouring of emotion at being really heard by one's partner, sometimes after years of disconnection. It is truly one of the most powerful experiences in life.

Listening Empty and Mirroring make it possible for us to forge and strengthen the partnering aspect of our relationship. With true Soul Partnering, we are connected in mind, heart, soul, word, and deed. All parts of each of us are aligned on having the greatest and highest good for both of us as individuals and for the two of us as a couple.

This is love magnified to the nth degree. *This is a force to be reckoned with.* Couples with true partnership are not susceptible to affairs, separation, or divorce. They cannot imagine being anywhere other than with one another because it is so deeply fulfilling to be connected in this way.

Mirroring allows you to be sure that what you heard is what the other person meant. It is not a short cut to hurry the conversation along, and can be challenging because it is so automatic to interpret what the other person is saying, rather than just get it as it is. Here, John and Jill were trying to communicate, but were not connecting.

> Jill: "After you left last night, I went into the bedroom and cried for about an hour. I felt so sad that you just walked out without working with me on our problems. It felt like you just gave up. That was the worst feeling—that I was all alone in this and I had lost my best friend."
>
> John: "After I left, you felt so sorry for yourself that you just went to bed and cried. You misjudged me, and thought that I didn't care and that made you feel awful. Once again, you felt like an abandoned little girl, alone and friendless, just like when your father left."

John, though he was making a genuine effort, was not mirroring the *essence* of Jill's communication, but his *interpretation* of her communication, based on his knowledge of her personal history. After some coaching, this is what he gave back the second time:

> John: "After I left, you felt terribly sad. You went to the bedroom and cried for an hour. It felt to you as though I had given up on us, on working out our relationship, and that made you feel so alone. Me walking out last night felt like losing your best friend. Did I hear you?"

This time, Jill gave an enthusiastic "Yes!" as she affirmed how good it felt to be really understood. The purpose of these exercises is *to create the experience of being understood in the relationship*. The way to do it is by attending to the essence of the speaker's communication and giving it back in a way that the person experiences being truly heard. That is listening empty and mirroring.

Through listening empty and mirroring, we give the gift of being understood and validated. The value of this gift is so enormous that it cannot be measured. With it, the possibilities are limitless; we deepen our connection and simultaneously grow and thrive as individuals within the boundaries of our love.

More Steps

Now that you are ready to communicate, here are the rest of the steps:

Speaker: Are you ready to listen empty?

This is actually a critical step. When you ask your partner if he is ready to listen, it requires him to stop and reflect on his willingness and ability to do so. When he answers that he is ready, he then assumes the responsibility for listening. This helps people to "get on line," almost like booting up your computer.

Listener: (LISTENING EMPTY) Yes, I am. What would you like to share with me?
Speaker: I want to share with you my thoughts and feelings about (topic). The way I see it…

(The way the Speaker expresses herself makes all the difference in how easy it is for the Listener to hear. In chapter 7 we'll cover how to speak in the most empowering way possible.)

IMPORTANT: Do this exercise in small "sound bites." Once a particular thought has been completed (a paragraph), the Speaker pauses and asks, "What did you hear so far?"

Listener: (MIRRORING) "What I hear you saying is…"

This is another critical step. To say, "You said…" implies that what I heard and believe that you said are the same as what you meant to say. On the other hand, to say, "What I *hear* you saying is…" assumes responsibility for my own listening and the reality that it may or may not be accurate, and leaves room for the Speaker to offer correction.

While the Listener mirrors, the Speaker pays attention to it, noticing if it feels like the Listener "got it."

> Listener: (Once done mirroring that part) "Did I hear you?"

This step is critical in that it allows both parties to check to see if they are on the same page. In everyday automatic, unconscious communication, this step is often skipped. Someone says something important in the relationship, the other person nods or says "uh huh," and both walk away believing that they have reached an understanding. I often hand out this quote on a piece of paper when I do workshops to illustrate this point:

> *I know that you believe you*
> *understand what you think I said*
> *BUT*
> *I am not sure you realize that*
> *what you heard is not what I meant.*

Because of the high likelihood of misunderstandings, it is critical to make sure that what you believe you heard is exactly what the Speaker meant to convey. If the Speaker indicates that you did not hear it correctly, ask: "Please tell me again." If it was correct, the Speaker says so:

> Speaker: "Yes, you did. Thank you for listening."
> Listener: "*What else* about that?" (Listener encourages the Speaker to continue about the topic.)

This particular phrase is critical. It is registered in the brain as permission to say whatever comes to mind.

Typically, we do not ask for more communication, or if we do, we say things like, "Is there anything else?" and "Is that all?" These are *close-ended questions*, meaning that there are only two possible responses: "yes" or "no."

The aim of these exercises is to encourage more opening up on the part of the speaker, and therefore, deeper understanding by the listener.

The Speaker continues to speak in "small bites," or paragraphs, pausing to ask, "What did you hear so far?" Listener continues to mirror each time and to check to see if he "got it." The listener continues to ask, "What else?" and "What else about that?" (Use these exact phrases.)

Continue repeating these steps until the Speaker says, "That's all for now on this topic," or, "I can't think of anything else right now." At that point, go into the wrap-up, or completion, of this part of the exercise. This acknowledgement part is also highly important and is often overlooked.

> Listener: "Thank you for sharing your thoughts and feelings with me."
> Speaker: "Thank you for listening."

Many couples at this point feel some sort of shift in their relationship: a greater degree of connection, perhaps a return to intimacy. Follow your hearts and do what feels natural: hug, kiss, make love, or simply hold one another.

When Your "Cup" Fills Up

From time to time while your partner is speaking, you may find your "cup" filling up. Suddenly something your partner says triggers you emotionally, and you begin reacting internally. You begin to argue with your partner internally (some people actually interrupt at this point to argue out loud) and to focus on your own thoughts, feelings, judgments, and opinions about what your partner is expressing.

This is where the "rubber meets the road"! It is easy to listen when you are calm and in agreement. The challenging part is the moment that you *strongly disagree and feel emotionally triggered.* STOP.

At this point, hold up your hand and say, "Please stop for a moment. My cup is getting full." Say this without blame or accusation toward your partner. Do not begin expressing what you are thinking at this time. You will have a chance to do that when you and your partner switch roles and he becomes the listener.

During your break, re-focus on your intention as the Listener. Once again, *CHOOSE* to consciously set aside (temporarily) your thoughts, feelings, and opinions about the topic or about your partner or what he is saying. Once again, remind yourself of your sole intention as the Listener: to *understand* your partner's thoughts, feelings, and point of view.

When you are calm once again, re-focused on your intention to listen empty, tell your partner, "I'm ready to listen empty to you. What else is there to say about that?" You may need to ask your partner to repeat the last part that you may have missed when your cup began filling up.

When the Speaker Does Not Feel "Heard"

Let's go back to the first stage of mirroring. If the Listener mirrors back something that does not feel like an accurate representation of what the speaker said, here is how to handle it.

> Speaker: "That's not quite it. This part is what I said …(indicates
>   what Listener got right)."
> Listener: "Please tell me again the part that I missed."
> Speaker: (shares again) "What did you hear this time?"
> Listener: "What I hear you saying is…"

Keep going with this until the Speaker says, "That's it!" During this exercise, the Speaker is *always right* about being heard correctly or not. The Listener's job is to continue mirroring until the Speaker feels heard.

If you try three times on the same thing and it is still not right, table the exercise for a while. Sometimes, even though we are trying very hard, we get stuck in a pattern and simply need a break.

When the Listener Is Not Ready to Listen

Now, let us go back to the very beginning of the exercise. Sometimes, when the Speaker says, "Are you ready to listen empty?" the Listener stops, pays attention to his inner sense of being emotionally prepared, and realizes that he is not. Remember that you must be in a rested, peaceful state with no immediate distractions in order to give the gift of listening empty.

When we did this exercise with Stan and Linda, Stan replied, "No, I'm not." I coached Linda to reverse roles at that point. Here is what happened.

> Linda: "What would you like to do about that?"
> Stan: "I would like to say some things that are in the way."
> Linda: "Okay."
> Stan: "Are you ready to listen empty?"
> Linda, after reflecting, "Yes."

Perhaps when Stan stated that he was not ready to listen, and that he would like to say some things that are in the way, Linda might have indicated that she could not listen to him. If that is the case, she must say so. Then, they must decide together if they will postpone the conversation (always re-schedule on the spot) or just take a short break (go walk around the block, stretch, meditate, get a cup of coffee, etc.) and resume.

> Stan: "I am not in a good place for this conversation. I have so much on my plate today, with my father ill, with the holidays coming up next week and all the work I have to catch up on before we leave town, and with the stress of being with your family. I just feel so overwhelmed right now."
> Linda: "What I hear you saying is that you have too much on your plate right now—work, the holidays, your father dying. Did I hear you?"
> Stan: "Yes."
> Linda: "What else about that?"
> Stan: "I don't know how I feel about my father. One part of me is very sad and another part of me knows it's just his time to go. I don't feel like I have the time to sort it all out."
> Linda: "What I hear you saying is that your emotions about your father are not clear. You feel sad one moment and the next you just realize it's his time. It's too much to try and sort that out right now. Did I hear you?"
> Stan: "Yes."

Linda: "What else?"

Stan: "Being around your family is so stressful. I don't know what to do with those relationships, with your mother and your sister. And I'm afraid to talk about it right now because I know I will have some work to do on it, and I just don't have the energy to take on any more work!"

Linda: "What I hear you saying is that you find being around my family too stressful right now, trying to figure out how to deal with my mother and my sister. Did I hear you?"

Sometimes, the listener leaves out parts of what was said, or adds things that the speaker did not say. When that happens, it is important for the speaker to acknowledge that he did not feel completely "heard." However, how he acknowledges that is critical as well.

Stan: "No."

By simply answering "No," Stan leaves the impression that Linda did not get anything that he said. Instead, I coached him to say,

Stan: "Yes, you got most of it, and there was more."

Linda: "What else did I not get?"

Stan: "The part about how scared I am to get into this right now. That I don't want to take on any more personal growth work. I just don't have the mental and emotional energy to do that."

Linda: "What I hear you saying is that it is too much right now for you to take on any 'work' having to do with your relationship with my family. You have way too much on your plate to do that, and it feels like if we get into this conversation you will be expected to do it anyway. Did I hear you?"

Stan: "Yes."

Linda: "What else?"

Stan: "No. That's all there is." He paused. "Thank you for listening."

At this point, Stan's face lit up, he smiled, and then he said, to Linda's surprise, "I'm ready to listen now."

Linda said in amazement, "It's so simple. Why didn't I realize this before? The resistance just melts away." Linda was then able to speak about her issue with Stan's full attention.

Resistance to Listening

What Linda was talking about, "the resistance," is one of the unconscious events that takes place in a distressed relationship. If we are angry, hurt, and fearful, it is usually because we do not feel listened to, understood, and honored in the relationship (i.e., you are not taking care of me and my needs). If our partner comes to us and asks for something, the knee-jerk response is to put up resistance. This is because it is not easy to give when we feel that our own emotional bank account is depleted.

Resistance takes many forms. "I'm too tired" is one, "Not now, maybe later" is another, and then there is the ever-popular, "What have you done for me lately?" Resistance may be overt, as in the above examples, or it may be covert, as in making agreements and then "forgetting" to follow through on them. Resistance may even take the form of consciously or unconsciously doing things that directly hurt our partners, such as staying out all hours and not calling, being unfaithful, or withholding affection.

Resistance to communication processes also happens when one person has a secret agenda that is not being met. For instance, when couples are dating, it is not unusual for them to have different timetables for commitment. One person is "gung-ho" for getting married as soon as possible, while the other is more cautious. The gung-ho partner often focuses only on that which proves that they are a great couple soon to be married, and is resistant to any communication process that would allow his partner to express her caution. This may leave the cautious person blocked, as the gung-ho partner refuses to hear anything that is contrary to his agenda to be married as soon as possible.

Over time, the person blocked in expressing herself may build up resentment and exhibit counter-resistance as a result. This only adds another block to the previous one. What may be a great relationship is eroded through the buildup of resentment and resistance to the flow of love.

When we decide to "forgive," i.e., to "give as we gave before," and give the gift of listening empty, we open the door to a renewed connection where love has been eroded. When we listen to, validate, and honor the other's expressions of need, we melt our partner's resistance just as the sun melts the snow. This can create miraculous results and support deep healing, often to the point that couples on the brink of divorce decide to stay together and work to improve their relationship.

If your partner is resistant to hearing all that you need to express, keep reading. In chapter 7 we will explore this phenomenon in greater detail.

Naming the Issues

These processes work best when practiced with real-life issues. Every relationship has them. To get started, I often recommend that couples work individually to create an "issues list." Each person identifies the issues (situations, partner's behavior, problems, etc.) that are the most troublesome on a repetitive or ongoing basis. Create your lists separately, then come together to discuss them.

The way you describe the issues to one another makes a huge difference in how you resolve them. In fact, the exercise of **naming the issues** provides another opportunity to create healing and deeper connection.

This exercise helps you clarify the issues in your relationship while each of you takes responsibility. Often couples "name their issues" in a way that casts blame toward one another. It is barbed, feels like an attack, and attempts to place all of the responsibility on the other person. This is almost never the case in a relationship—it is almost always the case that *no one is to blame and everyone is responsible.* Both partners participate in the dynamics of the relationship that contribute to the problem.

The classic example is the alcoholic and the codependent partner. Clearly, the person drinking is choosing to drink, and alcoholism is her issue. Murkier is her partner's role in her behavior. When the non-drinking partner's behavior contributes to the denial of the problem, we call this dynamic "enabling."

In relationships in which one partner engages in repetitive, destructive behavior, the enabling partner typically fails to take the necessary steps to create the *possibility* of change. To confront, speak the truth, urge treatment, and demonstrate unwillingness to tolerate the "status quo" can and often does lead to change. To make these steps is not easy. The enabling partner, ironically, often fears change just as much as the acting-out partner.

In naming the issues, we begin with this premise:

In every aspect of our relationship, in all the repetitive patterns of interaction, in all of our most positive and our most negative behaviors, there is one common denominator: *We are in it together!*

Regardless of who did what to whom, and when, where, and why, we are partners in every way in our relationship. We are *co-creating it together* at each and every moment, and there are no victims in our relationship. We are doing this as partners every step of the way.

The reality of relationships is that we are both contributors to every dynamic that we share, in everything from money management, to sex, to not putting the cap back on the toothpaste. Paradoxically, though we are both collaborators in our dynamics, it only takes one person to change the dynamics and open the possibility for positive, permanent change in the relationship.

Co-Creating Love

Naming the issues is a step toward changing those things in our partnership that no longer serve us. It is an effective way to "shine the light" on our dark areas.

By naming the issues powerfully, we side-step the usual trap of *complaining*, and instead create *powerful intentions* for our partnership.

There is a way to present issues in a relationship that is blaming (which creates resistance and defensiveness) and there is a way to do it that opens the door for growth (which creates partnership and cooperation). I describe the first way as "disempowering," meaning that the listener feels accused, blamed, and cut off from the flow of love. I describe the second way as "empowering," meaning that the listener feels a sense of partnership while being given straight talk.

Here are some examples of how this works:

Disempowering

The issue is that you are completely irresponsible about money! I can't talk to you about it at all—you are so immature and you don't have any understanding about how money works in the real world!

Empowering

The issue is that our communication about money is not working. My intention is to talk about it without all of the anger and upset feelings, so that we may understand one another about money management. Then, my intention is that we find a plan that works for us both and make it happen together. I want us to be peaceful and happy together about how we handle money.

Disempowering

Our sex life is terrible—you have not been interested in being intimate with me in months! I feel totally ripped off in this relationship because you are not the lover that you were in the beginning.

Empowering

The issue is that we seem to have lost the romance and passion that we once had together as a couple. My intention is for us to understand one another's needs and desires so that we may find our way back to being romantic and intimate once again.

Disempowering

You show more affection to our dogs than you do me! I really resent it that I'm the last person you say hello to when you come home, after the dogs, the kids, and even your mother!

Empowering

I'm deeply concerned about how we interact at the end of our workday. I miss the times when we only had eyes for each other, when we took time to reconnect and be close. I want to find a way for us to connect at the end of the workday as happy and joyful lovers.

EXERCISE: NAMING THE ISSUES

Do this part individually for yourself. *Do not show this first list to your partner.* First, describe the issues in the relationship, as you see them—do not edit how you say them. It's OK to think of them as your complaints for this part of the exercise. Some examples might be:

- He leaves his things lying around and expects me to pick up after him like I'm his mother!
- When I want to talk, he is never there. Television is much more important than listening to me.
- We almost never make love anymore. He's so selfish when he does approach me—just wanting a "quickie" and not taking time to give me what I need.
- She never has time to be with me. She's exhausted after work and I can't get her to stop cleaning up the house and just sit down with me!
- She lets the kids get away with murder! I keep telling her that she's spoiling them rotten but she never listens to me.
- She constantly nags me about the chores. I hate the way she doesn't trust me to take care of my commitments around the house!

Now, for each one, think about it as a *dynamic process*, not as a characteristic in your partner, and rewrite it accordingly. Instead of making it a *complaint*, make it *an intention for your relationship*. Our examples above are now transformed to:

- I would like to find a way that we can handle putting things away so that is more of a win for us both. I would like to have a system that does not involve either of us having to nag the other.
- I would like for us to have more time together at the end of the day for talking and listening to one another with no distractions. I want this to be time that we both agree upon so that it is not a sacrifice but is a joy.
- I want us to revive our romantic, lovemaking connection. I want that to be a top priority in our relationship and I intend to do whatever I can to reconnect with you in that way.
- I want more time connecting at the end of the day. I intend to make sure that you feel sufficiently supported about household

chores so that you can relax more with me and enjoy just being together.

- I want to be powerful partners in our role as parents. I intend to collaborate with you about how to decide on matters of discipline so that we are in agreement and our children feel empowered through our unity.
- I want us to become partners about household chores so that we are choosing our jobs and fulfilling them. I want to see us never fight again about such mundane things, and to have more energy to focus on loving one another.

Speaking the Issues

Now that you have transformed each issue into positive relationship intentions, it is time to speak them to your partner. Decide who will be the Speaker first. The Listener's job is to mirror the issue accurately (as expressed by the Speaker). Once that is done, the Listener asks, "Did I hear you?" The Speaker confirms that and asks, "Do you agree that this is an issue and to be my partner in this intention?" If the Listener says, "No," you put a mark beside that one and come back to it. Later, switch roles and have the person who does not see it as an issue speak about that while the other listens empty.

When you are done, you should have an agreed-upon *intentions list* for your relationship. Congratulations! Now you have an empowering way to bring positive change and growth into your Soul Partnership. That is how naming the issues works.

EXERCISE: LISTENING EMPTY AND MIRRORING

Now you can use your new intentions list to practice listening empty and mirroring. To recap, here is the communication exercise in its entirety:

Individually create an issues list, beginning with your complaints and transforming them into positive relationship intentions.

Review your relationship intentions list together, creating agreement wherever possible to work on these things together.

Each of you chooses one item that is midway on the emotional intensity scale.

Choose who will be the speaker first—have an issue ready to talk about.

The Listener consciously sets aside his own thoughts, feelings, and point of view, making it his job *only to understand* the Speaker and her point of view.

The Speaker asks, "Are you ready to listen empty?"

The Listener signifies readiness.

The Speaker begins, talking in reasonably short paragraphs. After each complete thought or idea has been expressed, the Speaker asks, "What did you hear so far?"

The Listener mirrors with, "What I hear you saying is…," concluding with, "Did I hear you so far?"

Once there is agreement (the Listener heard correctly), the Listener asks, "What else about that?"

The Speaker continues with another paragraph or complete thought.

The process is continued until the Speaker says in responses to the Listener's question ("What else about that?"), "That's all, there is no more." At this point, pause, and then the Listener asks, "What else?" Sometimes there is more! Continue until the Speaker is certain there is no more to say at this time.

The Speaker acknowledges the Listener for listening: "Thank you for listening to me. You did a great job!"

At this point, take a break, smile, congratulate one another, get a glass of water, hug, take deep breaths, or whatever feels appropriate. Prepare yourselves to switch roles by taking some sort of nurturing break. Now, begin all over again, this time with the former Listener doing the speaking about the same issue.

Once you have each shared about the issue, you are ready to go to the next step. Sometimes that means offering apologies (see chapter 9 for this extremely powerful process). Sometimes it means going straight to brainstorming and creating new solutions together (see chapter 11). Sometimes it simply means acknowledging one another for the struggles that you have experienced about this issue (see chapter 10).

Often the process of discussing issues in an empowering way, getting the truth on the table, and listening to one another with honor and appreciation is enough! It is so rare that we take the time or bring forward the skills to do this that when it happens, we are so filled with gratitude and fulfillment the issues simply dissolve. Sometimes the issues do not dissolve, but the emotional distress around them does, so that they assume new proportions and appear much more solvable than before.

What If It Looks Too Hard?

Sometimes, this all just seems to be a bit too much. It is so prescribed, not very spontaneous, and looks like lots of hard work. Why would you take this on?

Most couples when they are learning new processes such as these find them cumbersome. It is not unlike learning any new skill in life, whether it is driving a car or learning how to use a computer for the first time. Yes, there is a learning curve. Over time, however, it gets easier, more natural, and much more spontaneous. Eventually, you will find that you naturally listen empty and mirror without even being conscious of it or necessarily following all of the prescribed steps. The fulfillment and satisfaction of expressing ourselves fully and being really listened to is so attractive that you will be magnetized toward it even in everyday conversation.

In the beginning of your learning curve, be willing to experience it as awkward and uncomfortable. Carve out time for these exercises—I recommend two hours per week with no distractions until you feel confident using the skills. When practicing in the beginning, use your intentions list (issues renamed) for topics. Over time, some of the issues may dissolve without ever addressing them because you have created so much connection with regard to the other issues and so much success in resolving them. It is therefore OK and even good to let your intentions list evolve over time, naming and re-naming, and removing issues.

New Love Stories

As I have witnessed couples bringing these skills into their relationships, I have seen them create their own new, far more empowering love stories. Listening empty promotes deeper and more authentic communication. Mirroring renews intimacy. The heart-and-soul communion that takes place peels away the layers of hurts, resentments, and other blocks, revealing once again the essence of who we are for one another.

With our essence revealed, our stories shift and become empowering once again. Instead of seeing our partner as "the enemy," we see him as another human being who longs for connection just as we do. Instead of viewing our partner as someone we must fix, change, or drag through life, we are able to see her once again as a strong and capable person, the Soul Partner we chose. When we listen to and honor the other person's point of view, miracles happen, as in the case of Denise and Zach.

Denise was struggling with her partner of seven years, Zach. In her eyes, he was a "workaholic" who never took time to play. She believed that he viewed her as a frivolous person who failed to take responsibility. They argued endlessly about the division of work, who did what, and whose turn it was to do the next thing. He resented her time off to have lunch with girlfriends or get a massage, while she resented his endless drive to make more money.

Denise realized one day that her judgement of Zach for his way of approaching work was no different than his judgement of her for how she handled her leisure time. She decided to take a new approach with him. Instead of beginning with her point of view, she asked him about his. She opened this conversation with a concern (his working so much) and then asked a couple of open-ended questions about how he felt about that. What unfolded was an entirely different conversation than the ones they had had in the past.

With encouragement, Zach opened up about his feelings. It turned out that his age concerned him (mid-fifties) and the prospect of growing old with inadequate funds to take care of himself concerned him a great deal. He felt that he had few productive years to work as hard as he did and to bank the resulting money. Working hard was his way of trying to ensure a comfortable lifestyle in his old age.

Denise's compassion for Zach opened up as she listened to him talk about his fears and concerns. Instead of appearing like the cruel taskmaster, he now appeared like a vulnerable man who was doing the best he could. Their relationship became more tender and intimate after this open, honest, and loving dialogue, even though their work patterns didn't change.

Things to Remember

Listening empty is a gift, not an obligation. If we demand that our partner listens, and he is not in an emotional space to do so, we will most likely encounter resistance. If, however, we give the gift of listening to our partner and express that we would like the same gift in return at the appropriate time, we will most likely get what we want.

In order to open our partner's heart to want to give this gift, we must be willing to give it with no expectation in return. We must give, because we want our partner to have the gift, and trust that when the timing is right, we will find that gift coming back.

Listening empty must be chosen by both partners in order for it to work best. These processes cannot be forced; they must be allowed to evolve. Our job is to create the right conditions for them to occur, such as:

Letting go of resentment.

Recognizing our own and our partner's humanity, complete with our individual flaws, that has led to this point.

Recognizing that, in some way, we have both contributed to the dynamics of our relationship, and that it is up to us to do everything possible to create the possibility for change to occur.

Releasing blame toward our partner and ourselves.

Finding some way to accept conditions *as they are currently* and then setting new intentions for the future.

I recommend reading this chapter *three times* before you actually do the exercises. Read all the way through once together (one of you reads out loud), then once individually on your own, and then once more together (other person reads out loud).

If your relationship is full of pain at this time, see the listening exercise for distressed relationships at the end of the book.

Chapter Six
Compassionate and Intuitive Listening

I once witnessed an exercise in a personal growth seminar in which the leader quickly tossed an ordinary baseball to a volunteer several times. After the volunteer performed several tentative catches (and misses), the leader suggested that she focus on how many times the ball turned in the air as it was coming toward her. As she did so, she quit struggling—instead of tensing with each throw, she began to relax. Now, she was easily able to catch every single ball!

The exercise illustrated that when we focus on "trying hard to do it right" or on "making something happen," we are at our worst. We struggle, we fumble, we literally "drop the ball" in our lives.

When we focus on something other than the mechanics of the problem at hand, we enter an entirely different state, a zone that some have called "flow." In that state, we transcend the mechanical aspects of what we are doing and we operate intuitively and creatively. By attending to the number of times the ball turned in the air, the catcher began working intuitively rather than mechanically. Intuitive action is exponentially easier than action by rote or by following certain steps.

I saw this again when I studied ballroom dancing. At first, every step was mechanical as I focused on moving my body just so, remembering the steps, and attending to my posture (I'm sure I looked somewhat like the Tin Man in *The Wizard of Oz* in those days). My dance instructor assured me that one day I would develop "body memory." One day, I unconsciously got caught up in the magic of the music and the rhythm of the dance itself, and I "forgot" to worry about the steps or my body posture. I was dancing from body memory, and I was in the flow. I was truly dancing.

Intuitive Listening

In communication, there is a similar state that can be achieved, one in which we are transported back to the early days of our romance when we easily understood one another. We finished each other's sentences; we laughed at the same jokes. There was an almost magical connection that transported us out of the everyday and into the extraordinary. That is what ***intuitive listening*** does for a mature relationship.

Intuitive listening is more than following the steps of listening empty and mirroring. It *begins* with those necessary steps, like the dance steps in my story. If we practice them over and over, with our partner, and if we trust the process, one day we spontaneously move to a deeper level of listening that is no longer mechanical. There we find ourselves listening from intuition. We discover that there is more to our mate than the words he is sharing. We discover the *essence* of the person with whom we are sharing life. There, our relationship takes on a whole new quality of connection, love, and growth. How does this happen?

In the beginning with these skills, we primarily use our minds. We concentrate on the process itself, what the steps are, how to deal with the blocks, and how to get through them. It requires a great deal of mental focus to do this, and that is a function of the mind.

Eventually, the steps become automatic and no longer require concentration with the mind. Then, the *message itself* becomes primary, and the desire to understand this other human being is more important than getting the steps right. In this stage, following the steps is insignificant because the mechanics are receding into the background while the essence of the communication (and thus, of the other person) is moving into the foreground.

As it is with any new skill, whether it is dancing, or typing, or driving a car, the better we get at it, the less of our mind and concentration it requires. That is how our brains work with learning and skill development. The how-to's recede into the background, we move into "flow," and our intuitive processes take over.

Our Essence

The true aim of all communication is connection, which happens when we understand, grasp, and validate the essence of someone else's thoughts, feelings, and point of view. An even deeper, more profound connection occurs when we "get" the *essence of one another*.

It is from our essence that our creativity, self-expression, joy, and fulfillment in life flow. When I am in touch with *who I am* in the matter of my life, great things invariably happen. When I help my clients rediscover their essence, their lives sort out, their relationships improve, and they experience greater well-being and fulfillment overall. That is the power of connection to essence.

Modern life does not promote the experience of essence, in us or in our relationships with one another. Someone once said that most of us are operating like the "human doing" rather than the "human being."

One of the most challenging pieces of homework I give to my clients is to simply take *thirty minutes per day* to just be—to relax, breathe deeply, meditate, or engage in a spiritual exercise such as prayer. Modern human beings often resist such an exercise because we have not done it in so long (if ever!) that we are fearful. Getting in touch with one's self, or soul essence, after perhaps years of not doing so, sometimes initially brings up pain—the pain of lost connection with *who I am*.

In relationships, this lack of awareness of essence leaves us far too much in the logical, practical side of ourselves so that we skip over attending to the qualities that make us unique and so appealing to one another. Over time, we have forgotten who we are and we spend our time focusing on our roles and the rules that we invent for ourselves (e.g., "I must be perfect!").

In relationships, we make up a similar picture of the other person (often through internal stories) and no longer attend to the exciting process of discovery. This, along with so many other aspects of modern life, takes us away from our essence and leaves our connection lifeless and mechanical. Losing touch with essence individually and in our relationships affects far more than the quality of our relationships. It affects our well-being in general and even our ability to resist or recover from disease.

Author and renowned cancer specialist Dr. Mitchell L. Gaynor, in his book *The Healing Essence*, describes essence as embodying a "healing power" that exists within every person.[7] Dr. Gaynor discovered that if he could help his patients reconnect with their sense of essence, they were able to bring tremendous healing powers to bear upon their health issues. Those patients who practiced the meditations he taught them and who were willing to consider the spiritual implications of their disease had a much higher than expected recovery rate.

Recovering Essence

I was once going about my day when I encountered a very difficult person. This person was irritable and out of sorts. Nothing seemed to make her happy, and she blamed her unhappiness on everyone and everything around her. I tried to rationalize with her. I tried to persuade her to see things my way, but she just did not seem to want to listen.

Finally, in frustration, I said to her, "OK, nothing I'm doing seems to be working. Why don't you tell me what you need?" She answered, "I need you to listen to me." I said, "OK. I'm listening. What are you feeling?" and she said, "I'm angry because…" She had lots to say about feeling angry.

Then she said, "I'm sad because…" and I asked her to tell me more. She had lots of sad stories to tell. I let her talk about them all.

Then she said, "This is what I want…" I listened and I honored her feelings, and I didn't try to do anything about them. Finally, when everything had been said (I know this because I asked her, "Is there anything else?" and she said, with great relief, "No, that's all"), I thanked her for telling me how she feels.

That difficult person was myself. That day, I needed to stop and listen to her, honor her feelings, and make sure she knew I loved her.

There was a time in my life when I almost never listened to myself, to my true thoughts, feelings, wishes, and desires. I was so separated from who I was and therefore from my essence that my life was an endless series of dramas with no sense of coherence. Disconnected from who I was, I was powerless to direct my life or to understand how to derive fulfillment and satisfaction in living each day.

My recovery began, continued, and will always be, in attending to my essence first, all else in life second. I cannot give to others what I do not have for myself. I cannot love my partner any more than I love and care for myself. I cannot listen to, respect, understand, or "get" his essence if I do not get my own.

Recovery of essence, and therefore recovery of the ability to love and be loved, begins with the self. When was the last time you listened to yourself? Honored all of your feelings, right or wrong, positive or negative?

Perhaps you could start with the most difficult person of all, yourself, and maybe you could give yourself the gift of listening empty. Then, maybe you could give yourself the most powerful healing agent of all: full acceptance of yourself *exactly as you are,* in all of your humanity and imperfections, warts and all.

In seeing and honoring all parts of ourselves, we create healing within our hearts and spirits, and then we are able to extend that to others. This enables us to connect to our Soul Partner in the deepest, most fulfilling way.

I suggest that if you do not already, you begin to set aside thirty minutes per day *just for yourself.* Use that time for relaxing, deep breathing, spiritual exercise, meditating, or whatever allows you to simply be with yourself and reconnect with your essence. Make this time sacrosanct and inviolate. Enroll your partner and your family in the importance of this exercise for yourself. Do it regularly, especially when you do not want to. Over time, I promise that you will begin to see phenomenal positive changes in your life.

Essence in Relationships

Intuitive listening brings us back to the place of connecting from our essence, the way we were in the beginning of the relationship. Intuitive listening is not the same as analyzing or interpreting. It comes from the heart and soul, not the mind. It involves compassion and is non-judgmental and caring.

Intuitive listening goes beyond the words our partner is speaking and delves into his or her experience as a human being. It is expansive, creative, flexible, and spontaneous.

Trying to explain how to listen intuitively is like trying to explain the exact nature of love, which is inexplicable and always remains mysterious and subjective.

What we can do is *point to*, or indicate, what love might be. We can draw distinctions, and we can name some of the components of love, as the majority of us understand it. It is the same way with intuitive listening.

NOT Just the Facts

One important distinction about listening intuitively, is that it is very different than listening in order to "get the facts." What does that mean?

When we are endeavoring to understand our partner, it is typical for us to go first toward the literal, or factual, analysis of what we are hearing. In so doing, we may skip over the real message in the situation.

For example, when Nicole told George, "You make me happy," he became fearful that she believed he was the source of her happiness and that she would therefore become dependent on him. He interpreted her words literally, rather than getting the message that she loved him. He responded by talking about his ex-wife's emotional dependence on him and how uncomfortable he was with that. Nicole interpreted George's words as him comparing her to other women in his past and became angry.

George and Nicole initially were emotionally "hooked" when they interpreted one another's words literally rather than intuitively. George thought Nicole was making him solely responsible for her well-being, and Nicole thought George was failing to see her for who she was.

As they continued talking and began listening more closely (intuitively), they realized the deeper truth that each was trying to express—that they *both* wanted a relationship based on autonomy and interdependence. On a deeper level than their initial words, they were, *in essence*, expressing identical wishes and desires. From there, they easily cleared things up and were able to express and "get" their love for each other.

Often, as I am listening to couples in my office, I am struck by the similarity of their underlying messages. Paradoxically, I witness them struggling to express themselves and believing themselves to be worlds apart in their values, views, wishes, and desires. What is missing is not that they want the same things, but that they are blocked in expressing their thoughts and hearing one another so that they experience their true connection.

The Space between the Words

The practice of meditation takes us beyond our day-to-day constant stream of inner self-talk so that we are no longer "in our thoughts," but are connected to something much greater. Some describe it as a spiritual or holy state of mind and body. Others describe it as a peaceful, calm state.

In meditation, we find the *space between the thoughts*, or what some have called the place of no-thought. In that place, we are limitless, we are our essence, and we are present to our deepest truths.

Meditation has tremendous emotional and physical benefits. It often provides relief from innumerable stresses and stress-related diseases. It also parallels what happens when we listen intuitively.

Somewhere in between the words that my beloved is speaking lies his truth. If I listen, first to what he is saying, then to what he is *not* saying, then to *who he is* with regard to what he is expressing, I begin to get close to the true message. How do I do that?

To listen intuitively is not an exercise of will or a matter of following steps. It is more a matter of *giving certain things up* in order to allow something new to emerge. In meditation, we give up the attachment to our thoughts. Some practices teach that we view our thoughts like words marching across a movie screen. Yes, those are my thoughts, but I do not have to latch onto them, dwell on them, and make them my reality at this time. Not an easy practice in a world that prizes rational thought above all else!

In listening intuitively, we give up the attachment to our own interpretations, judgments, or analyses. We give up the attachment to the mechanics of listening empty and mirroring, although we paradoxically continue to practice those steps somewhere in the background. We give up our own reactions, letting them go when we feel them, or even before we feel them. We listen from heart, soul, and a genuine desire to understand the essence of the other person.

By letting go of these things, we open ourselves to that which lies in the space between the words themselves. We open ourselves to our partner's true essence. In so doing, we are able to not only listen intuitively, but also our mirroring takes on that same quality. This is what David discovered in one of his interactions with Esther.

David, wanting to discuss an issue in his relationship with Esther, found that she was becoming increasingly defensive in the conversation. He stopped talking and began to use his intuition. He mirrored her emotions: "I can see that you are feeling defensive. I don't wish to make you feel that way. Let's go in a different direction with this conversation." From there, he was able to reassure her of his love and devotion and they were able to collaborate in solving the issue.

People are not always verbal with their thoughts and emotions. Intuitive listening enables us to "hear" what our partners are not saying and steer the conversation in directions that are more productive. This is especially important when deciding the right timing for communication.

For example, just because I am in the mood for a conversation, and I am ready to listen empty to my partner, does not mean that he is ready and able to verbalize. By listening intuitively, I can give the gift of mirroring his mood or his emotions. Some examples of what I might say at that time are:

"It seems that you are feeling out of sorts and not ready to talk."

"It looks like you would rather be quiet for now."

"It seems like you just want to be left alone, maybe have some private down time."

"Perhaps you don't have the right words at this moment to say how you feel. How about if we talk about it some other time, when you are ready?"

Giving Up Judgment

To listen intuitively, we surrender, or give up, judgment and interpretation. One day, Joseph was endeavoring to listen empty to Stephanie. The context: just prior to this conversation, Joseph had become afraid of going to the next level of commitment and, in fear, had abruptly exited the relationship for a few weeks. Here, he was giving Stephanie the opportunity to express her feelings about what those two weeks were like for her. Later, he said that although he felt very close to her, she had expressed hesitation about being intimate with him until she could feel more trusting. His judgment and interpretation: "Seems like she's playing a game with me."

I challenged Joseph to question his interpretation. When he could see that Stephanie was fearful of his leaving again, he was able to let go of his own feelings of being manipulated and feel compassion for her. He realized that he wanted to help her feel safe again, to really be there for her.

The miracle of giving up our interpretations and listening intuitively is that it automatically creates compassion. That is because underneath it all, we all carry the same basic fears, the same basic desires, and the same capacity for healing and growth. Underneath it all, between the words, we are truly connected in our similarity as human beings. That is the truth that intuitive listening reveals and that is the pathway to the greatest gift we can provide in our relationships: *compassionate listening.*

Surrendering Being Right

Perhaps the most important thing that we must surrender in order to listen intuitively and compassionately, is one of our most powerful addictions as humans: being right!

Remember that we are constantly creating stories about our lives, the people we love, our relationships, and ourselves. The problem, however, is not the stories themselves, but our inflexibility about them.

When we decide that the stories we hold so dear are *the truth, the whole truth, and nothing but the truth*, we close ourselves off from further learning and growth. When we do this, we adopt the stance of being "right" about the ways in which we perceive others and the world around us. Being right, we must therefore conclude that others are "wrong" if they do not agree with us. *This automatically creates enormous blocks in our relationships.*

It is impossible for us to agree at all times. It is highly unlikely that a relationship between two equals who are empowered to express themselves fully is never going to contain disagreement. Sooner or later, all Soul Partners face the inevitable clash of ideas that comes from being unique individuals.

I used the term "addicted" earlier in reference to being right because it is that dramatic. It is not just that we *want* to be right—it is that we *cannot tolerate* being wrong! Being right protects us from feeling vulnerable and confused, and shields us from the experience of our wounded childhood egos.

In our closest relationship, that with our Soul Partner, being right often stands solidly in the way of being connected, and therefore, fulfilled and happy.

True understanding, and therefore connection, occurs when we are able to express ourselves fully and find that place where our most fundamental values intersect. To do that, we have to give up being right. Someone once posed the question, "Do you want to be right or do you want to be happy?"

In giving up being right, without surrendering our point of view, we open the door to lively, spirited discussion. If I can speak my truth, you can speak yours, and we are flexible in our listening and compassionate with one another, we can be creative, inventive, and supportive of one another in our growth and in structuring our lives together. Our relationship takes on an excitement and sense of adventure that makes our connection so valuable we cannot imagine being apart.

Being Right and Having a Point of View

One of the core aspects of being human is that we each have our own point of view. Two people can look at *exactly the same thing* and see something different.

In relationships, it is not only possible to have different points of view about the same thing, it is desirable. By remaining open, we keep our connection fresh and lively, and we gain the benefit of the wisdom that our partner was put in our lives to share with us.

By recognizing the desirability of differing points of view, we release the emotional blocks that prevent us from a deeper level of intimacy. How do we do that?

EXERCISE: BEING RIGHT

Here is an exercise to do individually and then to share with your partner. First, take paper and pen, when you are alone, and ask yourself:

What am I "being right" about in my relationship? Now, separate your responses into two categories: 1) About my partner or our relationship, 2) About certain underlying values or beliefs (generalizations).

An example of this exercise might look like this:

What I Am Being Right About

My Partner/Relationship Underlying Beliefs: He doesn't pay attention to my needs Men are insensitive and uncaring She is irrational when it comes to her emotions It is impossible to understand a woman's emotions He is so sloppy and messy Men are like little boys. She neglects my sexual needs Once you marry a woman, sex goes out the window He is so co-dependent with his mother Men who are too close to their mothers never grow up I don't feel the same excitement with her that I once did If the "zing" goes out of the relationship, you can never get it back He has no clue about my sexual needs Men only care about satisfying themselves sexually

As you can see, this list can go on and on. Keep going until you run out of things to say. Be willing to sound negative to yourself—don't sugarcoat this exercise!

Once you have completed the exercise, sit down together and share your lists, making sure that you do them one at a time and practice listening empty and mirroring. For this part of the exercise, *put new words in front of each item*, so that you introduce the *element of doubt*. Those words are: "Sometimes" and "I'm not sure if." This part of the exercise looks like this:

"*Sometimes* I feel that you don't pay attention to my needs. *I'm not sure if it is true* that all men are insensitive and uncaring."

"*Sometimes you seem* irrational when it comes to your emotions. *It may not be true* that it is impossible to understand a woman's emotions."

When you have gone through your entire list with one another, introducing the element of doubt, stop and ask yourself: *Am I willing to give up being right about these and other thoughts and beliefs that I hold about my partner?* Remind yourself: *I do not have to give up my point of view in order to do this.*

If your answer is "yes," then affirm that to one another, something like this:

"I can see that sharing different points of view with each other can be really good for us. I want to be more open to what you have to say in the future."

Now you have opened an entirely new door in your relationship! Thank one another for being willing to be so much more open and vulnerable together.

Giving Up "What I Want to Hear"

One very significant block to intuitive listening is being attached to what we *want to hear*, rather than being truly open to what the other person is attempting to say. This especially comes up when one person is trying to express the need for change.

Over and over, Peter attempted to tell his wife, Karen, that he was unhappy in their relationship and why. Each time he brought up the subject, she reacted emotionally, or she ended the conversation. He tried two different therapists, hoping that a third party could help her listen, but she refused to go back to therapy.

Peter, fearful of Karen's reactions, backed down each time, holding back from expressing his full truth: that if things did not change between them he would not stay in the marriage. Eventually, Peter "shut down," and began the process of divorce, to Karen's shock and dismay.

Throughout their separation and divorce, Karen made repeated efforts to reconnect with Peter, but she never asked him to talk about his unhappiness in their relationship, or how he was feeling, or what his needs were.

If Karen had been willing to hear Peter's message, rather than avoiding it because she did not want to hear it, new possibilities might have opened up. They might have parted by mutual agreement and with respect, or they would have forged a much deeper connection based on really hearing and understanding one another. Instead, they parted bitter and angry.

In a Soul Partnership, we must be willing to speak and to hear the truth. Is this scary at times? Absolutely. Is it emotionally risky? Yes, but only in the sense that you may decide to redefine the *nature* of your connection, based on greater understanding. Expressing the truth cannot break a real soul connection, though it may contribute to the decision to change its form.

Listening: The Gift of Release

Paradoxically, even if our partner expresses doubts about our relationship, by giving up our attachment to what we want to hear and by hearing the truth, we open the possibility for those feelings to change. This is due to another interesting phenomenon in human communication:

> *Sometimes, there are things to express that actually change once we express them.*

> *Likewise, if those things are* not *expressed, they become an internal reality that solidifies into "truth" and then guides our course of action.*

How does this happen? Communication is so much more than the words we speak, beginning in the heart, mind, spirit, and even the body. First, there are sensations, impressions, and emotional imprints; from them, we experience perceptions, thoughts, judgments, beliefs, and interpretations. These things feed into our stories, which then influence what we say, how we say it, and to whom we say it. This process, which usually goes on unconsciously, powerfully influences behavior and choice of action.

Distorted perceptions damage connections between human beings, but they do not have to happen. At the point that sensations, impressions, and imprints are beginning to solidify into thought and emotion, we have the opportunity to bring them out into the light of day, before we act on them. Often, when that happens, they are revealed for what they are—false perceptions but not the truth.

The reality is that *whatever we think, feel, and believe is subject to reevaluation*. When we express it, it is actually experienced in a different way than when we merely think about it or keep it to ourselves. Sometimes, the difference is so dramatic that even deep-seated beliefs or intense feelings shift simply by expressing them out loud.

What this means in our relationships is that it is extremely important to constantly give our partner the opportunity to express his truth. In fact, it is one of the greatest gifts we can give, both to our partner, and to ourselves! By encouraging our partner to express thoughts and feelings that may be difficult for us to hear, we allow the possibility of releasing false perceptions that may block our connection.

For example, it is normal in the course of our lives to feel attracted to others outside our primary connection. It is not necessary, and often it is false, to indulge in those feelings in secret. In fact, it is the secretive nature of attraction to others that often causes the feelings to grow and to solidify into an internal reality that demands action. That is how affairs are often begun.

One way to affair-proof your relationship is to have an agreement to always disclose your attraction to others, no matter how uncomfortable it is to do so. If you also agree to never act on those feelings, and if you agree to keep no secrets, you will most likely find that this strengthens your relationship. How? The power of the attraction diminishes by expressing it out loud. In this, as in all of your interactions with your partner, the element of compassion will sustain you and empower your connection.

Listening with Compassion

When things are good between us, when we are connected in love and feel no threat to our sense of security, compassion is easy. It is when we are stressed and feel our emotional needs aren't being met that compassion is so challenging. Yet, listening with compassion is essential at all times in a relationship in order for it to work. We do that through taking time to understand our partner from his point of view, even when things are not going well between us.

The partner who at a distance appears one way appears another way up close and with personal contact. That is the way it is when we connect. When we are truly connected, we cannot help but feel love and compassion. Anger and judgment are only possible when we are disconnected from one another.

Connection leads to compassion, and compassion creates connection. It is an amazing and miraculous circle of positive energy when we allow it to flow in our relationships.

We create compassion when we set aside judgment and open ourselves to seeing the other person's humanity. We experience compassion when we listen empty and honor the other's experience.

Creating Compassion

In highly stressed relationships, where anger and ill will run the show, sometimes a loss will pull the couple back together. This is because grief is an emotional state that often allows us to put down our emotional walls and connect more easily and with greater compassion.

After a devastating loss, such as the death of a friend or family member, there is often a deeper focus on those things that truly matter in life. We spend more time with family and friends. We are more spiritually directed. Our grievances now seem petty and we release them more easily. Though we would not have chosen this path consciously, it is a huge wake-up call for our lives and our ability to experience and express compassion.

In our relationships, we do not have to wait for circumstances such as loss to smack us in the face and wake up our sense of compassion. We have the power to create the circumstances for compassion to come forth naturally and spontaneously. We have the ability to create and live in this state every day of our lives, if we choose to do so.

Actively Creating Compassion

In relationships, compassion is blocked to the degree that we perceive ourselves as different from others. The truth about people is that most of them are fundamentally good, honorable, and worthy. When we peel away the stories and the ways we appear different on the surface, we find that we are very much alike. We are all working on the same things, whether conscious of it or not.

We are all striving to learn how to love ourselves better, to be more connected in spirit, and to live honest lives in the pursuit of fulfillment. We are all yearning for lives that reflect our soul's mission and purpose. We are all longing for more connection to God and to one another. We are also deeply afraid of failing to live up to our own expectations, of being revealed for our flaws and imperfections, and of being discovered as fearful.

We are all afraid on some level, of things that we can and cannot name, and we are covering it up. We walk around with plastic smiles and, when queried, say things like, "I'm fine!" whether it is true or not.

The Truth about Your Partner

Your partner is afraid, just as are you. Chances are, he is not conscious of that fear, just as most of the time, you are not conscious of yours.

When your partner behaves badly, it is *always* motivated by fear. When he hurts you, lets you down, and runs away from intimacy, it is usually not deliberate. Even if it is, it is not truly vicious in nature, though it may feel that way to you.

When your partner disconnects from you, it is because he is terrified of being "found out" that he is imperfect. When he sabotages your love in those unique ways of which only he is capable, it is not with the desire to break your heart. It is because he is afraid. Fear leads to closure of the heart. It leads to self-protection and sometimes to lashing out at others.

When we recognize our own humanity, and our own fears, then we are able to see them in our partners. When we inventory our own flaws and imperfections (without self-criticism), then we are able to see the wonderful humanity of others without judgment. When we "own up" to the mistakes we have made in the past, including the ways we have hurt others, and when we forgive ourselves for those mistakes, we are naturally forgiving toward our partners.

Dealing with an Angry Partner

Sometimes, no matter how hard we try, we cannot seem to grasp why our partner is angry or what to do to help him calm down. When this happens, the best you can do is stay centered in compassion. Anger always stems from hurt, and hurt stems from fear. Therefore, when an angry partner confronts us, we are actually in the presence of a fearful human being.

Keeping that in mind, we can often defuse the situation by listening compassionately and mirroring the anger. "I can really hear how angry you are. Tell me what's wrong. I want to listen." Getting angry and defensive in return never works!

Anger sometimes serves the purpose of getting a partner to "show up." If our partner is angry with us, it may be because we have not been emotionally available in some way. The solution: show up so BIG that your partner no longer needs the anger. Sit in front of your beloved, make eye contact, focus totally on what he is saying. Be completely emotionally present and available for however long it takes to handle the situation.

Another thing that helps is to keep in mind that most of the anger, though it seems to be about us, is in reality a reflection of the other person's deepest issues. Therefore, we can take it less personally, without closing off to what our partner has to say. Sometimes, it helps to request that the other person speak in a less critical way.

"I know you are angry, and I want to hear you out. However, it's hard to listen to so much criticism at one time. Could you try to put it in a more gentle way?"

A powerful way to defuse our partner's anger is to diligently look for the truth about ourselves in what we are being told. Almost always, there is some truth we can acknowledge and own up to. When we do so, we let our partner know that we truly care about her grievances and that we are willing to take responsibility for whatever imbalance exists in the relationship.

It is not easy to avoid feeling attacked when our partner is angry. A way to counteract those feelings is to ask ourselves, "What are my partner's true intentions?" In this way, with intuition, we are able to refocus on the deep realization that our partner is not truly intent on hurting us.

Sometimes, anger comes from a partner because of an emotional imbalance in that person and through no responsibility of ours. Our partner may be going through something biochemical, perhaps a hormone imbalance or illness. It could be anger stemming out of another life circumstance, such as the loss of a job. The best time to defuse that kind of anger is before it explodes. How do we do that?

We can approach our partner at a time when we are both feeling calm, and bring up the issue of anger and how best to handle it. We can gently (without blaming) let our partner know how it feels when she explodes in our direction.

We can ask for her to tell us how best to calm her down at those times. Often, people have the most amazing and simple solutions to offer if we ask and thereby stimulate the creative and collaborative process.

EXERCISE:
CREATING COMPASSION

If you want to open up compassion in your relationship, this exercise will assist you in that intention. Individually, do the following self-inventory. Look back on your life without self-blame and without fear of admitting your own humanity:

> **List the regrets that you have:** things that you have done that you wish you had not; things that you have not done that you wish you had.
>
> **List the guilts that you have:** things that you have done that you feel guilt or shame about, including any people who may have been harmed by your actions.
>
> **List your fears:** things that you sometimes worry about; things that you dread; things in life that you are afraid of happening to you or to someone you love; things that might be wonderful but that you are not sure you can fully embrace (such as success, however you define that).

Once you have done your inventories separately, set aside time to share them. Even if you have shared these events and stories before, do it again, this time listening empty (with compassion) and mirroring. Speak slowly and allow any feelings you may have to come up.

This is how the exercise looked for Tony and Susan:

> Tony: One of the deepest regrets that I have is that I moved away from my ex-wife and my children several years ago. Because of this, I missed out on so much of my children's lives growing up, and I can never recover that time. My heart aches over what we missed together.

Susan: What I hear you saying is that one of your greatest regrets is not being there on a day-to-day basis to participate in your children's lives while they were growing up. You missed out on the little things in their lives that are in the past and can't be recovered. You feel deeply sad about missing out on...

Tony: One of the things I feel guilty about is the time that I quit speaking to my dad for two years. I was so angry with him for not being there for me when I was growing up that I just cut him out. Even though we got past that, I know that it hurt him deeply and it cost us dearly in the short time we had left. I didn't realize that he would die of cancer just a few short months after we healed our separation...

Susan: What I hear you saying is that you feel guilty about cutting your dad out of your life for two years. You were hurt about his not being there for you, so you shut him out, not knowing that you had so little time left with him. Even though you made amends before he died, it hurts deeply to know how much he was hurt by that and by how much time the two of you lost...

Tony: One of my fears is that the people I love will realize how flawed I am and will leave me. Even though you and my kids tell me every day how much you love me, I am still terrified that one day you will wake up and see me for how imperfect I am and leave. I guess I have that fear because I have done that to others...

Susan: What I hear you saying is that one of your deepest fears is that you will be abandoned by those you love in the way that you believe you have abandoned others. You are afraid that we will see how imperfect you are and lose our love for you and just leave.

Take turns in the exercise so that one of you shares a regret, guilt, or fear, and then the other does one. STOP the exercise if you are not able to listen with compassion every step of the way. Resume in a few hours or days when you are ready to listen in that way.

When you finish sharing your lists, share what you feel in your heart toward one another at this moment. Allow your compassion to grow and express it in words, touch, eye contact, and whatever way seems loving and appropriate.

Chapter Seven
Speaking to Empower

In the past, there were numerous boundaries around what was OK to say and what was not. This served many purposes, among them to provide a degree of psychological protection. Allowing people to "save face" was important and valued. Keeping the "status quo" and maintaining cohesion through adopting society's rules was prized. Individual self-expression, especially when it went against the grain, was not.

In families, children were taught to "be seen and not heard," women were taught to defer to their husband's ideas and wishes and to withhold their own, and men were taught to spare women's feelings at all costs. Though these standards were not always upheld, their prevalence nevertheless effectively created a noncommunicative approach to human relationships, especially that between men and women.

All of this began to change in the mid-twentieth century. Women had had a taste of freedom, and yearned for more, the human potential movement was gathering momentum, and it became acceptable in society for a person to seek psychological counseling for life issues. The baby boomers who grew up listening to rock 'n' roll were unwilling to stifle themselves and submit to authority. Almost overnight, the "be careful of what you say" rule was tossed away, and "say anything" was our new mantra.

Say Anything

Because the old societal boundaries were found to be too restricting for modern life, we hastened to the other extreme. Yearning for self-expression, we dedicated ourselves to saying whatever our thoughts and feelings were. If we experienced anger, we "let it out." If we felt sad, we learned that it was okay to cry in front of others.

Many of the results of the "say anything" revolution have been very positive. There is no question that members of groups that were repressed in the past needed the freedom to speak up and be heard. Women, minorities, and children's advocates have gained a voice that was vitally needed to correct injustices and prevent future harm.

Socially, it is now possible to talk and connect with friends on a deeper and more rewarding level than was possible just a few decades ago. Though I do not have children of my own, I am often a witness to what seems to me to be an amazing level of self-expression that is afforded to little ones today. No doubt, men and women today have far more freedom to interact openly and honestly in their relationships with one another.

On the other side of the coin, however, we have perhaps lost something for our relationships. In prizing self-expression, we have forgotten that there may be an unwanted effect on the other person from our hastily uttered words. In venting whatever our emotions, we have lost sight of the value of letting someone "save face" or of being tender with another person's sensitivities. We have, to some degree, lost the art of diplomacy.

Restoring Balance

In families, we know that it is not possible to feel emotionally and psychologically safe if everyone has permission to say whatever comes to mind, however harsh or critical. Likewise, it is not possible to have emotional and psychological health if no one has permission to voice displeasure or to express disagreement.

Somewhere in between the "no talk" rule and the "say anything" paradigm is a state of balance. As with so many things in life, the real race is to the middle. Being able to express one's thoughts, feelings, ideas, and creative energy is essential to life, health, and the pursuit of happiness. Likewise, having boundaries around our self-expression is essential to relationship harmony and emotional safety with a partner. Bringing together these two potentially contradictory paradigms is both the challenge and the opportunity of Soul Partners.

First, Do No Harm

An intention that I often encourage couples to set about their communication processes is first to *do no harm*. This means that, before we open our mouth to speak to our partner, we resolve to be mindful of our choice of words, considering what might be the best way to deliver the communication so that it is not unnecessarily painful to the listener.

Setting this intention often creates amazing changes in a relationship. First, it raises the awareness that we have in the past done emotional damage in our relationships by giving ourselves too much permission to speak thoughtlessly and carelessly. Second, it invites a mindset of being attentive to the effect of our words on those we love.

A point of clarification is important here. Setting the intention to do no harm is not the same thing as deciding to withhold vital information from your partner just because you know that it will create an upset. Later, we will look at the effects of withholding important things that impact our partners.

What We Don't Know That We Don't Know

Providing feedback to one's partner is not only valuable but also necessary. One of the higher purposes of a Soul Partnership is being a mirror to one another. We trust our partner to let us know when we are behaving in a way that may not be a reflection of our best intentions. Though we may monitor ourselves closely, we are certain to miss vital information that can help us grow. This is because we all possess what is known as our psychological "blind spot," or to put it another way, "what we don't know that we don't know."

There are things that *we know that we know*—that which is in our conscious awareness. This includes all that we learned in school, from our parents and mentors, from books and other life experience, about ourselves, and about life in general.

Then there are the things that *we know that we don't know*. This includes the things we have not taken the time to learn, nor do we have a desire to learn, so we invite others who have this expertise to assist us if necessary. The mechanics of my car is one of these areas for me.

Then there are the things that *we don't know that we don't know*. This includes those things we are not conscious of, both about ourselves and about life. Since we have no conscious awareness about them, we do not seek to learn about them, not until someone in our lives brings them to our awareness.

Some of the materials in our blind spot are areas of our lives in need of correction. Often, a great deal of it is what I call the "hidden pot of gold," or assets and gifts that we do not see in ourselves or utilize fully.

Relationships with others—love, family, business, and friendships—help us see into this blind spot so that we can look at life and ourselves from a new perspective.

I will always be grateful to the people in my life who have made a difference to me in this way. One friend many years ago pointed out to me that I was being unnecessarily abrupt and demanding with a service person at a restaurant. She let me know that she found it difficult to go out with me because I behaved that way frequently. I was shocked! This behavior was not in my conscious awareness, and her comments enabled me to reflect, bringing up memories of similar behavior in adult family members growing up. Once I realized what was happening and why, I was able to make a new choice.

No one knows us better than our love mate does. This is the person who is with us morning and night, who sees deeply into who we are, with all of our gifts and assets, and with all of our flaws. One of the reasons we feel so vulnerable with our mate is that this person sees the parts of us of which we may not even be aware.

Our Soul Partner, knowing us so well, has the greatest capacity to uplift and empower us, or to deeply wound, by revealing what we don't know that we don't know. Likewise, we have the same influence with our partner. To the degree that we are allowed into our loved one's blind spot, we hold the keys to reflect in a way that fosters growth or to do the opposite.

Projections Revisited

We move into a mental and emotional state of empowerment toward our partner when we are clear about our own issues. It is impossible to hold a critical thought toward another when I am aware of my own flaws. This does not mean that I put myself down in order to remember that I am no better than others. It means that I do an honest evaluation of my own personal inventory from time to time, recognizing my own humanity, forgiving myself my mistakes, resolving to do better, and moving forward with renewed energy. This kind of process allows us to release negative energy toward ourselves and to be far less judgmental of others.

Before we can provide useful feedback to our partner, we must be able to separate our projections from our partner's blind spot. This means that before we leap into feedback, we stop and do an assessment of ourselves. It also means that we take time to evaluate what we wish to say to our partners so that we can create the best possible way to say it.

The following sections contain some methods to assist you in this endeavor. Use them, as they seem appropriate, whenever you feel irritated, annoyed, or judgmental toward your partner, or are tempted to criticize, control, or lash out. Use them when you want to create a state of love, cooperation, partnership, and growth with your partner.

Emptying the Trash

You have had a bad day, week, or month. Your temper is short, you feel depressed, irritable, and your emotional resources are wearing thin. Yet there are things to be handled, conversations you need to have with your partner, some of which may not be easy. Stop, take a deep breath, and do this exercise first! Do it to restore inner balance and then bring balance to your relationship.

When we are stressed, especially if that stress is extended over a long period of time and we do not practice regular release (through diet, exercise, meditation, etc.), our system builds up emotional "poison" that may contaminate our lives and our relationships. Often, the buildup takes the form of thoughts, feelings, and stories that impede our ability to relate. It is like the stuff that you put in your trash can. If you don't empty it, it just piles higher and higher, and whew! Does it stink!

EXERCISE: EMPTYING THE TRASH

Take some time for yourself with no distractions. Have paper and a pen, and put on soothing music. Close your eyes and take several slow, deep breaths. Now, open your eyes and begin writing down words that fit your emotional state over the past few days. Use actual feeling words, such as "angry, sad, irritable, and afraid." Keep going until you have captured on paper the full range of your recent emotional state.

Now, go back to the beginning of the list, and begin a sentence using the first word on your list:

"I feel angry because…"

Finish the sentence on paper without stopping to think about it or to edit what you say. Even if it makes no sense to you, write it down. Keep going until nothing more comes out, then go to the next word.

"I feel afraid because…"

"I feel sad because…"

Keep going until you have gone through your entire list of feeling words, and if more feelings come up, go through those as well. When you finish your list, if you do not feel significant emotional relief, go to the next step.

Now, begin with your first emotional word, only this time do the exercises *out loud.* "I feel angry because…" and so on until you go through the entire list. Do this even if you feel you are repeating the things you wrote earlier.

Most people cannot get through the entire exercise because somewhere along the way they experience a change in emotional state. Spontaneously, you may feel that your emotional load is lighter, or that the intensity of your emotions has lessened. Sometimes, people experience a change in perspective with this exercise. Having vented the emotions, they are able to see a situation or their lives more clearly.

This exercise works on an old principal of human emotions: *that which we can acknowledge and speak about (or write about) loses its power over us.* This is why so many people who have survived painful life ordeals choose to write or speak about their experiences. This is also what the power of twelve-step programs is all about. It is the heart of why psychotherapy helps so many people.

We need to express our deepest thoughts and feelings. We need to do it in a way that creates release for ourselves and does no harm to others. Then, we are able to be in an emotional, psychological, and spiritual state of balance.

Expressing Anger to Your Partner

Sometimes, we experience feelings as a result of our partner's behavior that push an emotional button. The result: anger. This is a natural part of being so close to someone and of being human. As Soul Partners, we have the ability to step on one another's emotional toes in a way no other persons do.

There are two ways we typically handle anger in a relationship, neither of which works well over time. One is to immediately express the anger, complete with raised voice, gestures, expletives, etc., while in a state of being emotionally triggered. The stories I have heard of couples who "acted out" their anger toward one another while being emotionally triggered would keep a soap opera storyline going for years! Clearly, allowing ourselves to explode in anger toward our partner creates emotional damage and solves nothing.

The other typical way of handling anger is to hold it inside and not express it. Over time, these feelings turn into resentment that can simmer for years and that can trigger unconscious acts of retribution.

Gary was deeply remorseful about an affair he had, but recalled that five years earlier, his wife had decided to quit working, putting all the financial responsibility on Gary, without collaboration or conversation regarding the larger picture of their lives.

The reality of the financial burden for him as sole provider, having just bought and decorated a large home, left Gary resentful, but he hoped that Jennifer would go back to work after a few months off. Months stretched into years, and his resentment grew, but he held back the true expression of his emotions, repressing them until they "popped out" and he had an affair.

By not expressing his true feelings, Gary denied his wife and himself the process of working through a difficult issue. By pretending that everything was fine, he left Jennifer operating from a false premise: "Yes, he would like it if I went back to work, but it's OK if I don't as long as he is able to pay the bills."

Had Gary been more forthcoming about his real feelings, they might have been able to talk openly and honestly about their points of view. Perhaps he might have seen things differently and been more at peace with her decision. Perhaps she could have seen things differently and either opted for a down-grade in lifestyle or going back to work. Either, way, this couple would have had the opportunity to repair their sense of partnership, salvage their love, and have a stronger, healthier marriage as a result.

Exploding in anger and withholding anger do not work in a Soul Partnership. Again, the race is to the middle, in learning to express anger in a healthy way.

Empowering Anger

When expressed appropriately, anger can be a "wakeup call" in a Soul Partnership. Spoken in the right way, it can highlight an imbalance, creating the opportunity to get back in balance. It can open our eyes to the ways that we may have taken our partner for granted. It can startle us out of compla-cency and negative habits or even inject some energy and life into a connec-tion that has grown stagnant.

As an authentic self-expression, anger is quite functional in a Soul Partnership. It is potent and powerful, to be respected and utilized wisely and carefully. To be fully functioning human beings, we must feel it, make friends with it, express it, and accept it as part of our life energy.

In this part of the book, I am going to offer slightly different coaching to men and to women about the expression of anger in a relationship. We are still in the process of correcting massive imbalances between men and women that have persisted for centuries. The use and abuse of anger in the past has left certain psychological and spiritual scars that must be addressed in order for this tool to be wisely wielded in our current Soul Partnerships.

Anger for Men

Society has traditionally overempowered men and underempowered women. Any time a section of society has less power, there is the opportunity for abuse.

In the past, there were few repercussions for those men who used or abused women. If a man was angry with his wife and violent toward her, the rest of his community tended to look the other way. While most men may have treated their female partners with respect and love, those who did not were generally not held accountable.

Even today, it is a struggle for women who are abused to protect themselves. Our laws offer some support, but fall short of preventing the escalation of abuse. Many women die at the hands of their abusive partners, often after repeated appeals to law enforcement to protect them. Collectively, we still have a long way to go to create a world in which women can feel safe.

When I walk out of a shopping mall at night, I am acutely aware of my vulnerability. I am vigilant and anxious until I get in my car and get the doors locked. These feelings of fear and vulnerability in a situation like that are something that most women identify with but that few men do. The reality is that we, as women, are frequent targets of the rage of men who are not psychologically well.

What does this have to do with relationships between non-abusive and caring partners? There is a connection because these things form part of the backdrop, or context, of our society, and therefore, of our relationships.

Many times, I have observed the woman in the relationship express concern and fear if her male partner raises his voice to her. Even though she *logically knows* that he is not capable of ever striking her or physically harming her, nevertheless, it is a frightening event. (If she comes from a family where physical violence was used, it is even more frightening.)

Why this anxiety and fear, if she is with a non-violent partner? Because the reality of our world is that women are not truly safe. Because underneath it all, most women carry the knowledge of our vulnerability by virtue of our smaller bodies and the lack of sufficient protection (e.g., inadequate consequences for male violence toward women and inadequate action to prevent violence when we are threatened). These realities cannot help but seep into our consciousness when we are confronted with an angry partner who is 20 to 50 percent larger than us physically.

A non-violent man may have difficulty understanding this phenomenon. Why, he may ask, would my partner ever be afraid of me? If he takes it personally, he may have trouble connecting with his compassion.

It is not personal. The reality of the world and women's fears may have no direct connection to this relationship. You, as a man, may be a perfectly safe partner to her. Yet, you, as a man, have the job of being aware of her sense of vulnerability, and to be respectful of that.

Therefore, my coaching to men and their expressions of anger is this. One, be aware of your partner's greater feelings of vulnerability than your own. Realize that your anger may be frightening to her. Be extra vigilant about the repercussions of how you express anger.

Two, never raise your voice to her, period. It simply is not OK. Never, ever, call her names or put her down verbally. Never, ever threaten her in any way. Do not "get in her face," do not point at her while speaking in an angry tone, and never block her exit from a room. Verbal abuse is the first level of violence toward women.

Three, never, ever, raise your hand to any physical object in a harmful way in the presence of your mate. Never break things or throw things in front of her while you are angry. Property damage is the second level of violence.

Four, it goes without saying that it is NEVER OK to strike a woman, either with your hand or with an object. This applies even if she is hitting you or yelling at you. Why? Because you do not ever have the right to harm a woman physically unless you *absolutely must because your life is in danger*.

When you do feel angry toward your female mate, *work it off before you speak*. Exercise, drive around the block and yell while in your car, or do something calming such as meditation. Get the anger out of your system as much as possible so that when you go speak to your mate, you are calm and able to speak in a normal tone.

Do the exercises earlier in the book to make sure that you are not projecting some of your own issues onto her. Separate your emotional baggage from the current situation as best you can before you sit down to talk. In this way, you honor yourself and your partner even when you are angry.

Sometimes, when you want separate time to process your feelings of anger, your mate may object to your departure. She may feel you are running away from her and the situation. Make sure you "give notice" of your departure, make a promise to return within a period of time to talk, and offer reassurance. "I'm really upset right now and I don't know how much of it is me and how much is you. I need time to sort things out before we talk further. I promise I will be back by ___ and we will talk then or as soon as possible. I am committed to you and to our relationship. I promise we will work this out together."

The Nice Guy

Many men in our culture have been taught, or conditioned, to temper their anger toward women. Sometimes, those lessons have gone to the extreme. The result is that many men are afraid to fully express themselves and their truth to the women in their lives. They are afraid of "hurting" a woman by expressing things that are difficult or confrontational.

In John's family, women were revered, but in an overprotective way. As a result, he came away with the idea that it was very bad if a woman was upset or in emotional pain, and if she was, it was up to him to fix it.

John molded his behavior around women's emotions at the expense of his self-expression. His desire to be "the nice guy" made him far too anxious to please and very reluctant to speak his truth. Consequently, his relationships always developed into a particular dynamic.

John "took care" of a woman, buying her nice things, taking her on trips, courting her, and bending over backward to avoid saying or doing anything that might trigger negative emotions. His partner, on the other hand, learned early that if she got sufficiently emotional, she could, on the surface, get what she wanted.

If John had doubts or concerns about his partner or their relationship, he kept them to himself. He held back large parts of who he was and how he felt in order to "keep the peace." Thus, he was a partner who was physically present but emotionally absent. This did not escape the notice of John's partners. Each could feel his lack of real connection, and this triggered emotions of her own.

John inevitably found himself in a relationship with an angry woman. Her anger pushed him away, and his retreat angered her further. The disconnection eventually became unbearable, and one or the other would move out, break up, or file for divorce.

John decided after his second divorce that he wanted to break this pattern. Gradually he faced his fear of self-expression and women's emotions. He realized that in being the nice guy, he had denied both himself and his past partners the joy of an authentic relationship. He learned to express concerns to a woman, to ask for what he wanted, and to say "no" if something did not feel right to him. He gave up internalizing and blaming, and developed the habit of dialoging and exploring. He gave up his view of women as weak and in need of psychological protection, and cultivated the view of women as emotionally strong and capable. In reclaiming his self-expression, John recovered his ability to be truly intimate in a relationship.

Men's Empowerment with Women

If John's story sounds all too familiar, take heart. It is possible to be a loving, authentic partner to a woman without giving up who you are. One thing that helps is realizing the truth about women's emotions.

First, know that just because a woman expresses emotions does not mean that she is in need of "fixing." Often, women express emotions primarily as a release. It is a relief to us to vent emotions, whether through speaking in a strong and emotional way, or crying, or in some other way.

Second, just because women may be more vulnerable physically does not mean that we are weak. Our bodies may be smaller, but our minds and hearts are not.

Just because many of us seem more emotional on the surface does not mean we are in need of protection from men by holding back what they really think and feel. In fact, the opposite is true. Women are empowered by being with a man who expresses himself fully, holding nothing back. If he consistently speaks his truth, then we know he means it when he says, "I love you."

When a man is authentic, when he reveals who he really is to a woman, he creates a powerful foundation of emotional security and trust. The partner to this man does not have to worry about what he is not saying. She knows that if it is important, he will say it, and thus, she will have all the knowledge she needs to powerfully choose him and their relationship.

If you have been the nice guy, you can change your path by realizing that the woman in your life is strong and capable, more so than you may have given credit for her being. Treat her and talk to her with this recognition. Do not "soft soap" her. Do not hold back who you are or what you really think and feel.

If you are angry with her, tell her, "I am angry with you and here's why." Let her know what pleases you and what does not, without blaming. Ask for what you want, even if you do not always get it. Just the asking makes you more real to her.

If you are thinking about exiting the relationship, tell her. Do not hold back those thoughts to "spare her" the pain. Sooner or later, you *will* exit, either physically or emotionally, if you do not express those thoughts. Remember that human beings tend to act out that which they cannot acknowledge. By expressing those thoughts and giving her a chance to respond, you may actually discover that you have a better relationship. You may even find that there is no reason to exit, if you are willing to speak up and work things out with your partner.

Be willing to be uncomfortable in the service of opening up communication with your partner. Say what you really mean and mean what you say. Rock the boat, ruffle some feathers, and trust the process of communication to reveal what you both need to go forward.

Celebrate the nice guy in you, and celebrate all of the other things about you that are not so nice. Embrace all of who you are, and trust that your mate, if she really loves you, will accept all of you as well.

Women's Anger

Traditionally, women have been taught that there is no place for our anger. We have been conditioned to submit without question to men's wishes and desires, even when that resulted in our harm. Now, in our culture, we are empowered enough to begin expressing our true feelings, including those of anger.

Most of us have not had adequate modeling of how to express anger appropriately. Thus, most of us go to one extreme or the other in dealing with this difficult emotion.

One extreme is to use our extraordinary verbal ability to battle a male partner. Being a writer, I have a fair amount of those skills. I learned early in life that I could pretty much run circles around most men verbally, and I am somewhat embarrassed to say that I have used this to my advantage at times.

Because we have not historically been empowered, we have resorted at times to the "verbal advantage" to gain power in a relationship. A woman's words, when spoken in a certain manner, can truly cut her partner down in a matter of seconds. A woman's words can also provoke and inflame her partner.

The other extreme is to hold back what we feel, submerging it and letting it grow into resentment and disconnection. When we are angry and quiet, we either develop poor health or depression (anger turned inward) or we "act it out," through affairs, addictions (food, alcohol, drugs, or spending), and other non-functioning behavior.

The first thing we must do before we can express anger wisely as women is to live a self-empowered life. We must feel strong and capable and that we have choices for our lives before we can stand up for ourselves. To be an equal partner in our own eyes first empowers us to speak our truth. Then, and only then, can we use our anger wisely and release forever the controlling behaviors that do not serve us.

Use the inventory at the back of the book to assess where you are in living a self-empowered life (see "Women's Self-Empowerment Inventory"). Use that information to guide you toward making corrections in your life path. To the degree that we feel empowered as women, we are able to fully express ourselves to our partners, and to be effective Soul Partners.

Expressing Anger Wisely

As women, the first step in using anger wisely is to accept it as part of our emotional repertoire. It is normal to feel anger from time to time. Let that be a healthy reality.

Second, learn to separate issues of projection and emotional baggage from the current situation. Use the exercises in this book to help you with that.

Third, speak in a straightforward fashion to your mate. Instead of listing all of his faults, tell him "I'm angry with you and here's why." Rather than "going off" on him, and ranting and raving, learn to calm yourself before you speak to him. Do not "get in his face," pointing your finger and raising your voice.

Refrain from using your knowledge of your partner's vulnerabilities against him. This is a sure-fire way to undermine intimacy and damage love, sometimes permanently. It is also an abuse of emotional power that inflames and escalates the damage.

If he has done something truly unacceptable to you, reserve what you have to say until you have considered it very carefully. Look to see if you have done anything to contribute to the problem, and be willing to admit it. Later, we will look at how to confront your partner in a loving yet effective manner.

The same rules that apply for men also apply for women with regard to expressing anger. It is not OK to yell, use verbal put-downs, or threaten. It is not OK to damage property. It is never OK to strike, unless you are in danger and must protect yourself.

In a nutshell, let anger be a motivator for positive change, not a weapon. Be indignant when appropriate. Be strong and assertive, not vicious and punitive. Stand up for yourself without putting your partner down. Be powerful without being overpowering.

Rage

If you are in a state of rage (uncontrolled anger), you are at risk for a dangerous emotional escalation with your partner. We feel rage when we perceive that the other person has done something unacceptable and that the consequences to us are *unbearable*. Whether or not that is true, once we feel enraged, it is impossible to communicate in any kind of constructive way.

Rage left unchecked leads to behavior that destroys relationships and endangers life. Rage is anger that is extremely out of balance. It is vital that you learn to identify it and do whatever it takes to release the emotional pressure cooker in a constructive way. You are enraged if you:

- Feel hatred toward your partner or someone else
- Have fantasies of doing harm to another person
- Have thoughts that dwell on getting revenge

You are dangerously enraged if you have a plan to harm someone else. It is one thing to have a temporary experience of these feelings. Though rage is on the extreme end of the continuum, it is nevertheless a part of the field of possibilities of human emotion and therefore normal. However, *it is another thing to move toward action or to harbor the feelings over an extended period of time.* If you are having these kinds of feelings and thoughts, seek professional help immediately! Never confront your partner while feeling enraged without expert guidance.

There are three simple rules to follow for healthy anger expression. They will guide you toward emotional healing and release.

Rule One: *no harm to self.*
Rule Two: *no harm to others.*
Rule Three: *no harm to property.*

If you follow these three rules, you will be able to change your emotional state from rage to anger to resentment to acceptance and, finally, to forgiveness.

Empowering Confrontation

In every healthy relationship, there are times when we are called upon to challenge one another. As your partner, I exercise the right to challenge you when I believe:

- The way you are perceiving something seems distorted
- The way you are behaving does not seem true to who you are individually or who you are in our relationship
- The way you are behaving affects you, me, or our children in a harmful or potentially harmful way
- The way you are behaving makes our relationship unworkable for me

Effective confrontation has certain key characteristics, without which it can be psychologically or emotionally intrusive. Use this checklist *before* you confront your partner.

Confrontation is empowering when it is:

____ Motivated by love and the desire to contribute to the other person

____ Done in a timely manner with an intention to work things out (not as you are walking out the door)

____ Unselfish, or, if there is some personal gain at stake, to acknowledge that up front; e.g., "I want you to quit smoking because I want you to be healthier and live longer, and also because it will be better for me."

____ Carefully considered so that the way it is spoken is compassionate and gentle

____ Used very rarely—it becomes less effective over time if we use it for every little issue, such as being a critical nit-picker

____ Spoken from the point of view of first person, not as universal truth; e.g., " I think…" or "I feel…" rather than "Everyone knows…"

____ Expressed in a way that allows the other person to have another point of view; e.g., "this is how it seems to me…"

____ Carries no demands; focuses instead on collaborative problem-solving

So, how does this work? The following is an example, keeping in mind that communication is a creative process. Use these phrases as guides, taking into account your own unique self-expression. The *intention* is what is important, and if you let that guide you, the best words will always come to you.

Your partner is behaving in some way that distresses you. Try this:

"I want to talk to you about sharing our responsibilities as parents." (Straightforward statement of the issue.)

"I'm feeling burdened and stressed these days, and I'm not sure that we are collaborating the best way." (Straightforward statement of your own point of view.)

"What do you think is happening in our division of responsibilities as parents?" (Invitation to hear his point of view.)

You have accomplished two things at this point. One, you have expressed what the issue is without attacking your partner. Two, you have encouraged your partner to express his point of view. *These are the first steps in an empowering confrontation.* You open the topic, make a statement or two (not much at this point) about your position, then ask an open-ended question. Your partner can now express his point of view. This does two things:

1) It allows you to get the "full story" from your partner before you challenge him. Be flexible and open at this point—you may discover something new!
2) It establishes a dialogue, not a one-way confrontation that leaves no room for disagreement.

Once your partner has expressed his point of view, you can address his thinking. *Only when you have a complete understanding of your partner's point of view do you have the right to challenge it.* Again, keep in mind what you are trying to accomplish. Now, mirror, make sure you heard correctly, and then express your point of view. Take into account what you have heard.

"Well, that's interesting. The way you see it, since I am home all day and you are at work, therefore, I have more energy to deal with the kids, even at the end of the day." (Mirroring)

"I can see how you might think that." (Honoring his point of view, even if you do not agree with it.)

"You are not here all day to see how much I do, so you may be under the impression that I'm having lots of leisure time. I have a different point of view about this. Are you ready to listen to it?" (Asking him to listen empty)

Now you can express the issue from your own point of view and you can ask him to Mirror what he hears. At this point, you will be in a dialogue—a powerful process for your partnership.

Take your time with the dialogue, and do not expect instant insight, change, or results from your partner. Realize that change takes time and must come from within the individual. Later, we will look at how to make requests of your partner.

Don't underestimate the accomplishment at this point. To have a real dialogue about a controversial topic, with each person freely expressing his/her thoughts and view, is tremendous. This opens up many new possibilities for your relationship and for your partnership.

Discussing Issues

Remember the listening empty exercise in chapter 5? Verbalizing the issues makes all the difference in your success. The basic guidelines for discussing issues are as follows. When it is your turn to speak:

- Use "I" statements, avoiding any sentence that begins with the word "you"
- Use the phrases "it seems to me" and "from my point of view" when you state your opinion; that way, it leaves room for your partner to have a different point of view
- Speak gently; make sure that you do not spew anger and resentment as you express yourself
- Speak passionately if appropriate; infuse your words with your spirit in a way that does not step on your partner
- Stop periodically and give your partner an opportunity to mirror; try not to pack too much material into one speech as that can be overwhelming
- Add lots of acknowledgment of your partner from time to time; this makes your critical feedback easier to digest

Remember as you speak, that hearing feedback from your partner is not easy. Most couples avoid doing this like the "relationship plague" because it can be so psychologically and emotionally stressful. Therefore, keep your compassion in the forefront and err in the direction of moderation.

Years ago, I participated in a speaker training group. Part of our practice was to give feedback to the speaker. Our rule was this: for every suggestion of change, we offered three positive acknowledgments. The reason for this is simple: *it is highly stressful for human beings to hear critical feedback*. Most of us need several acknowledgments for each piece of criticism. This applies even more so in love relationships, where our sensitivity is even greater. In order for critical feedback to be helpful, we must infuse it with lots of acknowledgment. In chapter 10, we will look at how to do that.

Overcoming Critical Feedback

One of the reasons that we are critical to our partners is because we are treating ourselves in the same way. If I am accepting of my humanity and myself then I am automatically more accepting of my partner. Thus, if we wish to heal our critical expressions to our partner, we must begin in the same place that everything else begins: with ourselves. The following is an intention I encourage my clients to set and that has served me as well:

> *"I recognize in myself a magnificent soul. My intention is to remember that each day and to do my best to bring forth the highest and greatest expression of Who I Am in everything I do and say. I recognize my humanity. My intention is to accept all parts of myself as a person in process of remembering my soul's greatness. I recognize the humanity and the greatness of others. My intention is to accept each person, just as I accept myself. In my relationships, my intention is to express myself fully and in a way that encourages the highest and greatest good in myself and in all those whose lives I touch."*

What Is Mine and What Is Yours

The other dynamic of criticism is that it usually comes from fear. In love relationships, we criticize our partners to cover up our fear of being hurt. It is our vulnerability to criticism that we are attempting to protect. If I can point my finger at you, then I can put off the day that you point your finger at me, revealing me in all of my shortcomings and failures.

When you feel tempted to criticize your partner, stop and do this exercise. On paper, begin by listing all of the criticisms that you are holding in your mind and heart about your partner. For example:

"I don't like it that my partner:

- Is so messy around the house
- Has gained twenty pounds
- Misplaces things
- Doesn't always pay the bills on time

When you have listed everything that comes to mind, go back to the first one and ask yourself:

What am I afraid of if my partner is messy? How does that affect me? You might in this instance have an answer such as this:

The way it affects me is that I feel uncomfortable when things are out of place. I am afraid that I will have to clean up after her or that I will have to be uncomfortable all of the time.

Write your responses for each criticism, being as honest with yourself as you possibly can be. Now, beginning with the first item again, go a step further with this question:

What do I see in *myself* as a result of this situation?

You might then acknowledge:

I see my own rigidity. I like to have things done my way and I get very uncomfortable when others around me insist on doing things their way.

Continue through your list for each item, acknowledging what you see in yourself as a reflection. Now you are ready to be responsible for your own responses to the things your partner does. *Now, you have separated what is yours from what is your partner's.*

This does not mean that you do not address the issues with your partner. You may still want to ask your partner to be less messy. The difference is that you will be asking from an entirely different emotional place. Rather than being angry, critical, and blaming, you can be straightforward and honest.

Instead of:

"You are so messy! I get really sick of seeing your clothes lying all over the house. And why can't you put things away after you get them out?"

You can say:

"I want to talk to you about keeping things neat around the house. I realize that you and I have different standards about this. I get uncomfortable much sooner than you do when things are left lying around and not put away. I don't expect you to feel differently, but I would like to ask your help. It feels really good to me to look around at a neat environment. It would be so helpful to me if you would be more attentive to that and try to put things away."

Alternatively, after acknowledging your feelings about it, you could propose hiring a cleaning service. The solution is not as important as the (self) honesty in the way you express the issue. Acknowledging that it is your own issue of discomfort removes the dynamic of blame, making it much more likely that your partner will respond in a helpful manner.

What works in discussing issues is *staying with my truth*, rather than taking a stab at yours. This keeps me honest, open, self-expressed, compassionate, loving, and powerful as a Soul Partner.

Resistance

When we choose to confront one another, we may consciously or unconsciously provoke resistance. What does that mean?

Resistance is what we feel when we do not want to look at something in a new way (or at all). Resistance is what happens when someone or something outside of us intrudes into our current view of ourselves or our lives. Resistance is psychological protection from *too much change too quickly*. It is natural—it is a part of the human condition.

Resistance takes many forms. It may appear as a reluctance to have one of "those talks" that our partner is demanding. It may appear as "forgetting" that we planned a talk, or being late for a talk. It may appear as a feeling of anxiety or discomfort, a "knot in the stomach" when the other person brings up a certain subject.

Resistance also may be experienced as a sudden, irrational feeling of mistrust in someone who is perfectly trustworthy. It is a sudden perception that the other person does not have my best interest at heart, even though I know that is untrue about this person. Suddenly, my partner may be viewed as an "enemy" to be pushed away or fought with. Resistance leads to misinterpretation, misperceptions, and power struggles.

Resistance may also occur as neglecting to do the things that nurture our relationship or connection. We make promises or have certain agreements, and when the time comes to fulfill them, we simply do not. Then we may make excuses and make new promises, only to repeat the pattern. This will continue until we stop and look inside to find out what the resistance is about.

Resistance is a signal that something important is happening. It is a sign that we are entering emotional territory that contains old wounds. This is not a bad thing, contrary to the way it may feel. It is sort of like pulling off a bandage—it hurts! However, it is necessary in order to let the wound get some air and to heal at a deeper level.

When we feel resistant, we can either fight the feelings, or we can learn to welcome it. When we embrace our own resistance, an amazing thing happens—it goes away. In fact, the sooner we can simply acknowledge, "I feel uncomfortable about this," the sooner we begin to realize why, gain greater self-knowledge, and can give more to our relationship.

The next time you feel suddenly, irrationally suspicious of your partner; the next time you notice that you have been sabotaging your partner's efforts to talk with you about certain issues; the next time you fail to do something that you promised your partner you would do, or notice that you are "shutting down" emotionally, stop and ask yourself: What do I feel so uncomfortable about *right now?*

Stay with this question until you have the answer from yourself. Be fearless in your search for insight. You will be rewarded!

Overcoming Your Partner's Resistance

What if my partner is resistant? This, too, is a signal, telling me that I may be going too fast for him. I am already two miles down the road emotionally, while he is just beginning to realize that there is an issue. I always know this is happening in my own relationship when I catch myself presenting solutions to problems he has not even acknowledged.

The first step in melting our partner's resistance is to *be compassionate*. When we realize we have experienced the same feelings, though perhaps about other issues, we see ourselves in the same boat. There is no need to judge when we recognize our mutual humanity. I am just as afraid as he is of too much change too quickly. It is just as scary to me when he points out my vulnerabilities as it is to him when I do that.

The bottom line is that *we are both working on the same issues in different forms*.

The next step in melting your partner's resistance is to express your highest and greatest intention. For example:

"Sweetheart, I want to talk about something with you. But first, I want you to know that I love you very much. I think the world of you and hold you in highest esteem. I realize that some of the things I am about to say may sound critical, and perhaps they are, but that is not my intention. My intention is to clear the air about some things, and to sort out our responsibilities. What I really want is for us to be loving partners about these issues and whatever else is bothering either one of us."

Say this in your own words. Spend some time putting together your opening comments so that the message comes through to your partner loud and clear:

I love you. This conversation is about deepening our relationship and our love. That is my intention, even if I make mistakes along the way. Please help me in this endeavor.

Now your partner is less likely to begin putting up defenses at the beginning of the conversation. By being openhearted, we increase the likelihood for our partner to be open as well. So much more gets accomplished this way than in an atmosphere of fear, resistance, and emotional barricading.

Sometimes, people say, "My partner should *know* my intentions—I have proven over and over that I am a loving person. I should not have to say that every time I want to discuss an issue!" My answer to that is, so what?

Yes, most of us have loving intentions most of the time, but this does not give us license to speak in any way and expect our partners to automatically get it. The reality is that relationships are tough! No matter how loving I am, I must realize that my partner is living in his own universe, and that may not include a minute-to-minute awareness of my intentions. Therefore, I have a responsibility to look for ways to express myself to him in a way that makes it easier for him to open up to me.

What if I am *not* truly intentional about having an openhearted conversation? What if my heart is closed? What if I am not sure that I love this person anymore?

If you are having strong doubts about your relationship, then this is not the time to confront your mate about the particulars of her behavior that are bothering you. This is the time to process your fear and doubt. The last chapter of the book presents the framework for recreating commitment in a love relationship. I strongly recommend that you explore that issue before you confront your partner.

For a confrontation to be truly effective, it must come from love and concern. It must be in the *context* of a true commitment to the relationship and from the perspective of *personal accountability*.

This means that in everything I confront my partner with, *I am willing to acknowledge my part. Yes, it is true that I do not like things messy. Yes, I want your assistance in keeping our home nice.*

Yes, you are drinking to excess. Yes, I have ignored this issue for too long, thereby giving you the false impression that it is OK with me.

Yes, you are distancing from me by watching too much television. Yes, I have given you the false impression that it is OK by hanging around you and bringing your dinner to you so that you can continue to sit there doing that.

Yes, you are spending way too much on our credit cards. Yes, I have silently paid the bills way too long, allowing my resentment to grow. Yes, I have used this as an excuse to be emotionally distant from you as punishment to you and as relief for myself.

I have let my fear of confrontation stand in the way of being open, honest, and direct with you. I have let my fear of losing you stand in the way of asking for what I want. I have let my own insecurity prevent me from standing up to you. I have let my own self-criticism keep me from being compassionate when I confront you.

Today, I acknowledge that I am bigger than my fears. Today, I acknowledge that you are bigger than your behavior.

Today, I place our long-term fulfillment and satisfaction above the short-term relief of avoiding the issues. Today, I speak up and speak out, and I invite you to do the same. I open my heart, my ears, and my soul to the possibility of what we can create together.

The possibility that emerges from being personally accountable in any confrontation is the power to choose something new. We have the ability to stand back, take a fresh look at what we are cocreating, and choose another way of relating, if we do not like what we see.

It is like that old saying about the stick. On one end is the complaint about the issue, and on the other is personal responsibility. You cannot pick up just one end of the stick. When you pick up the complaint end, you cannot help but also lift the responsibility end.

For every dissatisfaction in life that we have, there also exists the opportunity to create something new. Nowhere is this truer than in relationships. In order to turn our complaints into opportunities, we must develop and devote ourselves to total honesty with our partners.

The exercise, no matter the issue, is to open up the possibility for a dialogue. We do that by asking for and encouraging our partner's self-expression. We melt our partner's resistance by being compassionate and by speaking in a way that creates emotional safety.

Most important of all, we create the conditions for deep connection and the possibility of positive change when we recognize our partner's magnificence underneath it all.

Chapter Eight
Honesty and Letting Go

Once upon a time, men and women were taught to be dishonest with one another. Women were told to suppress their true thoughts, feelings, and desires, and men were taught to hide their behavior. Everyone pretended that everything was okay, whether it was or not.

If a woman sensed that her husband was being unfaithful, she might choose to ignore the signs, not confront him, and let him believe that he had successfully hidden it from her. If a man suspected that his wife did not really love him, he might close his eyes to those signs, choosing to focus on work or the children rather than confront her. In these and a myriad of other ways, couples in the past collaborated to be less than forthcoming with one another.

The purpose served by the mutual collusion not to be honest in relationships was to *stay together at all costs*. Because divorce was unacceptable and women were financially dependent, many couples chose the path of withholding in order to get their needs met.

Even today, it is a challenge to be completely honest in a relationship because the truth can be threatening, especially when it threatens the relationship itself, such as one partner having serious doubts about feelings for the other.

When we fall in love, we make an emotional investment in the relationship. As time goes on, that investment grows. Getting married, having children, buying property, and blending finances are all natural steps toward greater and greater interdependence. All of these things serve to bond and to bind us together, which is a positive thing that enables us to get through tough times.

On the other side of the coin lies our fear of separating or of losing "the investment." It is not easy to distinguish interdependency (we rely upon one another in mutually beneficial ways) from dependency (we are together because we are afraid to be alone). Thus, we can easily develop the habit of not being totally honest in service of keeping things together, especially when there are children involved.

On the surface, this strategy works. The old adage, "what you don't know won't hurt you," seems to fit here. On a heart and soul level, this leads to one of the worst and most damaging myths about relationships.

The myth is: *It is possible to lie or withhold and still have a loving relationship.*

The reality is: *The failure to be honest with one's partner destroys connection and love.*

The simple reason is that trust and dishonesty cannot coexist, and without trust, a relationship loses its core. Trust is so vital to healthy love that there is virtually no scenario in which a relationship can thrive without it.

Trust flows directly out of a dedication to honesty, integrity, and authenticity. This dedication begins with self and extends to others. I cannot be truthful with you if I am lying to myself. I cannot be a real partner to you unless I am being true to who I am and expressing that to you.

Trust flows out of a dedication to self-care. This means that I trust myself to take care of myself, regardless of how others may let me down, hurt me, or abandon me. If I have that much self-trust, I am able to discern more easily where and how to place my trust. I am also empowered to be honest with others, to "let the chips fall where they will." This is because I realize that the worst abandonment of all is to abandon myself, and this I will not do.

Trust flows out of a genuine spirit of love and contribution. "I am with you and I give my heart to you because I want to, not because I am afraid of being alone. I give to you because it is an expression of who I am and of the love in my heart, not in order to get you to take care of me or give me (the illusion of) security."

Trust flows out of a belief in the power of intuition and out of honoring that in self and others. This means that if I am in a balanced state in my life, and I get emotionally close to another person and alarm bells begin going off internally, I listen to that.

Intuition and Honesty

Because I believe in the power of intuition, I honor the ability of others to sense the truth of a situation. I know that I can never truly deceive another person, because the fundamental universal principles apply. One of those principles, that we are all connected, makes it impossible for any lie that I tell to go undetected.

Sometimes people say, "If my partner never finds out that I am lying about something, how can it hurt him?" This question reflects the false belief that we are not connected on any level other than superficial. Nothing could be further from the truth.

Science now confirms what we have believed on the level of spirit for a long time: that we are connected in ways that are not clear to us with the naked eye. In one amazing trial study, a researcher was able to type words onto a computer screen using the power of thought combined with "adaptive brain interface technology."[8] This study shows us that thoughts are more than words inside our heads. Thoughts are energy, and that energy can and does create an effect outside of us.

In psychology and in recovery work, we know that thoughts, beliefs, and feelings are powerful energy sources that are deeply felt by those who are close to us. In families, there is no question that the spoken and unspoken thoughts, feelings, and beliefs of all family members affect everyone. When we study family patterns, time and again we find the repetition of certain behaviors over generations. The fascinating thing is that we see this even when the behavior has been kept secret.

Secrets and Lies

Keeping secrets and telling lies are the symptoms of imbalance in our souls and in our relationships. The most troubled families are those in which family members hold secrets and lie to one another on a daily basis.

On the surface, lying covers up those things about us that we find embarrassing or shameful. It also serves to shield us from the immediate consequences for our thoughts, feelings, and behavior.

On a deeper level, lying covers up fear, primarily the fear of losing control. Lying comes from attempting to control the uncontrollable. This is very obvious when one partner attempts to cover up an affair in order to hold onto two relationships at the same time.

The truth is that we have no real control over the outcomes of our relationships or over the choices of any person in our life. In reality, lying accomplishes nothing in the way of living a fulfilling and rewarding life. In fact, it makes us absolutely miserable deep down inside, so much that we lose our self in the process of maintaining the falsehood.

This is the real consequence of lying: the loss of self. The more we lie to others, the more we are forced to lie to ourselves. The more we do that, the greater the disconnection from who we are, and thus, from our soul and our soul's highest and greatest good. Disconnected from who we are, we have no capability to really connect with another person.

The other consequence of lying is that it is saying, in essence, "My fear is greater than my desire to be fully alive." It is caving in to fear. We become weak in the emotional muscle of courage, so that with every new challenging circumstance, we deepen the damage to self. Over time, we lose self-esteem, self-respect, and even self-love. I have witnessed deep self-loathing in individuals who habitually deceive themselves and those they purport to love.

Withholding

To withhold in a relationship means to hold back from expressing thoughts, feelings, and information that are important for a partner to know and that are vital to self-expression. To withhold is to make a choice to not say what needs to be said.

Withholding, like lying, is a way to attempt control over another person or the outcome of a situation. In addition, like lying, on a deeper level, withholding is an act of fear.

Withholding has a strong impact in a love relationship. When one person "holds back" from expressing vital information, the other person feels something in response to that. The feelings in response to a partner's withholding may be experienced as intuitions or hunches, or it may be felt as raw emotion, including fear, insecurity, anger, feeling off-balance, anxiety, and despair, just to name a few. Often, the emotions are not accompanied with clear insight, leaving the person confused and struggling to understand without real information.

Withholding may take many forms, from the smallest issues on a day-to-day basis to life-altering issues. At the moment of truth, when one of us puts something on the table, so to speak, and is looking for truth in return, we have a choice. We can respond from the greatest and highest part of ourselves, the part that is dedicated to truth and being courageous in its expression. That is one choice. The other choice is to succumb to fear, to doubt that we could ever be really loved for who we are, and to say whatever it takes to "get by," rather than speaking our truth. As with lying, the choice to withhold in a relationship has far-reaching effects.

Filling in the Blanks

An interesting thing about human beings is that we dislike a void of information. This means that if what we know about something is incomplete, we tend to seek to fill that void. In relationships, this means that we work very hard to understand our partners when we sense that the picture is incomplete, often to the point that we construct a false reality and then build our lives on top of that.

This means that we make day-to-day decisions, small choices, and life-altering choices, based on false information. Without the truth on our side, we do not possess the clarity to make choices that are in our greatest and highest good.

Without living together in truth, we flounder in our relationship. We operate on false premises, interact about things that do not matter, and sweep massive issues under the rug. We wander about, emotionally disconnected from one another and feeling unfulfilled. In this state, we are wide open to affairs, separation, and divorce.

This is the effect of lying and withholding in relationships: that all parties involved are robbed of the opportunity to live in truth. To live in truth and authentic self-expression is one of life's greatest gifts. Why would we want to take that away from those we purport to love and from ourselves? In a word: fear.

Why We Lie and Withhold

We lie and withhold the truth because we are deeply afraid of losing control and of confronting our worst fears: the fear of abandonment and rejection.

These fears, when we deny and suppress them, bubble up in the form of deception. Underneath them is the fear that who I am is not good enough for my partner.

We do not break the cycle of lying, withholding, and deceiving until we confront these fears and learn to be strong in the face of life's reality: that we do not have real control over the outcomes of our relationships. People come and go. They love us, leave us, and eventually die. That is life.

The opportunity of loving someone is not to hold onto that person to create a false sense of security, but rather, to express ourselves, make a difference in life, and be the best that we can be. The bottom line: we must love ourselves enough to live an authentic life if we are to have authentic relationships.

Honesty and Soul Partnership

The reality is that it is impossible to have a true partnership without honesty. Being Soul Partners means that we work together, as equals, for the growth of our spirits and for the greater good of the relationship. We cannot possibly be effective in this way unless we know where we truly stand with one another, and that takes a tremendous amount of loving, openhearted communication.

We also can never experience what real love is until we are living in truth. If I construct a false picture of myself and then sell you on it, how do I have an experience of being loved by you? You are expressing love for the portrait I have painted, not for the real me.

Without honesty, a relationship cannot be any more than an arrangement. There was a time when "arranged marriages" were the rule, and love matches were the exception. In Western culture, we have tried to move away from that way of pairing up in favor of choosing our partner based on love and the desire for a "soul mate."

The interesting thing is that we are still creating arranged marriages in our culture, though we pretend that they are love matches. An arranged relationship is one in which we consciously or unconsciously set up a bargain: I will give you this and in exchange, you will give me that. What we sometimes bargain with are withholding truth in exchange for the illusion of security.

Often relationships begin with love, but then the day comes when we are faced with a truth that we do not want to express or acknowledge, a truth that threatens the very foundation of our relationship. At the point of choice (to say what needs to be said or to withhold), the tempting path is not to say, not to confront, and to hope that the issue will magically go away.

Telling the Truth

The reality of speaking our truth in a love relationship is that it sometimes hurts. It hurts because it threatens the basis of our being together, exposes us for who and what we are as fallible human beings, and shatters our illusions.

It takes courage to speak the truth in a relationship, especially when doing so means putting the relationship itself at risk.

When we tell the truth, we learn about what is important to us in life, and we make discoveries about ourselves. We need the reactions of those we love when we behave in ways that betray our partner's trust. It is essential to our growth. For example, people who have affairs and never get "found out" never quite get it about why that does not work in relationships.

Deception blocks our growth. The truth moves us forward in the evolution of our spirit.

If there has been a pattern of deceit, it can be changed. The steps may be difficult, and often the case is that we have huge blind spots that contribute to the problem. If this is you, begin with the exercises in this book and seek professional help if you get stuck.

From Deception to Honesty

If we have not been fully honest with our partner, there is much to consider before taking action. How do we decide what to say, how to say it, and when to say it? The following are some suggestions for moving through this process:

First, spend some time with yourself and do some soul-searching. The following are some questions to ask of yourself. Either write or journal about them or reflect upon them.

What secrets am I holding from my partner?

Why am I keeping these secrets? (my rationalization and my fears)

What do I really gain by having these secrets in my relationship? (i.e., what is the emotional payoff)

How do I really know that it is in my partner's best interest to withhold my secrets?

What is the cost to me for keeping these secrets? (e.g., integrity, self-esteem, personal and spiritual growth, etc.)

For each secret, ask yourself:

What false beliefs or false reality am I possibly encouraging my partner to have as a result of this lie/withhold?

What cost(s) do I have in my relationship as a result of this lie/withhold?

What might be possible in my life and in my relationship from telling the truth?

If you work with yourself on these questions and you still do not have clarity, I suggest you seek help from a professional to help you sort out what your truth is and what to do about it. Keep in mind that human beings in general are uncomfortable with the notion of total honesty in a relationship, so you may want to ask questions about the person's values with regard to that before you work with that person.

In deciding what to do about the secrets and lies in your relationship, it is vital that you consider your real intentions. If you have no intention of staying

Honesty and Letting Go 165

with your partner and working things out, it may serve no purpose to unburden yourself of all your deceptions. Your partner is likely to feel deeply wounded but lack the emotional safety net of your continued love and support. If you have every intention of staying with your partner, then "coming clean" can be very powerful for your relationship.

If you decide that in order for your partnership to go forward and be healthy it is time to reveal the lies and withholds, these are some guidelines:

Choose a time and place with no distractions and with lots of time for processing. You may need hours to go through this conversation and to allow your partner to have emotional reactions and ask questions.

Set the intention up front to give your partner all the time he needs for his reactions. This part is unpredictable and uncontrollable, so it is important that you release all notions of a "happy ending" at this point.

Realize that this may be an extended process, and that you may need help for getting through it. Don't expect instant miracles!

Set the intention right up front to be a loving partner for however long it takes for her to work through her feelings.

Let go of needing your partner to forgive you. This is something that cannot be controlled—it must spontaneously arise in that person when it is right for her.

Though you may realize (and be right) that your partner has colluded with you to "keep the secrets" or has contributed to the behavior via certain relationship dynamics, now is not the time to talk about this. Take full responsibility for your part, and trust that in time, your partner will take responsibility for his.

Don't make excuses for what you did, even though you may have made those choices from pain. That is not your partner's to process, it is yours. Healing is possible in the relationship only through being fully responsible for you and for your choices.

Practice patience and get set for the long haul. Remember, your lies and withholds have created the real damage. Your partner's reactions are appropriate to the betrayal and must be honored however they are expressed.

If you are coming from love, that is, truly caring about your partner and what she may be going through, that will go a long way toward the healing process.

The Choice of Honesty

I am not here to tell you that you must reveal all of your secrets to your partner today. Nor am I here to be the "poster child" for truth and honesty, as if I have never told a lie or withheld important information in a relationship.

I am here to say that every single time I have been less than forthcoming with a partner, I have failed to get what I really wanted. Through these experiences, I have discovered that withholding who I am and not revealing my truth has gotten me dishonest, unfulfilling connections that did not withstand the test of time.

I decided that I wanted more than an arrangement, a relationship that appears to provide security at the expense of my self-expression. I wanted more than someone to fill the empty spaces in my life at the expense of our growth.

I wanted a true Soul Partnership, a relationship of equals who are striving to be the best that they can be. I wanted a relationship based on honesty and choice. I discovered that there were things I had to give up in order to have what I wanted, such as the illusion of security.

It is a choice for each individual and each couple to make. What do you want? What are you willing to give up in order to have what you want?

Love and Honesty

Studies show that many couples would rather end their relationship than have truly open and honest communication. Why? Because opening up your heart to another human being is emotionally risky. What if she does not honor the language and message of your soul? What if he finds something unlovable about you in that moment? To truly open up and communicate honestly, we make ourselves highly vulnerable. To do that with a partner, who is not fully trusted, or perhaps not even trustworthy, may seem riskier than it is worth. Yet not to do so, to choose to stay closed, is to shut down the possibility of growth on a personal level and within the relationship. Love simply cannot blossom where there is fear of self-disclosure. Real love, Soul Partner love, special, deep, and enduring, cannot occur in denial of self-expression.

True partnership, Soul Partnership, cannot be created without full self-expression of both persons. This is the mission of today's love relationships: to find a way, to find the courage, to be truly open and honest with one another, and thus to discover the true possibilities of being together and traveling through this lifetime side by side.

The irony is that most couples experience a greater level of intimacy when they express what is in their innermost hearts and souls to one another, even if there are vast differences in their point of view. If the process of communicating openly and honestly is honored fully, with many hours spent revealing true thoughts and feelings, what eventually emerges is a core truth that is remarkably similar between two people. It is this: "I want to love and honor myself, as a spiritual being in a physical experience, and I want to receive the love you give for who I am, and I want to love you in the fullest measure as well." Very rarely do couples discover truths between them that make it impossible to continue the relationship, and in those cases, they were headed for separation anyway.

Does this mean that all love relationships should continue? No, certainly not. Many times, couples discover that their needs collide so dramatically and so painfully that they choose not to do their soul's work with one another. It is a very legitimate choice to move forward and look for another partner at that point, particularly with dating relationships.

For married couples, it is important to honor the commitment you made to one another by doing everything in your power to revitalize your relationship *prior* to indulging in thoughts of leaving. Most married couples do not know how to honor this process. They allow resentments and hurts to build over time until the love in their hearts is squashed by the weight of these things. Then, they say to themselves, "I do not love my wife/husband any longer, and since love is the basic reason to be married, therefore I need to leave him/her and move on." They announce to their spouse that it is over, often blind-siding that other person, who had no idea that separation and divorce were options being placed on the table. The incomplete communication process leaves both parties devastated.

The reality is that you do not know the true potential of your relationship until you are willing to spend literally hours communicating openly and honestly with your partner. You do not know what you really have together until you plant both feet firmly IN the relationship, create as much emotional safety as possible, and open up all the way.

Letting Go

In order to empower a relationship through honesty, we must be willing to let go of the end result.

You may have noticed in this chapter the expression "the illusion of security." That is because one of the greatest myths about relationships is that it is possible to achieve total physical, financial, and emotional security through love. The problem with this belief is that it relies on the ability to predict and control the future.

Love is a dynamic process and energy. Like life itself, it is not the same from one day to the next. Love grows when it is real and nurtured. Love expands over time when it is genuine. We love one another differently in ten years than we love today because our love is contained in the thousands of experiences and stories that we share. As life changes over time, so does our love.

Love is not a thing that we can capture, put in a box, and store in the closet on a shelf. Love is energy, and when real, is freely given and shared. Love is far more than attachment (I need you), although it may include some elements of attachment.

The kind of love that encourages the growth of our spirit is given and shared with little expectation. It is based on the desire to walk through life together, not on the need for security.

To choose this kind of love means that we recognize our fundamental lack of control over another person. It means that we view our partner as someone to connect and share life with, not as someone whose job it is to make our lives OK. It also means that we both recognize that each day together is a choice, not an obligation. We know that it is possible that one of us could experience a change of heart about this love. Although there would be grief on that day, there would also be truth, because we set it up that way.

Ultimately, *a relationship is a choice,* and that is the foundation of Soul Partnership. Our choice is one that is based in the experience of love, the dedication to the behavior of love, and the commitment to honesty and integrity. What a powerful foundation, but it is only possible when both people are fully informed about what they are choosing. If it is Soul Partnership that you desire, and your partner does also, then the following communication exercise may be an appropriate next step.

EXERCISE: CHOOSING HONESTY

A word of caution about the exercise: this may be emotionally stressful. Do not attempt it unless you are both clear about your responsibility for your own well-being. Do not do this exercise:

- In an exhausted, emotionally depleted, angry, or chemically altered state
- If you are in the midst of a significant loss
- If you have a significant power imbalance in the relationship (e.g., one of you is more dependent on the other emotionally or financially; one of you is halfway out the door). The exception is this: if the person who is one-down wants to do the exercise and feels emotionally strong and stable enough to do so.
- If one of you is suffering from an emotional or psychological disorder

Do this exercise:

- As a way of opening up your communication to a deeper level
- Because you love one another and want a stronger Soul Partnership
- To practice the emotional muscle of listening empty and honoring one another's thoughts and feelings
- To practice letting go and surrendering control
- To deepen your sense of trust in one another

Schedule this at a time with no interruptions. You will need two to four hours. Sit across from one another, make eye contact, and take turns speaking the following commitment to one another (in these or your own words):

"Today, I declare my commitment to being fully honest with you, my Soul Partner. My intention today and always in our relationship is to speak openly to you about my thoughts and feelings, especially when those things have an impact on you and on our relationship together. I promise to do so in a loving and compassionate manner."

Decide who will be the speaker first. As the listener, ask your partner the following question, and listen to the answer:

"What do you want to tell me?"

Listen empty, and stop the exercise if you get "full." Pause, set aside your own thoughts, feelings, and reactions, and ask the question once again. Keep going until the other person, in response to the question says, "blank." Then ask, "What else do you want to tell me?" When you get the next "blank" response, pause and ask once more, "What do you want to tell me?" When you get the third "blank," pause and ask, "Is there more?" When your partner says, "No, that's all," pause and then go to this next question.

Ask: "What are you afraid to tell me?"

Listen empty, remembering to stop if you get "full," as above. Keep going until the other person, in response to the question says, "blank." Then ask, "What else are you afraid to tell me?" When you get the next "blank" response, pause and ask once more, "What are you afraid to tell me?" When you get the third "blank," pause and ask, "Is there more?" When your partner says, "No, that's all," pause and then thank your partner for sharing so openly. Then switch roles.

After you have both shared, take a few minutes to acknowledge one another for being so open, honest, and courageous. If you are still feeling energetic, go to the next step. If not, do that at a later-scheduled time.

Now, reflecting back on what your partner shared, write down any perceptions that you may have about issues that were raised. One at a time, go over your list and "check out" your perceptions:

"I heard you say that...did I hear you correctly?" (If yes) "Is this an issue that we need to talk about more for our relationship?" (If yes, put a mark beside it to indicate that it needs more discussion. If no, ask for clarification and then mirror that.)

In this way, you may discover that some things are expressed as a way of "emptying the trash" and do not require more processing. Other things highlight issues that you need to discuss further. Use this as a taking off point for future heart and soul discussions, using the tools of listening empty and mirroring, listening intuitively, and listening compassionately.

The Choice to Withhold

One partner in a relationship may refuse to open up to the other. He/she may have thoughts, feelings, or emotions that she feels too vulnerable to share. He may have secrets about his past, about another relationship or attraction to someone else, doubts about the current relationship, or whatever, that he is afraid will hurt you if he expresses it. She may have an addiction in which she is indulging secretly (e.g., drinking to excess privately).

These communication processes only work to the extent that both partners are willing to be open and honest. Both parties must be willing to take the risk that what they have to say may "rock the boat." Both must be willing to let the secrets come out in the open. If you have things that you do not want your partner to know, then you will be unable to derive satisfaction from these communication processes or a deepening of your intimacy and connection with your partner. If you hold back important feelings or information from your partner, then you will sabotage the process, perhaps creating even more damage than already exists in the relationship.

If your partner is holding back from you, you may not be immediately aware that that is what is happening. You may have to extrapolate from the lack of communication that he/she is not telling you the complete truth. Signs that your partner may be holding back vital information include:

- Frequent responses to your questions such as "I don't know" and "I'm not sure."
- Often feeling frustrated at the end of your conversations. Not feeling satisfied after you talk, sort of like eating a meal and still feeling hungry afterwards.
- Outright refusals to talk such as "I don't want to discuss it" or "I don't know and I don't want to talk about it."
- Postponements of communication with no follow up. "Not now, I'm busy watching this show." "I don't want to talk about it right now." "Not tonight, I'm too tired."

- Accusations and blaming when you attempt to bring up an issue. "Why do you always have to bring this up?" "You are always harping on that!" "Oh, here we go again!" "You're just jealous! That's why you always want to talk about my secretary!" "That's your problem —I have nothing to say to you!" "Maybe you should go talk to your therapist about it!"

Perhaps your partner is holding back because she does not feel safe opening up with you. Take this inventory, being completely honest with yourself, to see if you have perhaps contributed to that feeling. In the past, when your partner has attempted to talk to you about an issue, have you:

- Gotten angry or hurt, drawing attention away from what your partner has to say and toward your own feelings?
- Gotten defensive, interrupting with your own point view before he finishes expressing his?
- Invalidated her point of view (e.g., saying things like "You're wrong!" or "That's so stupid" or "How can you say that?" or "That's not what happened at all!")?
- Refused to listen with your full attention (e.g., "I can read the paper and hear you at the same time" or not making eye contact, or walking away while he is talking, or doing other tasks while she is speaking to you)?
- Invalidated his feelings (e.g., "You have no right to be upset about that" or "You don't really feel that way" or "That's ridiculous for you to feel that way")?
- Refused to listen any longer because you do not want to hear what he is saying; walked out of the room or hung up the telephone in the middle of a conversation because it is not going your way?
- Had to be right no matter what? Refused to admit you were wrong or offer an apology when it is clearly your responsibility that something went badly?
- Overpowered your partner? After she expressed a few words or sentences, you "took over" the conversation rather than encouraging her to say more?

If these sound familiar to you, then you may have unconsciously sabotaged your own desire for an open and honest partnership. Once these patterns get deeply ingrained, it takes time and healing to undo them and choose new ones. In the next chapter, we will look at some ways to make amends for the past and to create healing in the relationship and open up new possibilities for the future.

Meanwhile, one of the most healing things you can do is simply acknowledge to your partner the things you can see you may have done to inhibit his self-expression. This is healing for you because it puts you squarely in the position of personal responsibility. It is healing for your partner because it releases him from being blamed for not opening up, thereby opening up a new possibility.

Getting Things Done, Getting Needs Met

In every Soul Partnership, there is a time to connect and there is a time to get things done. Yes, it is important to attend to the business of loving one another, but what about the practical matters? Who is going to empty the trash, clean the dishes, make the bed? Who is going to get up this time to feed the baby? How do you decide who does what and when and where and why?

Then there are our emotional needs. What about when we feel frustrated? What about when we want something our partner is not giving us? How do we get our needs met when he does not automatically take care of them?

Remember, in the past, men and women's roles were more clearly defined. She made the bed and got up to feed the baby. He earned the money. She cooked and he mowed the lawn. That was just the way it was. There was little to discuss or "work out." As for emotional needs, most couples simply did not have the insight or awareness to focus on that, so they did not generally have that kind of discussion.

Now, of course, who does what is up for grabs. This means that we have to consciously choose, making decisions about the division of chores together. Likewise, our relationships have evolved into a new paradigm that requires our focus on emotional and spiritual needs, so those conversations are even more crucial.

As with everything else, there are ways to talk about "who does what" that deepen your connection and love. Likewise, there are ways to discuss these matters that create separation and disharmony. What is important is not so much what you do as it is how you go about it.

Command and Control

One way to try to get what we need is to attempt to control others with overt or covert manipulation. We may withdraw love and affection, pout, shut down emotionally, and even threaten to leave; we may nag, whine, persuade, bring up the same topics repeatedly, and refuse to take "no" for an answer; we may raise our voice, make demands, and attempt to force our will.

None of this behavior gets us what we truly want. By controlling, we may get some satisfaction right now, but it is not fulfilling in the long run.

By controlling, we act out the fear that our partner either does not know how or does not want to do what is in the best interest of our relationship, the anxiety that things will not happen soon enough, or that if we let go, they will not happen at all.

Controlling behavior covers up a multitude of fears and a mountain of anxiety. In a relationship, it stands solidly in the way of our connection.

Going Beyond Command and Control

All roads lead to the same dark place at the center of our being. As souls having a human experience, we long for connection. Simultaneously, we fear connection as surrender of freedom and as the forerunner to loss and abandonment. When we love and connect, we take the risk of being abandoned. When we attach and bond, we take the risk of losing who we are, not because the other person has the power to take that away, but because we often surrender it in order to keep the other person around.

Ironically, our controlling behaviors bring about that which we fear. Eventually, our partner gets tired of it and withdraws. Ultimately, the yearning for control (or the illusion thereof) creates the greatest loss of control.

The truth about control is that all it accomplishes is to buy time. It puts off the inevitable: facing and dealing with the core truth that *in our relationships, as in life, we have no real control.*

One of the greatest challenges in life is to embrace this truth, to realize that our relationships are a gift. They are not owed to us. They are given to us and for what period of time, we do not know. Though we may yearn for lifelong love with one partner, we never know if that is the nature of the love that we have, not until we get to the end of our lives.

We cannot know the outcome of any relationship because it involves another person, another soul with its own singular life path, which may or may not coincide with ours.

Likewise, if my soul's journey demands that I go in a direction that my partner does not want to share with me, then it is my choice to move on if that is what I want. For our relationship to be truly empowering, we must recognize that fundamental truth together. We must grant to one another at all times the freedom to take an alternative life path, even if that means that we separate.

This is the reality of relationships, though we desperately rail against it!

Because we deny this fundamental truth, we cling too tightly to our relationships. Out of fear of loss, we deny our true selves, we withhold, we lie, we manipulate and control, and in so doing, we create the very thing we do not want—a relationship that does not support either of us. We either begin a slow emotional death together, or one of us one day stands up and shouts, "Enough is enough!"

The interesting thing at this point is that, typically, the baby gets thrown out with the bath water. Most couples allow their lack of honesty, lack of self-expression, and lack of freedom to build up into a toxic mountain of resentment. Their stories about the relationship become twisted and full of negative meaning under the weight of so much suppression. On the day of liberation, the compulsion is to run from the entire relationship, yet this is exactly the opposite of what is needed.

The real liberation, the one that is desperately needed, is the one from fear. Fear is the true enemy, not our partner, in almost every case.

Liberated from the fear of loss, we are empowered to speak openly and honestly. Liberated from the fear of abandonment, we can express ourselves fully, yet with kindness and compassion toward the other.

Released from the fear of making mistakes, we can be flexible and creative, collaborating to invent multitudes of ways to recharge our love batteries together. Released from the irrational fear of loss of freedom, we can make a true commitment, one that is based in choice and love, not guilt and obligation.

When couples realize that they have given up too much in service of their connection, this can be a grand opportunity! It is the opportunity to recreate their love authentically, through full self-disclosure, full self-expression, and thus, eyes-wide-open choice. With this kind of framework, the need for control melts away.

Because it is so critical, I say again:

You do not know what is available with your partner until you are willing to set aside fear and control, to express yourself fully, and to make it safe for the other person to do the same. You do not know what you are capable of together until you spend hours and hours in heart-and-soul communion. You do not know what your relationship can really be until you dedicate yourself to this process.

When you do that, and give it lots of time, and you discover that you are not on the same path, your partner will most likely agree. You will earn your way out of the relationship by honoring the process of full communication with your partner. Only then are we truly free to go forward and create something new and different.

If we leap too suddenly out of the relationship, blaming our feelings of unhappiness and our lack of self-expression on our partner, chances are we will attract someone else with whom to act out once again this drama. That is because the lesson is still unlearned: the lesson of what real love is about.

When the need for self-expression becomes so great that we cannot deny it, we are poised for real and authentic love. If we take that awareness back into the relationship, dedicating ourselves to open and honest communication, to being who we really are, and to seeing our partner for who he really is, miracles can happen.

In taking responsibility for our own lack of self-expression, for our own fears and insecurities, and for our own unhappiness, we open a powerful door between our hearts for authentic connection. Where that will lead, there is no guarantee. However, one place that it is sure to lead is into growth. We will either grow together in real love, or we will grow in understanding and release one another in lifelong friendship.

Chapter Nine
Apology and Forgiveness

One of the greatest opportunities for Soul Partners is to assist one another in deep emotional healing. That opportunity, ironically, arises out of some of our most painful interactions.

We choose one another on both a conscious and unconscious level, and this results in a particular relationship dynamic. Who I am connects with my partner at the level of soul, who he is, so that we can help one another be more of who we are. The challenge is that on the level of humanity we sometimes clash. The paradox is that in that clash lies our opportunity.

This is how it works. We meet, we fall in love, we see our greatness, and time passes. Eventually, we lose sight of the greatness, view our humanity, and the illusion falls apart. Now we discover the human package that the soul of the person we love contains. We begin to interact in ways to embrace that reality, avoid it, or attempt to change it. Most couples start with some combination of avoiding and attempting to change.

Real love unfolds when we accept that reality, and embrace the person on a deeper level. The challenge and the opportunity of Soul Partners is to learn how to interact in ways that bring forth the truth, for us individually and for us as a couple. This is not an easy path, but it is infinitely rewarding.

Along the way in this journey, we are bound to make mistakes with each other. Lots of them. Accept this now, and you will have an easier path.

The pitfall is to think that your partner is making all the mistakes and that you are doing great. This is not possible in a deeply connected relationship. Your connection, if it contains energy and spirit, necessitates that you be a mirror for one another, both in your greatness and in your humanity.

Things are very difficult in a relationship when one person points the finger at the other. Things are impossible when both persons point the finger. Blame creates resistance, which leads to more of the same. To hold someone accountable, on the other hand, opens the door to a new way of thinking, feeling, and behaving.

Before we can authentically hold our partner accountable, we must hold ourselves accountable. I always tell my clients this: when you have thoroughly cleaned up your side of the relationship, then you are entitled to look over at your partner's behavior and ask for change. Holding ourselves accountable requires that we strengthen our ability to make amends for the mistakes that we are bound to make.

Making Amends

One of the most potent concepts to come out of the twelve-step programs is that of making amends. I had the privilege of participating in that process several years ago when a former partner called me out of the blue. After years of struggle with addiction, he was working the twelve-step program. He called to apologize to me for the ways that he allowed his addictions to destroy our relationship. It was one of the most moving and powerful conversations of my life. There were tears, stories with gaps that were filled in, and forgiveness. At the end of the conversation, I felt this one dark place in my heart finally heal.

The power of apology and forgiveness for Soul Partners is immense. Remember the way your hearts danced together in the beginning of your love? That is what is available with apology and forgiveness: the recovery of the Dancing Heart. What flows from that is freedom of love and spirit, as well as renewed energy in your connection.

Resentment

What stands squarely in the way of the Dancing Heart is anger and resentment. My partner does something that I do not like (or fails to do something that I want), and I feel anger. If I do not find a way to achieve closure with that incident, it sticks in my mind and heart. If it sticks there for a long time, and especially if it is added to with future similar incidents, it becomes resentment.

Resentment is the buildup of little or big hurts and angers that are not resolved. Resentment represents all of the negative emotions we fail to achieve closure with in the relationship. It is like the little clumps of dirt that are swept under the rug rather than cleaned away. At first it is hardly noticeable, but eventually it becomes a mountain.

Resentment distorts our perceptions. It is like a cloud or fog through which we attempt to view our partner and the relationship. We cannot see clearly through the fog of resentment. A distorted relationship is viewed as a liability, not an asset. The danger is that we may toss away the relationship while in that fog, not realizing that someday down the road, the fog will clear, and we may see that we tossed away a treasure.

Even worse, we may stay in the relationship without clearing away the fog. This distortion leads to all manner of unloving behavior and lack of satisfaction.

Resentment is such a toxic emotion that it is imperative we find ways to release it. The paradox is that often we cling to resentment, either because we do not know how to resolve it, or because we do not want to.

The Power of Resentment

Holding onto resentment actually plays a role in relationships, one that appears to be productive initially but that is not in the long run. This is because of two things: the illusions of power and of forgetting.

Maintaining resentment with a partner who has "done me wrong" temporarily provides a feeling of power. If I am angry with you, I cannot be intimate or vulnerable with you, and that feels safer. You cannot hurt me again while I am in this emotional state (or so the feeling goes).

Sometimes, holding on to resentment for a period of time can help a couple re-balance. Carrie and Paul discovered this after Paul pulled away from

Carrie in confusion over his level of commitment. This couple had been together for almost two years when Paul experienced an "emotional shut-down." This was his pattern: to connect, then to pull away in fear at some point. For Carrie, who had abandonment issues from her earlier life, this was a huge betrayal of the commitment he had already extended. At first, she was deeply hurt, then pain gave way to anger, and that turned to emotional detachment and resentment. By the time the fog lifted for Paul and he realized that he was losing a treasure, Carrie was deep into resentment.

Prior to this, Carrie and Paul's relationship had been tilted the other way. Carrie wanted a greater level of commitment than he, and therefore experienced less power in the relationship. Now, Paul was scrambling to retrieve Carrie, sending flowers daily and asking her to marry him. Carrie's experience now was that she held the greater level of power, and she was reluctant to surrender it.

The shift of power was probably necessary for this couple. The challenge is for them to find a place of equal, authentic power. How does that happen? Carrie must find a way to forgive Paul, and he must keep his heart open and vulnerable. For both, the path is letting go of the illusion of what is the true source of power in relationships.

The illusion is that our power in love comes from the other person. If you love me in sufficient quantity and in the specific ways I want, then I feel powerful. If you do not, then I lose power.

Authentic Power in Relationships

The reality is that true power, authentic power, comes from within, and is accessible when I hold myself responsible, love and care for myself, and acknowledge my gifts as well as my vulnerabilities. I am powerful when I focus on being a responsible, loving partner rather than focusing on what he does or does not do.

My true power lies in living my life as a self-expression, bringing forth my gifts and talents to make a difference where I can. I have far more to bring to my relationship when I focus on being connected spiritually, mentally, emotionally, and with friends and extended family. That is authentic power.

From the position of authentic power, I can look more objectively at my partner's behavior when he acts in ways that are hurtful. I can choose my responses based on strength rather than on feeling needy or one-down.

If I feel victimized by my partner's occasional less-than-loving actions, I am certain to feel devastated. On the other hand, I can recognize my partner's own issues and dynamics as the source of his behavior. I can hold constant my view of myself as a loving and lovable person, while considering what I may or may not have done to push my partner away. I do this, not in a self-blaming mode, but in a self-caring mode.

Now I have the opportunity to make amends if appropriate and to hear my partner's amends. From the unshakable authentic power that is within me, I am strong enough to be vulnerable enough to say, "I forgive you." I am powerful enough to say, "This is my part in what happened, and I apologize to you." I can hold my partner accountable by asking questions, understanding, and then choosing again how I wish to be related to him.

The Role of Memory in Forgiveness

I do not need memory erasure for this process. In fact, I do not want memory erasure because this would prevent me from seeing a pattern, if there is one. I want to be able to observe everything that happens in our relationship and to connect it to other things if that is appropriate. To do this, I must release two other relationship illusions.

The illusion is that to forgive our partner for transgressions gives permission to do it again. This myth leads to the perception that I have the power to prevent future negative behavior by being angry and by holding onto resentment. Only then, can I adequately "teach a lesson" to my partner.

How did we adopt this myth? It flows directly out of the other illusion: that the way it works is to "forgive and forget." If I forgive my partner, I must forget what he did. Yet, if I succeed in doing that, how do I hold him accountable for the future? This creates a problem.

I cannot create the dynamic of accountability in the relationship while at the same time attempt to "forget" what happened. Furthermore, I do not know how it is that humans can actually achieve deliberate memory erasure. The reality is that we do remember, and this is for a purpose.

Memory serves a relationship when we adopt certain ways of viewing what happened. It is potent for our connection when we use it to mirror, point things out compassionately, and identify patterns that need to be addressed.

Memory is a destructive tool when we use it to "throw in your face" what our partner did wrong in the past. To use this material against our partner (i.e., continually bring up past transgressions) is massively destructive. It is because of this dynamic and its power to maim that the idea of "forgive and forget" was born.

What we really need to "forget," i.e., release, is the anger and resentment. Only by doing so are we free to move forward and dance together in love once more. Our tool for that is the power of ***heart and soul forgiveness.***

Accountability and Blame

Every minute we spend blaming our partner for our discomfort or unhappiness is a minute we do not spend in the copartnering process of creating the life and the love we want. Blame is the opposite of accountability. Blaming lets us "off the hook" for being responsible. Blaming is like trying to drive down the road while staring in the rearview mirror—it keeps us mired in the past in a negative, draining way.

What we need is a focus on where we are going and what we are creating next. Once we start directing our thoughts and energy to what lies ahead, our spirits lift, we feel energized and enthused, and our lives improve.

I have spent my share of time in the blaming position, and I have found that it never, ever improves my life or my life situations. From those lessons, I have set new intentions. In any circumstance in which I feel that someone is "doing me wrong" I first allow myself to temporarily feel the full emotional impact. I do not deny myself that experience, as that would be unhealthy for me. I express what needs to be expressed without doing further damage, either to that person or to someone else. If necessary, I do whatever process I need to do to release the emotions: write letters that I don't mail, hit pillows, or just talk it out with a friend.

Then, I make it my goal to release the emotions of anger, resentment, and blame as quickly as possible so that I can move forward. This process has served me countless times.

The truth about love is that Soul Partners are both 100 percent accountable in the relationship. This means that I am 100 percent responsible and my partner is 100 percent responsible. That gives neither of us room to indulge in blame and resentment.

Sometimes, we let our grievances build into resentment and blame because the alternatives that hold authentic power are not easy. One is to hold the other person accountable, when the grievance is real. Another is to recognize our small grievances as petty and to endeavor to take care of some of our own needs. The last resort, not what we want but what is necessary for authentic power, is to be prepared to leave if the relationship is truly unworkable. If your partner absolutely refuses to work with you, or if there is ongoing abuse or neglect, you must consider the possibility of leaving. To not have this option is emotionally and mentally suicidal.

Being 100 percent responsible does not mean that it is totally up to you to do everything in the relationship to make it work. In fact, this creates a very unhealthy dynamic wherein one person is working very hard and the other is what I call a "lazy lover." An imbalance such as this feeds the resentment cycle.

If you are doing all the work of the relationship, the first thing to do is to *stop doing that!* You do not know what you have with a partner until you let things be as they are, make observations, check them out, communicate from your heart, and then decide. Being 100 percent responsible means speaking up, holding our partner accountable (once we have our own side of the dynamic as clean as possible), and seeing clearly what is happening.

Being 100 percent accountable means realizing that there are some things we must let go of in order to have what we want. No relationship takes care of every emotional need of both partners, but a good relationship takes care of most of them. This is because it takes emotional, spiritual, and psychological health to have a good relationship. Healthy people have fewer needs and are therefore less demanding in general. We have come full circle. To have a great relationship, we must be healthy, and to be healthy provides the foundation of good relating.

Resentment as a Wake-up Call

When we continually feel needy, angry, wounded, resentful, and unfulfilled in a relationship, this is a signal that something is not working. It is a wake-up call to look within for answers, not a reason to cast more blame. Either the relationship is so empty that it does not offer much connection, or we need more focus on getting our own needs met. Sometimes, it is both.

All the resentment in the world will not keep a reluctant partner. In fact, it will drive the person away more quickly.

What sometimes works is to do the opposite of what our emotions tell us. Rather than resent, forgive. Rather than lash out in anger, invite conversation. Rather than trying to change, extend acceptance. Sometimes, the reluctant partner is one who fears being controlled. The healing point, then, is to give acceptance for who he is.

When we recognize that we have been emotionally needy in the relationship, asking for more than we can possibly receive, the healing point is to take a step back and address our own needs. Sometimes, this is a wake-up call to get more connected to extended family and friends, to revive an old hobby, to go back to school, or to get more spiritually connected. It may mean going into recovery or getting therapy. Relationships sink under heavy emotional needs, and they thrive when we fill our own wells and then bring that abundance to the partnership.

Completion and Soul Partnership

Resentment is an indicator that a Soul Partnership has gone off-course. It tells us that it is time to step back, invest some time and intentions for healing. Often this involves devoting attention to some sort of process for completion.

Completion means, in essence, to bring back to a state of wholeness. It means piecing together the puzzle of what happened in the past so that it makes sense. It means that we find some way to view the events of the past so that they are purposeful and liberating.

A Soul Partnership, because it exists primarily for the purpose of personal and spiritual growth, demands the exercise of completion. It is not possible to have an ever expanding, constantly deepening, and soulful expression of love where resentment is held. Personal and spiritual growth is not available in a relationship that is mired in blame.

The Possibility of Completion

Completion exists as a possibility at all times within a Soul Partnership, and may be brought forward by attending to certain processes and factors, including the following:

- A state of mind, heart, and spirit that is self-contained (does not rely upon other's actions)
- The recognition that completion may be attained regardless of the status of the relationship (together or not)
- Acknowledgement of the facts of the events (self-honesty)
- Releasing any "story" that contributes to unnecessary emotional pain
- Release of blame, regret, and resentment
- Release of negative energy toward self and others
- Genuine apologies (where appropriate)
- Heart and soul forgiveness of self and others

Perhaps you feel your partner has done something so unforgivable that completion is impossible. You cannot imagine ever releasing your painful feelings or experiencing love toward your partner. Usually, that means it is early in your process and you have not had sufficient time to deal with emotions.

The heart has its own timetable for healing, and it cannot be forced. In fact, if you try to force yourself too soon into the path of completion, you may actually create an internal block. Rather than attempt to force your heart, it is better to encourage it in a healing direction.

In order to achieve completion with the past, we must closely attend to the rhythm of our hearts as we move through the healing process. We must also draw upon one of our most powerful tools to guide us.

Healing Intentions

What guides this process most powerfully, especially in a Soul Partnership, is our intentions. When my ex-husband moved out and initiated divorce, at first I was initially devastated. There were a few weeks when I focused solely on my grief and pain, consumed with anger and resentment. One day, I realized that I was in danger of becoming bitter about men and relationships. That was something

I did not want. I asked myself "What do I want in the future?" and decided that I needed a set of **guiding intentions** to aid me in the healing process.

I began by imagining at some distant future time that I would be fully recovered. I pictured what that might look like and how I might feel. I created a detailed image of my life in this future state. Then, I took a sheet of paper and I titled it "How I Will Know I Have Healed From This Divorce," and I made a list that contained items like this:

- I believe in the possibility of love and marriage again
- I wish my ex the best in life
- I no longer feel angry or resentful toward him
- I can see him in public with another woman and be OK
- I can speak to him without yelling or crying

I think I had about fifteen items on that page, all worded to specifically target my desired future state, in the present tense, as if I was already there. I put that page in my day planner and carried it there for several months. Periodically, I turned to the page and realized that I had reached another milestone, and I checked that item off. One by one, I completed the entire list, and on that day, I wrote a note of acknowledgment to myself. I declared myself "complete" with my marriage and divorce. That was a little over one year from the day my husband moved out.

I have been asked from time to time why I dedicated myself to this process. After all, I did not owe it to my ex to forgive him. My answer is this: I did not do it for him. I did it for me.

My observation is that a bitter heart does not attract love, either in the form of friendships or romantic relationships. I value and treasure my ability to love and trust: I consider them my greatest assets. I know full well that bitterness destroys these things.

I wanted, and set my intentions toward, a full return to a state of love, trust, hope, and belief in the possibility of great relationships. That is the power of the exercise: to return to a state of wholeness and completion, not because the other person gets "off the hook" but because I get my life back plus so much more.

Setting Healing Intentions

If you and your partner are struggling with resentment and pain, the first step is to set the intention to heal. This does not mean that you set the intention to stay together, rather, *to heal the pain in your connection* so that you can powerfully choose the future of your relationship. Begin with this exercise.

EXERCISE: SETTING HEALING INTENTIONS

Do this first part separately. Take some quiet time alone, and begin by envisioning all of the hurt and pain you are experiencing being poured into a large container. Now, imagine yourself placing the container to the side. It is still there, it is simply not your focus right now. Remind yourself that it will be there for you to pick up later if needed.

Now, imagine that you are gifted with the ability to see into the future. Picture yourself at a time down the road when all of this is behind you. (It is not important to know whether or not your partner is with you at that time.) Imagine that your heart is totally healed from these experiences and that you are living a fulfilling life.

Now, take a piece of paper and title the page with a statement that represents the desired result, something like this:

"How I Will Know That I Have Healed From ____"

Being very specific, list the things you will be doing and feeling that demonstrate your healing. State them in the present tense, as if you are already there.

Take a leap of faith and include several items about your relationship with your partner. Again, imagine that the two of you have healed all of this between you. List very specifically the ways you will be acting and feeling together that demonstrate this fact.

When you have finished your list, re-read it, and allow yourself to feel how you will feel in this future state. Close your eyes and bask in those feelings. In your own words, assure yourself that it is possible to be complete in this or any other relationship.

After you have done this exercise individually, come back together and share your lists. In your own words, state your intention to your partner to find some way of being complete in the relationship. If need be, acknowledge the fact that you do not know if that means you end up together as a couple or not. The intention to heal is your primary objective, and you trust that when that is accomplished, you will know what form your relationship needs to take.

If your relationship is in a highly toxic state right now, and you do not feel safe sharing, then wait until it seems more appropriate. The possibility of completion is to reach that state with or without your partner's participation. It can be very powerful for one partner to do so, often to the extent that the other person may release the corresponding toxic feelings and reach out again. Remember that we are deeply connected in a Soul Partnership. When one person "shifts" in emotional state, the other feels it and responds differently.

If your relationship is in a wounded state, doing this exercise energizes and speeds up the healing process. The unconscious mind is a powerful tool, and so is the soul, and setting intentions utilizes them. When we set healing intentions, we give permission to the deepest parts of ourselves to "let go" and "begin moving on." We "put the wheels in motion" so to speak, and the hardest part is done.

Laura and Jim had been together for eight years, but the past year was by far the most difficult. It was so difficult, in fact, that they were considering divorce. Both were angry and bitter, and the stage was clearly being set for a nasty battle with no winners. At my urging, they decided to set the intention to be complete with one another and their relationship prior to choosing whether or not to divorce.

Over the next few weeks, we explored what happened between them, finding points of responsibility for both partners. Later, apologies were extended and gradually, they forgave one another. This process restored Laura and Jim to their original state of care and respect. By taking time to thoroughly explore, accept responsibility, and heal, they sidestepped the usual trap that most couples fall into of rushing into divorce with bitter feelings. Now, two completely new possibilities are open. They may choose to go forward and have an entirely new marriage. They may choose to go forward and be friends for life. Either way, they have the gift of healing and completion and are thus far better prepared to love again.

The Healing Apology

Making apologies in relationships is not the norm. When we do "little things" that hurt our partner, we typically mumble something like "I'm sorry" or "Sorry about that" and just roll on. Many times couples don't address their infractions toward one another. It is simply assumed the other person magically knows it was not meant to be hurtful and therefore is OK with it.

The problem with this approach is that it denies human nature. Remember that our words and actions do wound, and in Soul Partnerships, they wound more deeply than in any other form of relationship. Thus, the little criticisms, caustic remarks, and unloving comments we let fly between us create a certain hardening of the heart. Being neglectful of the behaviors of love, or being mean-spirited in how we act toward one another creates barriers. We cannot be tender with one another when we never know when and where the next arrow will fly.

When they are genuinely delivered, apologies restore the heart to a tender state and also serve as a point of correction. When I stop and make an apology to my partner, it means that I am conscious of my actions. The more conscious we are about our own actions, the more likely we are to drop undesirable behaviors and pick up loving ones.

An apology is not the same as saying, "I'm sorry," which is a report of how I feel about what I did. An apology goes one step further. To say *I apologize for what I did* extends a particular energy toward the other person. It expresses more than regret. It expresses an acknowledgement that what I did affected you and that I recognize that.

To say "I apologize" makes me vulnerable to a certain extent. The feeling of vulnerability that comes with these words makes it more difficult to say and far more powerful as a healing tool in the relationship.

If my partner and I are dancing together and I step on his toes, I might say "Oh! I'm so sorry!" We will both laugh and keep dancing.

If my partner says he has a headache, I might say, "I'm so sorry you are feeling bad." He will feel that I sympathized with him (although he does not like a lot of that), and I will feel as though I expressed my compassion for his pain.

If I lash out at him verbally in anger and say something unloving, that situation demands more. It demands that I stop and take account of my own behavior, recognize it as toxic to our connection, and take responsibility for it. I would then spend a little time with my partner and talk about what I did, listen to how he felt about it, and offer him my apology.

Releasing Expectations

One of the most common mistakes we make when offering an apology is that, consciously or unconsciously, we offer an apology expecting that:

- The other person will automatically release resentment.
- The other person will instantly forgive.
- There will be no need to process the other person's emotions about what happened.
- The relationship will automatically return to its former state of love.

Offering an apology with expectations places a burden on the recipient. It requires an emotional payback, regardless of the other person's current state. Often, this kind of apology denies the necessity of emotional processing. Thus, it is not a healing experience. Instead, it can actually create further distortion, as in the case of Martin and Sally.

Sally knew she owed an apology to Martin for criticizing him in front of their friends one night. She felt guilty and remorseful. As they were driving home, she said, "I guess you're upset with me about how I spoke to you at dinner. Well, I apologize. I had a bad day and I guess I took it out on you." Sally hoped that this would end it, but instead, Martin came back with, "I guess your having a bad day gives you the excuse to rake me over the coals in front of my best friends."

Now, Sally felt defensive, and her guilt flared up again underneath. "I didn't say that. I said I apologize, what more do you want?"

Martin, not having had the space to express his feelings and filled with resentment, retorted, "Oh, so now that you've apologized, that makes it all OK?" From there, a nasty argument ensued. Both ended up emotionally wounded, and the incident at dinner sat there like a festering sore, still incomplete.

An apology with expectations and minus emotional processing usually creates resistance in the recipient. It contributes to an energy block that may lodge in place, standing in the way of a loving state.

To honor another person's emotional process fully, we must release all expectations. When we act in a way that is harmful to our connection or that causes pain to our partner, the very first point of healing is to recognize the significance of that withdrawal from the emotional bank account. Then, we must make it our goal simply to refill the account, knowing that the heart has its own timetable and that it may take a very long time. It is very powerful medicine to give back what has been taken away plus more and to give it unconditionally.

Heart and Soul Forgiveness

It is easy to forgive when transgressions are small. It is easy to forgive when the relationship is going great, our needs are being met most of the time, and love is flowing. Then, an apology is freely offered, forgiveness is quick, and we are on down the road dancing merrily once again. What about when that is not the case?

How do we forgive when we are deeply wounded? How do we release resentment when a partner continues to act in an unloving manner? How do we forgive the unforgivable?

Normally, forgiveness is granted conditionally—it is a bargain for future behavior, or it is granted when the behavior seems understandable. This is *not* heart and soul forgiveness, which is *larger than the circumstances, greater than the emotions involved*. It surpasses common understanding. It is unreasonable—others might not relate to it or approve of it.

Heart and soul forgiveness flows out of the intention to live life to the fullest and is necessary in order to fulfill the purpose of Soul Partnership. It leads us into healing and growth, demanding that we expand ourselves.

In order to forgive heart and soul, we must transcend our egos and be greater than our hurt. We must be committed to completion and carrying forward no toxic or negative energy. Most of all, *we must be willing to consider the possibility that everything that happens in our relationship is meaningful and purposeful toward our souls' growth.*

Understanding Purpose

Without a sense of purpose and meaning, our grievances in a relationship leave us wounded and floundering. They exist as stark reminders of our emotional and psychological frailties, putting us in touch with how little control we really have over what happens to us.

Without a sense of meaning, the unhappy incidents of the past in a Soul Partnership are too painful to bear. Thus, we either repress them (push them deep inside), deny them (pretend it did not happen or it was not that bad), or relive them over and over (neurosis). We stay, miserable and disconnected, or we ditch the relationship, taking the emotional baggage with us.

Heart and soul forgiveness offers the possibility of stepping out of this quagmire by adopting the stance that *our relationship is part of an overall life mission.* How do we do that?

Purpose provides power to our Soul Partnership just as it does to our lives. By infusing our connection with purpose and meaning, we rise above the petty grievances and small-minded behaviors of the past. We are empowered to be creative, flexible, and more loving, and to practice a level of forgiveness that was heretofore out of reach.

A Useful Story

The following is something I hold as my personal belief about my Soul Partnership. It empowers my life and is a point of view that I choose to adopt because it works for me. It is this:

Every circumstance in my Soul Partnership exists as a point of learning and growth. None of it is wrong or without purpose. If I look, I can see the meaning behind what is happening, not immediately in every case, but eventually. Therefore, regardless of what happens in this relationship, I am never the victim of anything. *At the level of soul, I am the cocreator of absolutely everything that takes place between my partner and me.* My partner and I are in a perfect dance that expresses who we are and that brings forth all of the right circumstances to move more deeply into who we want to be.

My useful story goes on to say that our souls deliberately chose one another to fulfill our life purposes, for however long we dance in this life together. Therefore, any time I (in my internal aggravation) start to indulge in thinking that certain things about him are not what I want, I remind myself that *I chose to be with him.* No one forced me to be here.

From this perspective, forgiveness is almost automatic, requiring little effort. I forgive because I am cocreator and a purpose is being served, because he is my partner and I am his, and because it is the only way to grow and expand our connection.

Whenever we act in ways that harm our connection, we have work to do to repair the damage. In fact, it is often during those times of doing repair in our relationships that we open to new levels of insight, intimacy, and love. Many couples report that their relationship is deepened and strengthened by going through hardship together and coming out on the other side.

To forgive in this way, by adopting a sense of purpose and meaning, is not the easiest path at first, as it requires setting aside a lot of old beliefs and patterns. I fully understand that it is not easily embraced or practiced. I encourage you to begin simply by having an open mind and heart to the concepts, and to seek insight for yourself. Colin Tipping, author and inspirational workshop leader, calls this kind of forgiveness "Radical Forgiveness."[9] If you are struggling with the concept of forgiveness or with lots of emotional baggage from the past, I highly recommend his book and seminars for deep-level healing.

Getting to Forgiveness

The following is a checklist to help you see if you are on track for heart and soul forgiveness. If you are struggling over forgiving your partner for a particular significant issue, begin by taking some clean paper and just write about the issue. Write everything there is to say, not editing or filtering what you write. (Even if you have done this exercise before, do it again to see where you currently stand.) Once you have done that, ask yourself the following questions and either write about your answers or reflect upon them:

1) Am I clear about the issue; do I know all the facts or do I need more information?

2) How much of what I have written is my own story and how much is "just the facts"?

3) Am I willing to acknowledge that a higher purpose is being served by these events, even if I do not know what it is? If so, what *might* be the purpose in my life of having this happen in my relationship? What *might* be the purpose in our relationship?

4) Am I willing to consider that I contributed in some way to the dynamics of this issue? If so, what is my part?

5) Am I willing to forgive my partner without the necessity of forgetting what happened? If so, am I willing to release all blame and resentment, and focus on the next steps for our relationship?

6) What is the appropriate thing regarding this issue to communicate to my partner at this time?

7) Most important: what are some of the things that I love and appreciate about my partner? (This last puts us back in our hearts after doing all of this processing.)

It may take hours, days, or weeks to go through this list of questions and complete them all. Often, this process alone is sufficient to release the resentment and nothing more needs to be done. Sometimes, once there is forgiveness, we can speak to our partner in a way that encourages collaboration, creativity, and connection.

Perhaps you do not have one huge issue you are struggling with. Maybe you have a whole list of grievances that add up to a mountain of resentment. This next exercise is for you.

EXERCISE: RELEASING RESENTMENTS

Begin by listing all of your resentments toward your partner. Make sure you write them down in behavioral terms, such as the following:

I resent Bill for:

- Not taking out the trash unless I ask
- Coming home late without calling to let me know he will be late
- Driving my car until it is out of gas
- Not giving me a hug and kiss when he comes home

When your list is as complete as it can be, read the whole thing over, then close your eyes, and ask yourself this question:

What is my *overriding resentment?* What is it that I am really angry with my partner for?

Let the answer float up into your awareness. Don't try to force it. Allow lots of time for you to simply understand.

The little things normally do not bother us that much if our connection is good. Usually, we get hung up on the little grievances because we do not feel connected to our partner on the level we desire (emotionally, spiritually, sexually, or mentally) because one or both of us has withdrawn in some way.

To complete the exercise, write about any insight or awareness you discovered. Do not be concerned if you did not get an answer to the last question. Keep asking it from time to time over the following days or weeks. If there is an overriding issue, it will come to you.

If not, this next part may help you release your resentment about the things your partner does (or does not do) that annoy you. Looking back over your list, ask yourself:

Which of these items have a *direct impact* on me (i.e., causes harm to me physically, financially, or emotionally)? (Put a star by those) How?

Of those that have a direct impact, which are important enough to address with my partner and which can I release? (Remember that it is not effective to make an issue of every little thing, but rather, to focus in on what really matters)

Now ask yourself:

Am I willing to forgive my partner for these things?

If so, what is the appropriate communication to my partner at this time? (Sometimes, it is powerful to apologize for "holding a grudge" over the little things.)

If you do not yet feel willing to forgive your partner, ask yourself this question:

What purpose does it serve for me to hold onto this resentment?

Be as honest is you can be about this question. The answers go directly to the heart of your well-being. Resentment, in the long run, harms the resentful person far more than it does the person who is resented.

Once you have forgiven as much as you can for now, set the intention to speak to your partner about the truly important issues, using the guidelines for listening empty, speaking to empower, and mirroring. Set the intention to complete those issues with your partner as soon as possible.

Powerful Relationship Completion

Remember the listening empty and mirroring exercises in chapter 5? With heart and soul forgiveness, we come full circle. Once a particular issue has been discussed on both sides and you have a full understanding of what has happened in the past, you are ready to "complete" the issue.

EXERCISE: ISSUE COMPLETION: APOLOGY AND FORGIVENESS

Do this first part separately on paper. Reflect on what your partner has shared about the issue, from his point of view. Reflect on her emotions, the ways that she felt wounded about the issue. Extend your compassion toward your partner. Look at your part of the dynamic of this issue in the relationship. Now, what are some things you can authentically apologize for to your partner with regard to this issue? Write them down one at a time, being as specific as possible, with the words "I apologize to you for..." in front of each item or at the top of the page as a reminder. Examples might be:

"I apologize to you, Cindy, for not being more understanding about your feelings of responsibility toward your mother. I apologize for trying to stop you from talking to her so much, rather than being a supportive sounding board for you."

"I apologize to you, Jim, for not thinking about your needs when you have had a hard day at work. I apologize for hitting you with all my problems the minute you walk in the door, rather than giving you some space to decompress."

Perhaps you feel that with this particular issue, you have done nothing wrong. Your partner is clearly the perpetrator, in fact, has stated as much. Still, there is some way that you have contributed to the dynamic, and searching for this will stretch your emotional capacity for love. Look to see if you can find some way to acknowledge that in the form of an apology. Examples might include:

"I apologize to you, Steve, for being so vicious to you when you were late getting home without letting me know. It was not called for and it did nothing useful toward dealing with the issue."

"I apologize to you, Marian, for withdrawing in silence from you for days at a time after your episodes of temper. I realize that that only escalated the damage rather than helping as a partner by addressing it with you and supporting you to get help."

Once you have completed your lists, begin speaking them, one at a time, taking turns. One person expresses an apology, and the other person looks to see, "Am I ready to forgive my partner for this?" If the answer is "yes," then communicate that. Say the words, "I forgive you for that."

Do this part slowly and deliberately, making lots of eye contact. Sometimes, couples want to rush through this part because it is not comfortable. The healing, however, is in allowing each word to sink in and to be felt throughout one's being. The words "I apologize to you for…" are enormously healing, when allowed to penetrate and go deep into the heart.

Likewise, the words "I forgive you" are also powerful medicine for the heart when allowed to sink in slowly. Take your time with this.

Next, each of you look to see if there is something that your partner has not apologized for that you would like. Write that down, then share it, one at a time. A request for an apology might look something like this:

"I would like your apology, George, for blaming me at times for our sex life not being great. I want you to acknowledge that doing that shuts down my desire to be a good lover to you."

"I would like your apology, Brenda, for criticizing the way I look. That really hurts, and shuts down my desire to work on losing weight."

This part of the exercise requires a great deal of compassion. It is not about blaming oneself for a partner's pain, but rather, reaching out in love to say, in essence, "I apologize for what I did that contributed to your distress."

If your partner's request for an apology is not exactly what you can say, then do your best to approximate it. The exercise is mainly about letting your partner know that you deeply care about his emotional well-being, that you want to do everything possible for her healing process.

Forgiving Oneself: Releasing Regret

One of the most potent parts of this exercise, and the part that brings it full circle, is to *forgive yourself* for whatever you are apologizing for. To not do so means carrying forward the element of regret, which is focused on the past, on actions that are done and cannot be changed.

As it is with forgiving others, so it is with forgiving oneself. I forgive myself, not to let myself "off the hook" or to magically "forget" what I did. I forgive myself so that I can carve out a new future based upon my highest and greatest intentions.

Therefore, when you apologize to your partner and you receive forgiveness, the next step is to stop and ask yourself: "Am I ready to forgive myself for this issue?" If so, communicate that. If you are the one being apologized to, you can support your partner in releasing regret by saying: "Do you forgive yourself for this?"

Keep going, one at a time, taking turns, until you complete your lists. Follow your hearts' energy when you are done. If you are feeling the desire to be intimate, follow that impulse. If you are feeling the desire to hold one another, follow that. If one person feels like making love and the other would just like being held, follow the lower impact impulse. Sometimes, just holding one another is the most potent completion.

Not Ready to Forgive

When your partner apologizes, it is vital that your forgiveness be authentic. Never fake forgiveness! This creates distortion in the relationship that is very difficult to undo.

Rather, take honest stock of yourself and where you are emotionally with the issue. Sometimes, it is too soon for forgiveness. You need more time for emotional processing. The next best thing you can do is to *set the intention to forgive*. In that case, tell your partner something like this:

"Thank you for that apology. It feels wonderful to hear you acknowledge your actions and to offer to make amends to me. I intend to forgive you because I know that is the only way for us to go forward. However, I need a little more time to express myself about this issue. Could we do that now?"

You might want to process your feelings separate from your partner. If so, communicate that: "I think I would like some time on my own to just deal with my feelings about this issue before we talk about forgiveness."

The exercise is not to have perfection in your process, but rather, to have honesty and compassion. Find your own way through these exercises. Look for and express the best way to achieve healing.

Forgiving the Unforgivable

Sometimes, the issue is so huge, the pain so deep, and the relationship is so dense with mistrust that it is no longer viable. Before you decide that this is so about your Soul Partnership, consider these thoughts:

There are two separate issues to resolve. One, what happened in the past—achieving closure, heart and soul forgiveness, and completion together. Two, the relationship dynamics leading up to that which, if not changed, may lead to a similar occurrence in the future.

Leaving a relationship before the pain is resolved usually results in creating the same dynamic again with someone new.

Once you complete the past, there may still be a significant imbalance in the relationship. I have observed that when there has been an affair, the other person often feels an almost overwhelming temptation to return the behavior. This might correct the imbalance, but it will not lead to Soul Partnership.

The point of healing is for

1) the transgressor to make amends and to be willing to put tremendous amounts into the emotional bank account for an extended period of time,
2) the transgressed to find a way to forgive and to extend trust again,
3) both parties to address their relationship dynamics and make significant changes together in how they relate. (You may need professional help for this.)

If these things cannot be accomplished together, it may be better to let go and move on. Often forgiveness comes down the road when we are no longer invested in the relationship. To stay together and remain resentful over months and years is toxic to both parties and accomplishes nothing.

What is the bottom line? When you apologize for your mistakes, forgive your partner's mistakes, forgive yourself for your mistakes, and empower your partner to forgive himself, you partner in deep healing for the heart and soul. Congratulations! You are participating in a powerful process to jet-propel your relationship into a brighter future. The next step is to infuse your relationship with positive energy on a day-to-day basis.

Overcoming Emotional Triggers

Being complete with an issue does not mean we will never have emotions about it again. Remember that painful events are stored in the brain along certain neural pathways. When something new happens that reminds us of the old event, we feel emotionally triggered and may relive the old feelings.

This does not mean that all of the healing work we did is now undone. It simply means we are feeling triggered. All there is to do is stop, honor the emotions in ourselves, and remind ourselves of the work we did and the forgiving state that we had before. The more we remember the state of forgiveness we had and the more we reinforce it, the less powerful the pathways to the old hurt in our brains. Over time, they can actually change so that we are triggered less and less, and someday, not at all. For particularly traumatic events, there are therapies now that assist in rapid recovery and dissolving those painful neural triggers.

What we are aiming for is release from the old emotions and neural patterns that stand in the way of recreating our loving connection. By setting the intention to heal and by forgiving our partner as we forgive ourselves, we depart from old ways of connecting in pain. Now we are in a position to infuse our relationship with positive, loving energy. In our softened, more open hearts, we have a place to put the emotions of love, gratitude, and appreciation for one another and for what we have.

Chapter Ten
Gratitude, Acknowledgment, and Appreciation

A relationship is a living, breathing entity, pure heart energy in motion. Every word we speak, every look, every facial expression, every motion when we are together, every action and behavior that impacts one another, our thoughts about one another, our daydreams, our hopes, wishes, desires, and fantasies—these are the components of the energy that is our love. The most powerful component by far of the energy of our love is our intentions.

All of this energy, by its very nature, is constantly evolving—changing shape and form, changing in quality, shifting from positive to negative and back again. It is a dynamic process, our love, and it is never completely the same from one moment to the next. In every moment, we have the opportunity to deepen and expand our love or to block and shrink it.

What Love Really Needs

Like any living entity, a love relationship requires certain elements in order to grow and thrive. It also must be protected from certain elements in order to live.

Love, in order to grow and thrive, must be protected from too much exposure to:

- Anger
- Resentment
- Critical words
- Judgmental thoughts and words
- Controlling behavior
- Fear

Love must be protected from *any* exposure to:
- Deceit
- Unfaithfulness
- Abuse of any kind

Love, in order to grow, must be given large doses of:
- Gratitude
- Acknowledgment and appreciation
- Thank-you's
- Loving action

If love were a garden, these last four elements would be the water and the minerals that support the growth of the plants. Like the garden, love requires nourishment. It cannot thrive by letting it sit there with no attention. In an unattended garden, weeds will choke out the plants. Likewise, an unattended relationship will stagnate and develop unpleasant qualities.

Active Love

Love is not the same as attachment. Attachment binds partners together, but that does not necessarily result in fulfillment. Attachment is *necessary* for love, but it is not *sufficient* for a Soul Partnership.

Attachment is passive rather than active, and it must be kept in balance. Too much of it (neediness) actually works against growth. Too little of it (detachment) leads to disconnection and sudden endings.

Real love is active, not passive, and requires attention and action, backed by genuine desire for the relationship and strong intention. In this chapter, we look at the behavior of love; specifically the actions that nourish love and support its growth. Some are actions that are done in private moments of reflection, while others are done with a partner. All of them are powerful to the degree that they flow out of our highest and greatest intentions.

The Intention to Love

Before we can take loving action, there must be alignment between the action and the intention. I once went to a counseling session with a man I had dated for a few weeks, at his request, for the purpose of his gaining some insight into a dynamic that he had experienced with several women, including me. While there were many things that were positive about that session, one thing did not fit for me. At one point, the therapist advised his client to "act as if" he loved a woman, whether he had those feelings or not, until he either developed them or realized they were not to be.

With no alignment between the action and the feelings, either the insincerity undermines the basis of the relationship and results in loss of trust, or the other person believes the actions and is blind-sided when the person suddenly withdraws with the realization that the feelings are not to be. Much more powerful would be simply to say, "I want to get to know you and see where this goes." Then, to align behavior with each stage of real emotional development.

Of course, a brand-new dating relationship is not the same as a well-established love relationship. In dating, the behavior of love is powerful when matched with the *intention to support the development of love.* Even though it may not work out, the sincere intention makes all the difference in how we decide to move forward or move on later.

In an established love relationship or marriage, feelings of love may be suppressed under months or years of neglect or emotional damage, and it may feel as though love has completely died. Therefore, the *intention to heal* is vital for the process. With this intention, loving behavior is sincere and aligned, even in a distressed relationship. This opens the door to attain completion with the past and thus create new possibilities for staying together. A heart unburdened of old grudges and pain often is free to experience newly the love that was always there.

It is a powerful and potent combination—the *intention to love* and purposeful, thoughtful, *loving behavior.* When all parts of us (mind, body, heart, and soul) are in agreement with this, love cannot help but win! Thus, the first step is to *set your intention to have the most loving, fulfilling relationship with your partner you possibly can*. Second, *study and take to heart the elements of the behavior of love*. Resolve to bring some kind of loving behavior into each and every day with your partner—to cherish and nurture your greatest treasure through your consistent and loving actions.

Gratitude

A good love relationship is a treasure. My partner and I, partly because of our relationship history prior to meeting one another, never tire of expressing our gratitude for having found each another and for what we share. We know what it is like to suffer through an unfulfilling relationship, and we know what it is like to wonder if real love will ever happen. One of our stated intentions is to be actively grateful for our love (never take one another for granted).

When love is flowing, it is easy to feel grateful. We exchange cards, toast one another over candlelit dinners, gaze into one another's eyes, and feel a profound sense of fullness.

What about when love is stressed? How easy is it to feel grateful when your lover ignores you, argues with you, and leaves his dirty socks on the floor? How easy is it to express gratitude when your partner is critical or fails in some way to meet your emotional needs?

Paradoxically, it is the times when we do not *feel* particularly grateful that gratitude is most important. In fact, it is a powerful healing tool to keep love alive and growing at every stage of a relationship.

Blocks to Gratitude

Gratitude is so vital to the growth of love that it stands out as clearly obvious that we express it in our relationships. Yet, gratitude is often left out of the picture in love. Why do we not feel and express gratitude easily and naturally, especially when going through tough times?

What stands in the way of the experience of gratitude is our very human tendency to project whatever troubles us onto the closest and easiest target: our beloved.

When I am in a state of dissatisfaction, I sometimes have the irrational thought that I would not be feeling this way if only he were doing something different. Now, my attention has shifted completely away from dealing with myself and onto my partner and what is "wrong" with him. That is projection in action! When I step back, usually after some sort of apology, I see that what is really creating the turmoil is me, not him.

In relationships, once we get past the blissful early stages, we find that we still must deal with the same issues that were there before we fell in love. We still have the job of creating balance within ourselves and in the way we manage all aspects of our life. Because we often set ourselves up to believe that finding the right person means finding total happiness, the natural tendency is to project onto our partners that which is not satisfying to us. In a nutshell, it is the expectation that a good relationship will take care of all of our needs that removes us from the experience of gratitude.

The truth is that no relationship can provide everything that we want. We choose our partners for the purpose of our growth, not for the purpose of achieving utter bliss every moment of every day.

Releasing unrealistic expectations makes room for the experience of gratitude. It also makes room for our partner to shine in our eyes and for our relationship to feel more satisfying for what it is.

We release unrealistic expectations when we:

- Recognize the true purpose of love: for growth and expansion
- Accept responsibility for our own satisfaction
- Assume accountability for creating our own happiness and then sharing that with our partner
- Focus more on what is good about our love than on what is not
- Accept responsibility for choosing this person
- Remember the positive reasons for that choice and focus on them
- Actively search for and create ways to experience fulfillment outside of the relationship (without disconnecting from our partner)

With the release of expectations that no relationship can fulfill, we are free to acknowledge all of the things we love about one another and about our relationship. We do this not just at times when we feel all warm and fuzzy inside, but at times when we feel challenged. How do we do that?

An Uncommon Gratitude

Gratitude as we normally understand it is a feeling that rises up from inside of us when we feel good. We do not create it, it just happens, and we have no control over when and how it will happen.

I have had the experience of this kind of gratitude more than once while on vacation in a beautiful place. Not long ago, my Soul Partner and I were dining on a terrace overlooking a spectacular garden while the sun was setting. We had spent the day hiking and observing animals in a nature reserve near the coast. That evening, my heart was suddenly filled with gratitude. I felt a deep and profound sense of "fullness" about life.

There is another kind of gratitude, one that can be created at will. It is uncommon, that is, greater than the ordinary. This kind of gratitude does not just "happen" to us. It is highly purposeful and intentional, and it is available at all times. Sometimes, it is created and experienced in the face of circumstances that are painful and difficult. Thus, it defies rational understanding. It can only be understood on the level of heart and soul.

Heart and soul gratitude is more than a feeling, it is an intention, a state of mind, and part of standing for something that is larger than the circumstances or even the feelings in our relationship. It is something that we have the power to create at any moment in time.

Creating Gratitude

We create heart and soul gratitude when we choose to step back from the flow of life and all of its challenges to take inventory of our most priceless treasure: our relationship. The following exercise will assist you in this process.

EXERCISE: CREATING HEART AND SOUL GRATITUDE

Carve out some time for yourself with no distractions. Play some soft music, light a candle if you want, and get comfortable. Have paper and pen handy. Close your eyes and take several deep breaths, allowing your thoughts about your day to drift pleasantly to the side.

Now, focus on your relationship with your partner. Remember when you met, the feelings of attraction that drew you to this person. Recall one of your best dates early in the relationship. Remember the sights, the sounds, the smell and feel of your beloved. Bask in those inner remembrances.

Now, focus on the qualities that drew you to this special person. Open your eyes and write them down. Be specific and keep writing until you can think of no more. Examples:

- Her sparkling eyes
- His warm and genuine smile
- Her intelligence
- His kindness
- The graceful way she moves
- That dimple in his chin

Now, close your eyes and focus again on your beloved. Think about all the little gifts of self-expression, word, and deed that he/she does each day. Open your eyes and write about those. Examples:

- The cards with those love notes he gives me
- The way she hugs me when I come in the door
- The foot rubs he gives me
- Her gifts of listening empty and mirroring
- The way he holds me when I am sad or scared
- The way (s)he makes love to me
- The little things he does for me without asking, like washing my car and repairing things around the house

Close your eyes once again, and this time focus on the innermost qualities of your partner that you admire and appreciate. On the deepest level, what are the qualities of your beloved's heart and soul that you connect with? Examples:

- He is a true giver
- She is the most thoughtful person I know

- He is committed to integrity and honesty
- She is a wise and strong woman
- He is gentle and caring with children and animals
- She is compassionate and loving
- He is a real go-getter
- She is ambitious

Re-read your entire list, this time putting the words "I am grateful for my partner who is… and who gives me…" in front of each one. Do this with your inner voice or (even more powerful) read it out loud; this allows the unconscious mind to hear the gratitude, reinforcing it on an even deeper level.

To make this exercise even more powerful, take your list, type it with a beautiful font, or handwrite it with colorful ink. Do whatever you want to make it attractive, and then put it somewhere that you have to see it daily. Some people like to keep it in a day-planner, some like to hang it on the wall. Make it a "working list," adding things to it over time. Spend five minutes each day reflecting on your partner's special qualities and what you are grateful for in the relationship. Notice how your heart fills with love.

Hungry for Acknowledgment

Acknowledgment is, in a nutshell, the expression "You are wonderful and here is how and why." To acknowledge someone is to reflect that person's greatness, to highlight the gift of that person's presence and the difference that it makes in our life.

Acknowledgment is vital to human beings, yet it often does not happen until someone dies. I have often thought that it would be wonderful if we could gather together for our loved ones and acknowledge them while they are alive as fully as we do after they pass on.

Why do we not easily and naturally acknowledge one another verbally? Why do we not ask for it or expect it? Most important, *why do we not give it to ourselves first?*

One reason is that acknowledgment is often confused with egotism. We hesitate to acknowledge ourselves because it might be perceived as "blowing my own horn." We steer away from giving it to ourselves because we do not want to be self-centered. We shy away from others' acknowledgments of us because it is uncomfortable.

Often we assume that others feel the same way. We hesitate to draw attention to them in a positive way because they may feel the same embarrassment that we feel internally when someone acknowledges us.

This is the dilemma. *Unless we are comfortable acknowledging ourselves, it is difficult for us to receive it. Furthermore, it is difficult to give that which we cannot receive.* This is a vicious circle, and the net result is that most of us walk around hungry for appreciation and acknowledgment yet not getting it. We exist in a state of discomfort with both giving and receiving acknowledgment, and we bring all of this to our love relationships.

Often, this is how affairs intrude into a relationship. Someone else gives the acknowledgment that we are missing, and we mistakenly believe that means we are with the wrong person and must switch. We forget that acknowledgment happens easily in the first blush of love, but naturally dies if not consciously attended to. Thus, we wind up in the same soup with the new person when the initial love high fades.

Making Room for Acknowledgment

The way out of this dynamic is to bring the elements of acknowledgment and appreciation into our relationship, and to do it consciously and purposefully.

Acknowledgment is available to us all, regardless of where we perceive ourselves to be in our development. Not only is it available, it is *essential to our growth*. Remember that we create more of that which we focus on. Therefore, when we receive acknowledgment from others, and when we acknowledge ourselves, we increase our positive energy and we reinforce that which is good and wonderful about us.

Bringing acknowledgment into our Soul Partnership supports our growth as individual human beings and as partners. It is practice in stopping to notice one another through the lens of love, then speaking it so that it reaches out and touches the heart of our beloved. It is a way to remind one another that *we are truly wonderful for exactly who we are.*

Giving Heart and Soul Acknowledgment

Acknowledgment is not the same as "pumping up" the ego. Genuine *heart and soul acknowledgment*:

- Recognizes and gives specific examples of true gifts and talents
- Highlights the intrinsic value of the person (i.e., lovable for *who you are*, not what you do)
- Touches and inspires the recipient

This kind of acknowledgment asks both the giver and the receiver to stretch emotionally, expanding into a larger sense of self. The following exercise helps you practice this in your relationship.

EXERCISE: GIVING HEART AND SOUL ACKNOWLEDGMENT

Using your gratitude list, write an acknowledgment for each item that reflects your partner's *innermost qualities* of greatness. Expand it into a couple of sentences that express your love for your partner and that include specifics about the item. For example:

Item: He is a giver

Acknowledgment: "I want to acknowledge you, (partner's name), for being the true giver that you are. (Include a specific example) I notice the way you select your nieces' and nephews' gifts for their birthdays. (Be descriptive) You really pour your heart into it! You take the time to find out what they really want so that each gift is personal and something they will really want! (Go deeper, make it personal to the relationship) I especially want to acknowledge you for being the true giver that you are to me. It constantly amazes me and touches my heart when you think of me and do something special just to please me. (Express your love) You are so wonderful in this way, and I am so lucky to share my life with you. I love you."

This acknowledgment could have been as simple as saying, "I want to acknowledge you for being a real giver." There is nothing wrong with leaving it at that. However, if you want to reach deeply into your partner's heart with your acknowledgment, then practice creating heart and soul acknowledgment. This takes time and loving energy—two gifts that very powerfully nourish a relationship. By going into greater depth and by being *specific* and *descriptive*, the acknowledgment is much more likely to reach our beloved.

Heart and soul acknowledgment on a regular basis is powerfully nourishing to our connection. If you want to super-charge your relationship with love, practice acknowledging one another in this way at least once per week. Make it part of your especially carved-out time together for nurturing your connection. Light candles, make lots of eye contact while you do it, perhaps share a glass of wine. Do it over a romantic dinner, or do it in your living room or bedroom after the kids are in bed. However you choose to do it, make it a regular part of your lives and your relationship.

Appreciation

To express appreciation is, in a nutshell, to say, "I appreciate you for what you do." The expression of appreciation is rare in love relationships. Normally, if we express appreciation at all, it is a hasty "thanks" delivered in passing. This is certainly a valuable practice and a great starting point.

More powerful is to step back, take notice *in detail* of our partner's gifts in the relationship, and then to express that verbally. To say "I appreciate what you did" in specific terms, sends the energy of gratitude straight from one heart to the other. This energy has a powerful and positive effect.

When we feel appreciated by our partner, we cannot help but want more of that. To be appreciated means to be recognized for our loving behavior, to be honored for that, and to be recognized as a loving human being.

Giving Heart and Soul Appreciation

More than a simple "thank you," ***heart and soul appreciation*** is:

- Stopping to notice *what our partner does* and *how it makes a difference*
- Giving specific examples to deepen the experience for the recipient
- Always sincere and genuine, never manufactured
- A way to deepen love, gratitude, and respect in a Soul Partnership

The following exercise shows how to do this.

EXERCISE: EXPRESSING HEART AND SOUL APPRECIATION

Using your gratitude list, focus on the items that reflect *what your partner does for you* in the relationship. One at a time, write an appreciation statement, using the following example as a guide.

Item: The little things he does for me without asking

Appreciation: "(Partner's name), I want you to know that I really appreciate the little things you do for me without my asking. (Give a specific example) Yesterday, when you got take-out for me because you knew I was working at my desk and didn't have time to stop and make something to eat, was so sweet! It was exactly what I needed, and you did it without my asking for it, just because you noticed what I needed. (Go deeper—how it makes a difference) I feel so loved by you when you do things like that. I feel free of anxiety about our relationship and energized to focus on my work. Thank you, honey. (Express your love) I am so lucky to have you. I love you."

Setting aside time each week to express heart and soul appreciation is deeply enriching and powerfully reinforcing, motivating us to continue doing the positive behaviors of love.

Saying "Thank You"

Saying "thank you" is a simple and quick way to infuse your day-to-day experiences with more gratitude and love. Ordinarily, we are more focused on what is wrong than what is right in our relationship. In order to be thankful, and to express it frequently, we must focus on what is right.

EXERCISE: EXPRESSING THANKS

Stop and pull out a sheet of paper right now. Think back over the past couple of days, and recall everything your partner did either directly for you or as a contribution in your lives together. Write down everything that comes to mind. Take time to really focus on the details and list them specifically.

Examples:

- Thank you for taking out the trash.
- Thank you for driving the kids to school.
- Thank you for working so hard to provide our financial resources.
- Thank you for hugging me before you left today.
- Thank you for snuggling with me in bed this morning.

When you complete your list for now, pick up the telephone, or go find your partner right now, and express your thanks.

Example: "(Partner's name), I want to thank you for some things. Thank you for…, and also, thank you for…" Be specific, make eye contact, and smile. When you are done, give your partner a hug or a kiss, and then get on with other things. You may leave an astonished person in your wake—that's OK! You have begun a new habit, one that I encourage you to make a lifelong behavior on a day-to-day basis. Notice what your partner does right, then say "Thanks!" just as soon as you do. Now, watch your relationship become more positive and loving.

All of these tools infuse a Soul Partnership with more of the essence of real love. For a relationship that is doing well, the result is a deepening and enrichment of your connection. Heart and soul gratitude, acknowledgment, appreciation, and thanks can also alter the dynamics of a relationship in trouble and put it back on course.

Appreciation as Agent for Positive Change

In a distressed relationship, appreciation can reverse the negative tide that often leads to divorce. Marilyn and Chris' story shows how this happens.

Initially, Marilyn's complaint was that Chris never helped her out around the house at the end of the day, and his complaint was that she was too critical and controlling. In an individual session, Chris stated that he did not believe that Marilyn wanted their marriage to work, and that he did not want to live that way and was considering divorce. Marilyn privately stated that she sensed her husband was losing the desire to be married to her. They decided to come in for couples' counseling and set the appointment.

Meanwhile, Marilyn did some soul-searching and decided that her behavior was creating a block with her husband. She set the intention to go "above and beyond" her usual ways of interacting, to be positive and appreciative instead of negative and critical. She overlooked the small things that usually irritated her, and instead of making an issue of them, she thanked him for what he did, refraining from berating him when he did not meet her expectations. She hugged him when she came in the door and she sat on the sofa for a few minutes talking with him before starting the kids' homework and making dinner.

Initially, Chris was resistant to her efforts. He was distant and unresponsive (holding onto resentment about the past) but eventually he softened under her persistent efforts to appreciate him. He began doing more for her and responding to her positively. He was warmer, more attentive, and much more involved in taking care of household chores. When they came in, Marilyn reported how astonished she was at how greatly Chris responded. "He's even doing things for me that I haven't asked him to do!" she beamed.

They were not quite out of the woods with their old patterns, however. In the midst of acknowledging their progress, they began to focus some of their attention on the negatives in the past. I introduced the exercise of acknowledgment and appreciation. Chris' first effort sounded like this:

"Marilyn, I want to thank you for being so nice to me lately. I appreciate you hugging and kissing me when you come home. It's nice to have you smile at me instead of yelling at me and barking orders at me like you did before…"

I stopped him, pointing out that tacking on statements about unpleasant things she had done before had the effect of diminishing the acknowledgment. In fact, an acknowledgment can be completely undone so that it has no positive effect by adding statements about the person's past misdeeds.

Chris' second attempt was much better. Marilyn reported that it felt really good to have him notice and acknowledge her for her efforts. Then, I asked her if there was more she wanted to hear. "Yes, I want to hear something about how he appreciates how hard it is for me to do these things. No one in my family modeled this kind of relationship, and old patterns are hard to break."

Chris came up with this acknowledgment: "Marilyn, I want you to know that I realize how hard it is for you to make these changes. I really appreciate you for doing this for me and for us, even though it takes a lot for you to do it. Thank you, honey."

At this, tears came into Marilyn's eyes, and I asked her how she was feeling. "It feels so good for him to recognize how hard I am trying, and to see that I really do want our marriage to work," she said. I asked Chris how he was feeling.

"It encourages me so much to know that she really wants our marriage to work," he said. At this point, they took each other's hands, tenderly thanked one another, then hugged.

Catch Each Other Doing Something Right

If your relationship has gone off-course and you want to restore the positive energy that has been lost, one way to do that is to look for excuses to acknowledge your partner. In every relationship, even the most distressed, there is something your partner is doing right. Find that one thing, or more, and highlight it with heart and soul acknowledgment and appreciation.

It is impossible to hold two opposing feelings at the exact same moment. Therefore, if you find one thing your partner is doing right, focus on that, then express it in a loving way, in that moment there is a positive feeling about the relationship. For those few minutes in time, there is no room for negative energy. Even the tiniest bit of positive energy can be added to and built upon.

This does not mean that acknowledging your partner is a cure-all. What it can do is contribute some positive energy to the emotional bank account of your relationship. Often, this can awaken long lost feelings of love between partners, giving them new energy to work on resolving their issues together.

Entitlement

One potential pitfall that couples can fall into is withholding gratitude, acknowledgment, appreciation, and thanks because you think that what your partner does is part of the job of the relationship and the family. Why should I thank him for taking out the trash when that is the only chore he does? Why should I feel grateful to her for taking care of the children today when that is her only job?

This kind of thinking creates an attitude of entitlement, rather than a sense of gratitude. Entitlement says, "You owe me," while gratitude says, "Everything that you do is a gift." When "What have you done for me lately?" becomes the theme of the relationship, love cannot thrive.

The problem is that emotional gifts, even ones that appear to be "our job," cannot be accurately tallied. There is no way to "even the score," so there is therefore no way of feeling satisfied or fulfilled. This method of dealing with a relationship creates a strong sense of dissatisfaction that will rapidly wither your love.

We release feelings of entitlement when we focus on the following truths about love:

- Love is not a bargain; it is a gift freely given.
- Each person in a relationship is there by choice.
- Commitment is a gift, not an obligation.
- Our true purpose in being together is to forward the growth of our souls, and this has nothing to do with score-keeping.
- *Everything* that our partner does to contribute to our lives is a gift of time, effort, and energy, and therefore worthy of acknowledgment.

Gratitude as a Healing Agent

When we are out of alignment in a love relationship, we are out of touch with feelings of gratitude. The interesting thing is that what makes us feel satisfied in a love relationship is not so much the sum total of what is good in it, but rather, *the sum total of what we notice*. If we focus on what is good and right between us, we add that up to equal a good relationship. If we focus on what is wrong, we automatically add that up to equal a bad relationship.

This is often how break-ups happen. We sometimes decide, consciously or unconsciously, to leave a relationship. The moment that happens, or sometime prior to the decision, our focus zeroes in on everything that is "not right" about our partner. We keep a running negative score, adding up the infractions one by one and filing them away in a drawer labeled "reasons to leave." Eventually, we attain some invisible "quota" and we leave, justified in that choice because of the evidence we have gathered. Thus, *we often create our own endings to love by the nature of our focus.*

It is possible to heal a relationship by changing focus and zeroing in on gratitude. It is possible to do this by doing everything in our power to heal the rift between us. This is real love, active in thought, intention, word, and deed.

If you are struggling to find something to feel grateful for in your relationship, spend some time in private meditation reflecting on these questions:

- Is it possible that I am *out of touch* with the gift of my partner's presence in my life because of the accumulation of old grievances?
- What am I holding against my partner? (Resentments, grudges)
- What purpose is it serving to hold onto that resentment?
- What new possibilities might there be in our relationship if I release those resentments?
- What new possibilities might there be in our relationship if I focus on what is good in my partner and our connection?
- What new possibilities might there be if I express my gratitude and appreciation to my partner?

If there is even one tiny bit of doubt about your intention to leave, it is worthwhile to stop, take inventory of thoughts, feelings, attitudes, and behaviors, and create a new intention. When we create the intention to heal, and then follow that up with loving behavior, the very least that we will achieve is closure.

With emotional completion, the possibility opens up for a return to love as romantic Soul Partners. Hearts *can* change. Love is not necessarily lost forever just because we have gone off-course. Our commitment is to give it everything we have before we sign off.

Authentic Self-Expression

In order for these tools to be effective, they must be freely and authentically given. Our expressions of gratitude and acknowledgement cannot be false or made up.

On the other hand, it is possible to stretch them. If I acknowledge my partner for something he has done once, but not lately, that is a stretch, not a falsehood. This reminds my partner of something he did successfully in the past, and now, being more conscious of it, he is more likely to do it again. My acknowledgment actually opens the possibility for more loving behavior from him.

This dynamic is possible because our connection and my appreciation matter to him. It works because my acknowledgment is genuine, not fake, motivated by love, not the desire to manipulate. If it were the latter, he would sense it on some level, and that distortion would undermine our love.

Have you ever received an acknowledgment from someone that felt phony or insincere? If so, then you know it is actually better to receive nothing than to be given a false gift. Therefore, before you use these tools in your relationship, check out your intentions. The following will guide your self-expression to be authentic and powerful in your connection:

- The intention to enrich the relationship
- The intention to stay in the relationship until everything possible has been done to reconnect
- Having honesty and integrity in all that I do
- Having genuine love and care for my partner, not just wanting my needs met by that person

Of all the tools explored in this book, by far the most powerful are the ones contained in this chapter. If you are able to do no more than follow these steps, your relationship is guaranteed to improve and be enriched.

Asking for Acknowledgment

There are times when it is not only appropriate but empowering to ask for acknowledgment. Perhaps we do something special or accomplish something important, and our partner, for whatever reason, does not notice. In that case, bring it to his attention. Do it in a positive way. Often, we are so focused on our own world that we miss things. We can support one another in being successful Soul Partners by saying, in essence, "I would so enjoy an acknowledgment from you for this."

Hungry for Acknowledgment

Sometimes, we are starved for acknowledgments due to a long history of not having it in our relationship. We may even recognize that our partner is so depleted (emotionally, physically, and/or spiritually) that it is unlikely she can give it. If that is the case, any request comes from neediness, setting us up for more disappointment.

Part of the healing process may be in learning to appreciate yourself. When we acknowledge our own greatness, we fill the inner well and do not feel quite so starved. Then we have more patience to bring to the process of learning how to give and receive it in the relationship.

EXERCISE: APPRECIATING MYSELF

This exercise repeats the gratitude exercise at the beginning of the chapter, only the person you are focusing on is you. Just repeat those same steps, focusing on all of the qualities, inner and outer, including things that you do, that make you special and that highlight your contribution to the people in your life.

When your list is complete, read it out loud, putting the words "I appreciate myself for…" in front of each one. Do this slowly, letting the words feed back to you and fill the well inside.

It can be very healing, also, to ask a close friend to write words of acknowledgment to you. One man I knew asked a close friend to make an audiotape of acknowledgments of him, which was enormously healing.

More Loving Behavior

This chapter is focused almost exclusively on the behavior of love through communication. However, there are many nonverbal ways to express gratitude, appreciation, and acknowledgment. The nonverbal ways we express love are tremendously powerful when they are aligned with our true intentions and are given freely from the heart (no expectations). If you want to water the garden of your love, make it a daily and weekly habit to look for ways to acknowledge your partner with acts of love. Sometimes, the simplest things are the most powerful, such as gifts of flowers, a card or note, going out on a special date, and loving touch such as a shoulder massage or foot rub.

Giving Great Love Gifts

Sometimes we give love gifts that are not received as such. Someone once said to me, "It isn't a gift unless someone wants it." What feels like love to one person does little for another, and vice versa. Therefore, part of our job in giving gifts to our partner is to make sure the gift is wanted. We miss the mark when we give gifts that reflect our own preferences and not the unique wants and needs of our partner.

In a heart and soul relationship, the focus is heavily on emotional gifts, but material gifts can be *symbolic* of our feelings of love and connection. When we notice what our partner loves and enjoys, and we go out of our way to look for the perfect thing that lights up the eyes of our beloved, we empower our love.

Take notice of your partner's likes and dislikes, the things that delight the soul of the one you love. When you are out shopping together, ask questions when you notice your partner looking at something. Make mental notes, spend time looking, and make it special when you give it.

Some people, and this is often true of men, do not enjoy material gifts nearly as much as they enjoy experiences. For this person, creating a special romantic experience is far more important than shopping for a new sweater or necktie.

For a deeper understanding of emotional love gifts that open your hearts, do the following exercise.

EXERCISE: UNDERSTANDING EMOTIONAL LOVE GIFTS

Over dinner, with lots of eye contact, take turns sharing the following statement, filling in the blank each time you repeat it:

"I love it when you..." (fill in with some action your lover does that touches your heart and makes you feel loved)

HINT: Try reaching back into your memory for something your lover did long ago, and state it in the present tense as well. In this way, you open the possibility for a return of loving behavior that may have been forgotten. (Make sure that you do not contaminate it by expressing regret that it's been so long since it last happened.)

For each one that your lover shares with you, make mental notes to *repeat that more often.* This is your "emotional gift list," the exact instructions for how to send loving energy to your partner. Each and every time we focus on giving our partner these gifts of acknowledgment, appreciation, and tokens of affection, we make huge deposits to the emotional bank account of our love. We fulfill a major purpose in being Soul Partners—to give fully of our hearts to the person we most cherish.

Chapter Eleven
Mission and Purpose

Having a sense of mission and purpose in life energizes all that we do. When our accomplishments reflect our values, we experience the joy of success as well as a deep sense of fulfillment. In our love relationships, a sense of accomplishment is also vital, and we create that by partnering to create a mutually fulfilling vision of how we want our lives to be.

Relationships are mutually satisfying to the degree that our deepest emotional needs are met. Though we commit ourselves to meeting many of our own needs, we also care for one another through honoring requests for emotional and other kinds of support. That is the "business of love"—dealing with all the daily matters that require collaboration and coordination. To "take care of business" and to best care for one another, we must learn how to ask for what we want and need in a constructive way.

Making Requests

In a nutshell, when we want something, we must *ask!* Our partner does not have the ability to read our mind. It is our job to communicate our wants and needs. In fact, we do a great disservice to the relationship by not doing so.

In a true love relationship, we want to give our partner what makes her happy, providing all the love and other gifts we possibly can. Knowing that your partner loves you and therefore *wants* to succeed with you, do you not want to help him in that endeavor?

We support our partner in being successful in the relationship when we:

Share our wants and needs without being demanding or nagging
Provide specifics about what we want without nitpicking
Express gratitude for what we have and refrain from criticism
Regularly acknowledge our partner and express appreciation and thanks
Express a spirit of cooperation and choice without using controlling behaviors

Requests are powerful when they are simply that and nothing more. A true request says: "Will you do this? It's OK if you can't or don't want to, but I would really appreciate your assistance."

With a demand, we feel that it is not OK for the other person to say "no." It is a demand when it comes from the feeling of need, and if there are consequences to the other person saying "no," such as retribution or emotional withdrawal.

Demands vs. Requests

The challenge in relationships is that we sometimes do not make these distinctions. Requests are expressed with the same importance as demands, and demands are disguised as requests.

Requests become demands when we do not feel partnership in the relationship. When it feels like I must beg for my partner's assistance or loving behavior, I may resort to making demands to get my needs met.

Through thousands of socializing experiences, from early family life to television and movies, we form a "template" or internal picture of how relationships are supposed to be. Initially, we feel that our beloved fits this picture perfectly. Later, when the illusion fades and reality sets in, we realize that our lover does not match the portrait of "real love" that we constructed earlier, a portrait to which we are strongly attached. Trouble is on the way.

At this stage of the relationship, we begin making demands of one another. Of course, the other person can never live up to this internal portrait, and that sets off resistance of one form or another.

In order for love to flow, we must take care of the business of life and love in a way that is satisfying to both partners. To do that, we must sort out our *real needs* from the needs that are flowing from early life experience and illusion. This requires some soul-searching. At the back of the book, there is a real needs inventory. Begin with that, then come back to this section.

Partnering vs. Power Struggle

In almost every relationship, there is the Asker and the Actor. One person gets his needs met by making requests and *asking* for emotional favors (the "Asker"). The other person tends to get her needs met through *action*: taking it or withholding it (the "Actor").

When the Actor wants greater sexual contact, he makes advances. When he wants more intimacy, he puts his arms around her and holds her. When the Actor wants to go out and have fun, he arranges plans for entertainment for them both.

When the Asker wants more intimacy, she asks him why he does not share his feelings more. When she wants more sexual contact, she asks him if he still finds her attractive. When she wants to be taken out more, she asks him to arrange their entertainment.

When the Actor is upset, she withdraws and diverts her attention to other things. When the Asker is upset, he says, "Can we talk?"

When the Actor feels the need for support in getting things done, she takes on all the tasks, works furiously, and hopes her partner will pitch in and match her level of giving. When the Asker wants help, he makes a hundred requests and gives his partner a list of to-do's.

The Asker often falls into the pattern of constantly making requests, many of them demands in disguise, and feeling frustrated that it is never enough. The Asker often expresses that, "I have to manage everything! If I didn't make these requests, nothing would ever happen."

The Actor often falls into the pattern of trying to please, feeling that it makes no difference and is never enough, and then becoming resistant and withdrawing. The Actor often expresses that, "I don't feel trusted! My partner thinks I am incompetent and incapable of doing anything right, just because I do it a different way or on a different timetable."

Couples often change roles—the Asker may be the Actor in another circumstance, and vice versa. Switching roles often does not get better results, however. In either case, we are often trying too hard to get our needs met, rather than allowing the giving and receiving to flow.

What is missing in all of these scenarios is partnership. The Asker and the Actor are trying to handle the flow of the business of love and life on a moment-to-moment (urgent) basis, setting them up for power struggle and lack of satisfaction. This is the equivalent of attempting to run a business totally from a task-oriented point of view, wherein everything is urgent, with no business plan, no strategic planning, and no mission statement. When everything is an emergency, everyone is stressed, and we are highly vulnerable to breakdowns.

A relationship is not a business, yet there are aspects of Soul Partnering that require some of the same perspective that successful executives take. If you want out of the power struggle, the way out is to take a couple of steps back, look at the whole picture of the relationship and the flow of life's demands, and make joint, collaborative, wise choices about who is responsible for what. *That* is the foundation of partnership.

Creating Partnership

The key element of Soul Partnership is partnership. In a nutshell, that is defined as *a collaborative relationship between equals that exists for a specific, well-defined purpose and to accomplish specific intentions and goals.* In a business context, this makes perfect sense and is easy to understand. In a love relationship, it is more difficult to see and to create.

The dynamic of *equal partnership* is a relatively new concept for love relationships. In the past, because men and women were not true equals, their "partnership" was defined by certain assumptions of purpose and goals. For instance, it was assumed that getting married and having a family was the goal and the primary purpose of getting together. The idea of our relationship as a vehicle for personal and spiritual growth did not enter the equation.

Now, the primary purpose that we seek to fulfill in a love relationship is connection with a Soul Partner for growth, life enhancement, and fulfillment. Getting married and having a family together is secondary to this primary purpose. Paradoxically, we sometimes attempt to fulfill this new purpose while at the same time trying to create a relationship from the old paradigms. This generally results in confusion, power struggle, and lack of fulfillment.

What we are seeking is to have our purpose together fully defined and then aligned with our intentions and goals on a day to day basis. Secondarily, we can much more easily and readily meet our needs for taking care of business, family harmony, and nurturing our children effectively when our partnership works.

Relationship Mission and Purpose

The first step in creating conscious Soul Partnership is to spend some time discussing your history together and putting the past behind you. In previous chapters, we covered all of the steps to do that, including naming the issues, listening empty and mirroring, apology and forgiveness, and gratitude and appreciation.

With emotional resolution about old grievances, the way is opened up for being truly creative and collaborative in our lives together. The next step in creating Soul Partnership is to design your own personal *mission and purpose statement.* This is a very powerful process but is effective only to the degree that we do it with little or no emotional baggage. Therefore, if you are still struggling with anger and resentment in your relationship, read this part but do not attempt it until you get some guidance to resolve past issues.

If you are uncertain about your commitment in the relationship, it may be too soon for this exercise. In chapter 12 we will examine Soul Partner commitment to assist you in being clear about that aspect of your connection. Meanwhile, your mission at this time may be centered on *discovery* about what form of relationship will be best for you.

EXERCISE: CREATING YOUR RELATIONSHIP MISSION STATEMENT

Carve out some time together with no distractions. (You will need several hours to go through these next few exercises.) Have the following items on hand:

- Several legal pads or spiral notebooks
- Several water-based colored markers; several writing pens
- One large (approx. 24" x 30") flip chart with sticky strip across the top

Begin by sitting facing each other, holding hands, and declaring your intentions for what you are about to do. For example:

"My intention, John, is to focus with you on our relationship so that we can bring out our most loving side. I intend to work with you to create a powerful and loving context for our relationship to guide us now and always."

"My intention, Susan, is to honor you and our relationship in every way possible. I intend to work with you to focus on our mission and purpose together so that we can be totally clear about that, for our good as individuals and for our relationship."

Step One: Values. On your legal pads (do this part separately), write down words and phrases that express the *core values* that are most important to you in your relationship. Some examples are: love, empowerment, adventure, romance, dedication to giving, prosperity, happiness, wellness, vitality, confidence, self-expression, and so on.

When you have each gone as far as you can with your lists separately, write all of them on the flip chart in color. Now, ask yourselves: What else? What other values are important to us in our relationship? Write on the chart any additional words and phrases until you can think of no more for now.

Do not be concerned if one of you contributes more phrases and words than the other does. It is not unusual for one person in the relationship to be more verbal than the other is and to find it easier to come up with these relationship values. Now, pull off this page of your flip-chart pad and stick it on a wall nearby for reference.

Step Two: Relationship Purpose. Getting clear about your relationship purpose is essential to conscious Soul Partnership. To do this, you may want to begin by acknowledging, for example:

- That our souls' journeys have brought us together for a higher purpose that is greater than meeting our emotional needs or creating a family together
- That in fulfilling that purpose we are called to bring forth something far greater than momentary satisfaction
- That with real love in our hearts and intentions to be the best, most loving partners possible, we are empowered to create an extraordinary relationship

With these acknowledgments, focus on how your relationship serves a purpose that is in your highest and greatest good and in the greatest good of those whose lives you touch. Rising above any pettiness that you have had in the past, looking at the larger picture of your lives, you are ready to declare your relationship purpose from this perspective.

In a nutshell, a purpose statement declares *why* we are together (other than to get our emotional needs met). By stepping back and considering the larger purpose of why we were attracted to one another and why we chose one another, we create a powerful context for our connection. This context acts as a reference point for everything we do and everything we say in our relationship.

Now, looking over the values that you are dedicated to in your relationship and taking them into account, in your own words, write a brief statement of purpose (why we are together). Do this separately on your own legal pad first. Some examples:

"Our purpose in being together is to support one another in the growth of our individual Spirits through the practice of loving behavior that expresses our most cherished values."

"Our purpose in being together is to have our relationship be a vehicle for nurturing our individual Souls to be the best that we can be, and a source of inspiration to those whose lives we touch."

Once you each have a purpose statement, read them aloud to each other, and then combine them to form one statement of purpose, using your flip-chart to brainstorm and rearrange words. Again, do not be concerned if the more verbal person finds this simple to do while the other may not. What is important is that you collaborate to create a joint purpose statement. Honor each person's words and include them all if possible. It is not unusual for one person to spontaneously express something that sounds right for both your hearts. How you get to your Purpose Statement is not nearly as important as the fact that you do.

Congratulations! You have already accomplished something extraordinary by declaring your purpose in being together. Though we may feel that we are aligned on our purpose, there is nevertheless something very powerful about writing it down and saying it out loud together.

Step Three: Relationship Intentions. In order to bring our purpose to life, we must set higher-order intentions that focus on the quality of our relationship. These intentions are the rudder of the "love ship" on which we sail, guiding us and keeping us on course.

Separately, on your legal pads, write your intentions for creating the best possible relationship. Examples are:

"My intention is to express gratitude and appreciation to my partner on a daily basis so that she feels cherished in our relationship."

"My intention is to actively seek to know my partner's emotional needs in our relationship and fulfill them whenever possible."

"My intention is to take excellent care of myself emotionally, physically, and spiritually, so that I have more to bring to my relationship with my partner."

When you have written all the intentions for your relationship that you can think of, stop and ask yourself, what else? Keep going until you can think of no more.

Now, one at a time, read your relationship intentions to one another. Write all of them on a clean page on the flip chart. In this way, you create a joint relationship intentions list for which you are both responsible.

Step Four: Mission. A mission statement basically states the things that you wish to accomplish together, such as raising your children to be happy, productive human beings, or making a difference in the world in some specific way. It also encompasses your commitment to one another and to the growth of your love together.

A purpose statement says *why* you are together, while a mission statement says *what you are dedicated to accomplishing* together. Looking at your intentions and, drawing from those and your value statements, create separate lists (on your legal pads) of what you want to accomplish in your relationship together. Focus this on spiritual, family, and relationship values, not the accumulation of wealth or material things (this part will be addressed later). Examples:

• To grow in soul's purpose through loving connection that teaches us to be better persons
• To raise children who are loving, responsible, productive, and self-actualized human beings that make a difference in the world in their own unique way
• To support one another in the fulfillment of our individual missions in this life

When you have written all of the desired accomplishments you can think of, read them aloud to one another. Again, write on a clean page of the flip chart those that you both desire.

Now, you are ready to bring all of this together to write your relationship mission statement. Looking over your purpose statement, your values and intentions lists, and your desired accomplishment list, put together sentences that express an empowering relationship mission. Take your time with this—it can be challenging. Do not be concerned if you cannot immediately get it just right—you can always revise and edit it later. What is important is getting something put together that has meaning for you both.

Some examples are:

"Our mission is to create a loving, inspiring relationship for the purpose of our souls' growth and for the purpose of raising our children to be happy, healthy, self-expressed human beings. We are dedicated to a focus on loving behavior that inspires others to love more deeply."

"Our mission is to create and maintain a loving, alive Soul Partnership that supports us in all of our endeavors in the world. Ultimately, our mission is to be the best that we can be as individuals and as Soul Partners."

When you have your completed relationship mission statement, type or write it in attractive letters, using colors if you want, and combine it with your relationship purpose statement on one page that you can mat, frame, and hang. Basically, it looks something like this:

Our Relationship Purpose
Our purpose in being together is to support one another in the growth of our individual spirits through the practice of loving behavior that expresses our most cherished values.

Our Relationship Mission
Our mission is to connect in Spirit so that our souls grow to the highest level possible in this life. We are dedicated to full and loving self-expression such that our relationship is empowering to us in all of our life's ambitions and to others whose lives we touch. Our commitment is to enrich and deepen our love through our consciousness of the behavior of love on a daily basis.

On a separate page, type or write your relationship intentions so that you can frame and display that as well. That might look like this:

Our Relationship Intentions

Our commitment is to support our mission and purpose together by fulfilling the following intentions:

To listen empty to one another on a regular basis so that we continually deepen our understanding of one another and how we can support each other in being the best that we can be.

To express gratitude and appreciation to one another on a daily basis so that we feel cherished in our relationship.

To actively seek to know one another's emotional needs in our relationship and fulfill them whenever possible.

To be creative in the ways that we express love to one another so that our relationship is kept fresh and alive.

To make it safe for one another to express ourselves.

To express ourselves to one another in ways that are empowering, straightforward, and honest.

To be available to one another when one of us is down or not feeling well, to really be there for one another.

To bring fun and adventure into our relationship and our lives together.

To actively look for ways to keep our romance alive and growing.

Congratulations! You have now accomplished something quite extraordinary. By collaborating to create your relationship mission and purpose statements, you have created the foundation of true partnership.

You have now elevated your relationship to the level of *conscious, intentional, creative Soul Partnership*. The power of this cannot be underestimated!

Each time you look on the wall in your home and see your mission and purpose statements, your souls register and reinforce them once more. Each time you pass by your relationship intentions, even though you do not stop to read them, your eyes pass the information along to the deepest parts of you, and they are reinforced.

When we collaborate to create these stated intentions together, we anchor them in our relationship and pave the way for a powerful journey of growth and discovery.

Relationship Life Goals

With a strong mission and purpose statement, and powerful relationship intentions, we have a solid foundation from which to construct life intentions and goals together.

It is not unusual for us to get caught up in our daily routines at the expense of long-term goals and dreams. As human beings with dreams and visions for our lives, we need long-range planning in order to make them happen. We also need short-term planning to handle the day-to-day tasks of our lives.

As Soul Partners, we need to bring together our individual dreams and form joint intentions and goals. One of the most frequent causes of conflict in relationships is lack of alignment on goals. One person is focused on one dream or goal and the other person is focused in an entirely different place.

On the other hand, when we are aligned on our visions and goals, our partnership is energized for the jobs we must perform, both within the home and without. This leads to feelings of accomplishment that we share, and our love is enhanced through those feelings.

I recommend that you spend time together focusing on your life intentions and goals at least once per year. Most people like to do it at the beginning of the year. Also, it is effective to periodically review your goals throughout the year to make sure you are on track. The following exercises will help you in this endeavor.

EXERCISE: SETTING POWERFUL LIFE INTENTIONS AND GOALS

Before you begin writing down your intentions and goals, review the basics of intentions and goals in chapter 3. Remember that:

1) Intentions are the rudder of the ship; goals are the destination.
2) Intentions must be aligned consciously and unconsciously.

3) Intentions must be in your highest and greatest good.

4) Goals are specific and measurable.

In your notebooks, separately, write your intentions for accomplishment for the remainder of this year. Focus on the areas of your life, such as relationship, career, family, health, finances, etc.

For each of these areas, look to see if you are currently experiencing problems or issues that are unresolved or that are in the process of being resolved. For each area, ask yourself: How do I want to grow? What do I want to accomplish? Then, set intentions based on your answers. The following example is not a complete list but provides a sense of how to create one.

My Intentions are:

1) To live an abundant and wealthy life and lifestyle

2) To fill my life with adventure and fun on a regular basis

3) To be spiritually connected on a daily basis

My Goals that support these Intentions are:

1) To increase my income by 25 percent this year through focusing on networking

2) To travel to Europe for an extended vacation, and to take several long weekend trips

3) To practice meditation, prayer, and spiritual reading every day

When you have put together your separate life intentions and goals, read them to each other and discuss them. Remember to listen empty and strive to understand your partner's desires and needs. Through dialogue and the intention to honor one another's deepest desires, put together your joint relationship intentions and goals statement for this year.

Now, looking over your intentions and goals, what *actions* do you need to commit yourself to taking? Talk about actions that you wish to take together, and ones that you need to take separately. Ask one another for support for being your best so that you can fulfill your intentions and goals. For example:

Intention: Live a healthy and active life and lifestyle.

Goal: Eat healthily and exercise on a daily basis.

Actions: Join a health club and work out at least three times per week. Go running four to five times per week. Buy a cookbook with healthy recipes. Go shopping on the weekend for healthy food and prepare things in advance.

Requests for support: Go walking together every morning. Cook together in the evenings instead of getting fast food. Buy healthy and nutritious snacks for the family, giving up unhealthy ones. Budget for health club membership dues, running shoes, and other sports attire. Spend less time watching television

Do this process for each of your intentions and goals. In this way, you create a plan for your lives together.

Remember that life happens while we are busy setting goals. Therefore, flexibility is a must! Be willing to alter your plans as life unfolds, always aiming for that which is in your greatest and highest good, as well as the best for your relationship and family. Regular reviews, monthly or quarterly, help you maintain alignment with the path of your life. Thus, at the end of the year, there is the experience of real accomplishment, both individually and as Soul Partners.

Creating Solutions for Issues

Being human beings, and not being perfect, we are bound to have personal and relational issues that challenge us and that strain our connection. In previous chapters, we covered the steps for getting complete with what has happened in the past in our relationship and with regard to certain repetitive issues. With those steps completed, we are prepared to put our creative energies together to find solutions to the issues that plague us.

The brainstorming exercise is for those times in our relationship that we need creative answers to our problems and issues, especially when we feel "stuck." In order to be truly effective and to prepare for this exercise, resolve to:

- Give up the need to be "right"
- Expect the unexpected—often the best solutions are not what our logical minds might have thought
- Focus on the best interest of the relationship and of your partner
- Be open-hearted
- Have fun—creative solution finding often brings out our more whimsical side

EXERCISE: BRAINSTORMING SOLUTIONS

The object of this exercise is to free our creative energy. We do that by removing the usual boundaries that limit our thinking (e.g., "shoulds," "should-nots," other's rules, our own rules, etc.).

Using a blank page in your flip chart, begin by stating the issue in an empowering way (see chapter 5, "Naming The Issues"). Then, give your-self permission to offer any and all solutions that come to mind for the issue. Do not edit these ideas as they emerge. Every idea is valid, and every solution is acceptable. Write them all on the flip chart page, no matter how seemingly absurd.

If you are coming up with all of the ideas and your partner is sitting with a blank look, stop for a moment and ask your partner to contribute. Sometimes, stepping back for a few minutes creates enough space for the other person's thoughts to flow. Ask your partner, "What are your thoughts on this?" Write all ideas from both persons on the flip chart, even the ones you know you will not use. By not editing at this point, you give yourself permission to be highly creative, thus encouraging the best ideas to come forward. Keep going until you cannot think of another idea. For example:

Issue: "We never have time alone together. The kids take all of our time and energy from the minute we get home at night until we go to work the next morning. We're exhausted!"

Brainstorming solutions:
- Lock ourselves in our bedroom in the evening and let the kids watch a movie or television while we have alone time.
- Send the kids to friends' homes on Friday nights.
- Wait until the kids go to bed to have quiet time together.
- Put the kids in bed earlier so we can have time together.
- Get up extra early in the mornings, before the kids, and share a cup of coffee in our room while we talk or snuggle.
- Take a weekend vacation without the kids once per quarter.
- Hire a housekeeper to come in once per week to take some of the burden off of us so that we have more energy.
- Have someone else pick up the kids from school and keep them in the evening while we meet for drinks and dinner alone together, once per week.

Once you have listed all the ideas you can think of, ask yourselves, "What else?" Often, more ideas will come up simply by asking this question. Keep going, and ask the question again, until you draw a complete blank.

Now, look over your list of ideas. There are some that will stand out as obviously not realistic. Go ahead, check those off, and congratulate yourselves for being so creative!

From the remainder of your ideas, choose the ones that look plausible and discuss them, remembering to listen empty and to mirror one another's thoughts and feelings. Through this dialogue, you should be able to choose a combination of ideas you are willing to implement.

Stretching

When we are creating new solutions to old problems, it is common to feel the sense of stretching outside of old boundaries. This may be somewhat uncomfortable, yet growth happens when we stretch outside our "comfort zones."

Often, couples go down a blind alley in their relationship by adhering to old plans, rules, and ways of doing things because they are familiar and therefore comfortable. "This is the way we have always done it," they say, even though the evidence is clear that change is needed.

If you are struggling with making a commitment to new behavior that takes you outside of your comfort zones, stop and review your relationship mission and purpose statements. Ask yourselves, "What might be the actions for us to take in order to bring forth our mission and purpose?" By refocusing on our higher purposes, we often find the energy to take actions that are momentarily uncomfortable but rewarding in the long run.

Assigning Tasks

What about the day-to-day stuff that requires collaboration? How do you decide who does the dishes, who does the laundry, and who mows the lawn? Remember that in today's relationships, everything is up for grabs. There is no room for assumptions—not if we want a truly loving relationship. There is no room for generalities—we must be specific. The only way to get these things done in harmony is by discussing them openly and honestly and creating joint, collaborative decisions.

E X E R C I S E :   C L A I M I N G   T A S K S

Step one in this exercise is to bring to conscious awareness the multitudes of tasks that must be done in order to make our homelife work. On a blank flip chart page, make headings across the top like this: daily, weekly, monthly, and periodically. Under each heading, begin listing all of the tasks that fall under that category. Keep going until you can think of no more. Keep asking, "What else?" until you get a mental blank. This part of the exercise looks something like this (not a complete list):

DAILY	WEEKLY	MONTHLY	PERIODICALLY
Wash dishes	Do laundry	Balance checkbook	Change oil in cars
Prepare breakfast and dinner	Go grocery shopping	Clip new recipes	Research healthy eating
Make the bed	Launder bedding	Pay bills	Dry-clean comforters
Put away clothes	Take in dry-cleaning; pick up	Recycle plastics and paper	Household repairs

When you have listed everything you can think of, one at a time, choose a task that you wish to be responsible for. One person chooses a task, then the other, and so on, until all are spoken for.

In this way, each person claims "ownership" of his or her tasks, making it far more likely that there will be commitment and follow-through. This exercise alone can remove much of the daily stress.

When you have claimed all of the tasks, make a new chart, with each person's tasks under his name. (You can do this exercise with children as well. It creates much greater family harmony!)

What about the tasks no one wants to be responsible for? Sometimes, couples disagree on household cleanliness chores. He says that the floors must be swept and vacuumed once per week, while she says every other day. Neither of them wants to do it the way the other wants it.

Sometimes there is an easy solution that does not involve change on the part of one person or the other. For example, one simple thing has saved many a relationship with the dilemma of disagreement over housekeeping chores: hire a house cleaner! Budget for it, view it as a "relationship saver," and just do it. There is absolutely nothing served by arguing over the cleaning chores. You are committed to much bigger things than that.

Sometimes the disagreement reflects a huge difference in personal standards. One person is a neatnik and the other is, well, not. First, recognize your differences without making each other wrong for your preferences and standards. Second, find a way to accept one another as you are. It is unlikely that the person who does not mind the mess is going to magically transform into someone who goes around cleaning all the time.

To get out of power struggle, take a step back and focus on your commitment to having a relationship that is satisfying to both partners. Collaborate to find solutions that are a win for both, even if it means hiring out certain chores.

Third, take this as an opportunity to learn from one another. The super neat person often needs to learn to be more relaxed and to enjoy the moment. The sloppy person often needs to learn more self-discipline. Realize that we are attracted to one another for these differences as they allow us to help each other grow.

Going through this exercise helps us create boundaries in our relationship. Clearly, we must be in alignment about who does what in order for our hearts to be free to focus on love and connection. By being conscious of all of the tasks around our home, we have greater appreciation for one another's hard work. By claiming our tasks and therefore taking on the responsibility for doing them, we leave no room for finger-pointing, controlling behavior, and resentment over things undone. We create true partnership for the "business" of life and love.

Changing Roles and Tasks

Remember that nothing stays the same and everything evolves. When you have a significant change in your life (having a child, changing jobs, going back to school, traveling for work, etc.) that affects the flow of life and work, sit down and do this exercise again. Leave nothing to the foggy realm of assumptions. Be crystal clear that now this change is occurring, here is how we will handle our lives together, as well as the flow of tasks.

The Power of Our Word

Being responsible and accountable in a love relationship means that we do as we say we will do, keeping our word with one another. It means that we understand the *power of our word* and how it affects all of our interactions.

When we set forth intentions and goals, and collaborate to map out the flow of our lives, we do so through the power of our word. We set into motion certain expectations and responsibilities in the relationship. This is not to be taken lightly.

If we fail to fulfill our promises, not because we could not but because we *neglected to do so,* we undermine our partner's trust, which is a direct affront to our connection. Therefore, we must consider very carefully the consequences before we make promises.

As with all things in life, a balance is required. To honor our relationship and to participate fully in the commitment to be a loving partner requires agreements and promises. To keep our word so that we build and maintain trust requires careful consideration that we can actually fulfill our promise. As is true of so many things about Soul Partnership, in this regard also we must balance our individual needs with the needs of the relationship.

Once we have made agreements and promises, our job is to fulfill them. When we see that we cannot, we must go back to the table, discuss it, brainstorm solutions, and make new agreements that empower our connection.

What if you find yourself being "unconscious" about your promises and therefore failing to fulfill them? Sometimes, this happens because we have overextended ourselves or are emotionally or physically depleted in some way. Depression, illness, stress, and fatigue can affect our ability to keep track of all of our commitments and fulfill them.

When we notice that we are not fulfilling our obligations in the relationship, that is a "caution flag" telling us it is time to go back to the drawing board (or flip chart) and redesign our lives. It takes two partners to do this, in the same way that it took two to create it in the first place. Use the exercises in this chapter as well as the listening empty and mirroring exercises.

When we notice that we are not fulfilling our relationship promises, it may be tempting to ignore it, hoping our partner does not notice. A more powerful way to handle this situation is to notice our behavior, stop and do some soul-searching, and bring it up to our partner.

Ask yourself, "Why did I not fulfill my promises?" Do not fall into the trap of searching for ways to blame your partner (e.g., "Well, she isn't doing her part!"). What your partner does or does not do is a separate issue. If you want to grow, keep the focus on you and your own choices and behavior. Then, speak about it responsibly to your partner.

Holding Our Partner Accountable

Sometimes, we find that we are holding up our end of the agreements but our partner is not. It may be tempting to "stick our head in the sand" and try to ignore that, or to get all steamed up and launch an attack. Neither of these works in a Soul Partnership.

Instead, carve out some time to gently confront your partner. Before you do, however, consider this distinction: *to hold someone accountable is not the same as attempting to control the person.* Instead, it is a conversation about the truth of a situation that creates the *possibility* for someone to see things differently and therefore, to alter behavior. How do we do that?

First, in a non-blaming way, introduce the issue or incident in which your partner did not keep his word. Second, state loving intentions for resolution and ask him for his partnership in solving the issue. In simple terms, describe the incident and then ask for his point of view about what happened. Do not adhere to every little detail of your own point of view. Aim for agreement on the basics of what happened.

Next, state in simple terms that you are concerned and are wondering what may be standing in the way of his honoring his agreements with you. As he talks about this, look for a picture of someone who is either taking on too much responsibility to honor all of it, or someone who is not committed to the relationship. Normally, you will find that it is the former, but regardless of which, you now have the real issue on the table. (Keep reading for what to do if the issue is lack of commitment.) Once you have the real issue before you, ask your partner, "What would you like to do about this so that we don't go through this again in the future?" This gives your partner the responsibility of creating his own solutions rather than doing that for him.

Often, a person's first response to this question is, "I don't know." Keep silent if that happens! By avoiding the temptation to jump in and provide solutions, you give your partner the opportunity to dig deeper. When we tell our partner what to do, we take away his "ownership" of the solutions, making it unlikely that he will follow through.

If your partner wants to participate with you in finding solutions, that is great. Collaboration works. Telling someone what to do does not.

What if your partner makes a new promise but you "sense" that it is not sincere or that it is a rehashing of previous broken promises? Gently let your partner know that you have heard this before and that you are wondering what will make it different this time.

Let your partner struggle with this. Only he can come to terms with the fact that he has undermined his own credibility through his past behavior; only he can recreate that trust by doing something different, and that comes from seeing things in a new way. When you hear your partner express a new insight, then you can begin to trust that there will be change.

What if your partner says, in essence, that he does not see the problem or the need for change? When one person says, in essence, "I am going to do what I want to do, regardless of how it affects you, and you can either like it or leave it," there is no possibility of Soul Partnership. The person may be less attached, which creates a power imbalance. The person may be unwilling to have a collaborative, creative relationship, preferring instead to operate from a different paradigm. Whatever the reason, the bottom line is the same: *no partnership*. Now that you know where you stand, you have a choice to make about that. In chapter 12, we will look at the choice of commitment and what it means in Soul Partnership.

Sometimes, a person expresses a "no partnership" statement, not realizing the consequences. Tell your partner gently but firmly where that leaves you, that there is no way to have a mutually satisfying relationship in that way.

This issue may be squarely in the other person's blind spot, so the feedback that it does not work for you may be a wake-up call. However, keep in mind that if someone does not fundamentally understand the concept of equal partnership, you may be taking on a long project in trying to teach him or her about it.

If a confrontation such as this leads to the issue of commitment, and your partner flatly states that he is not committed, there is no point in going further with the original issue. You must deal with the larger issue of commitment first. Only when both partners are firmly anchored in the relationship can you effectively hold each other to your promises and agreements.

In summary, to hold someone accountable includes:

- Introducing the issue, getting the facts on the table without blaming
- Inviting honest, open discussion
- Listening to the other point of view, asking open-ended questions, listening empty, mirroring, getting clarification.

- Expressing your own point of view, dialoging, creating full under-standing
- Asking partner to create or collaborate on a solution

If your partner does not offer a solution or is not willing to collaborate:

- Be willing to address fundamental relationship issues, such as lack of commitment or huge value differences
- Stay calm, engage in dialogue, and have the intention for a new possibility to open up through deeper understanding of the issue

Negative Behavior Patterns

Sometimes, broken promises and the behavior that sabotages our connection are signs of a deeper issue, part of an overall pattern. In this case, simply going through the confrontation process may not be enough. This calls for heart and soul communication on a deeper level.

When our partner exhibits repetitive behavior that sabotages our connection, we must take action. Not to do so sends the message it does not matter what we do that affects one another. Therefore, our relationship does not matter. To avoid confrontation is placing momentary comfort (because confrontation is not easy) ahead of long-term satisfaction and fulfillment for both partners.

Our primary intention for spiritual and personal growth demands that we take action to influence the course of our relationship by noticing patterns of negative behavior and then bringing them up to our partner in an empowering way. Remember that we all have "blind spots," and we therefore need one another to call attention to those aspects of ourselves that need healing and growth. We do a great service to our partner and to our relationship when we do so.

The basic steps for addressing negative behavior patterns are:

1) Carve out time for discussion with no interruptions.
2) State your loving intentions and be compassionate but firm.
3) Name the issue in empowering terms.

4) Ask for partner's point of view about the problem.

5) Listen empty and mirror what you hear.

6) Ask open-ended questions, get clarification.

7) Express your own point of view after asking partner to listen empty.

8) Ask for partner's commitment in solving the problem (see below).

9) Brainstorm solutions and create action steps.

In naming the issue, be sure to use terms such as "It seems to me that…" and "I have noticed…" Be gentle and patient, yet straightforward and honest. When you express your point of view, make sure that you discuss how the behavior affects you. (e.g., "When you stay out until 4:00 A.M. drinking and come home and pick a fight with me, I feel sad, confused, drained, and hurt.")

If your partner gets defensive, return to your loving intentions. "This is not easy to hear, sweetheart, and I want you to know that I am saying these things because I am deeply concerned about you and about our relationship." Keep coming back to your intentions over and over—it keeps the focus on your true purpose in having this discussion.

When you get to the point that you have agreement in *defining the issue,* and your partner acknowledges that it is a problem, *ask for a commitment* in solving it: "Susan, I want your help in solving this issue. Can you please tell me what your commitment is with regard to that?"

This is a critical question. Until your partner can express a commitment to change, nothing new will happen. It is vital to listen really empty at this point. Often at this juncture, someone makes a wishy-washy promise of some kind, everyone feels a little better, and that's the end of it. There is no real commitment and no real behavior change. This may start a vicious cycle of bad behavior, recriminations, more empty promises, and so on.

When we ask our partner for a commitment to change something, it is important to allow time for that to sink in. Most of us do not immediately leap into a new commitment that requires deeper awareness and therefore new behavior. Most of us need time to process what happened and to allow the commitment to "rise up" from deep inside. Only then is it genuine.

Therefore, it is helpful to notice that our partner is struggling to make the commitment. Then we can defer the promises until she has had time to process it. We know that the other person is struggling, but not yet there, when the words that he speaks begin with the words, "I'll try."

Someone once said, "Try is a lie." What that means is that those words indicate that some part of us is in doubt, not yet fully committed to the actions that are required in order to fulfill the promise. Therefore, it is unlikely to happen.

It is far better to defer the promises until they are real than it is to "buy into" false promises. How do we know which it is? Listening with intuition helps—really tuning in to what our partner is saying, and to what she is *not saying*. Listening without judgment, tuning into that "gut feel" for the conversation also helps. Then, check it out: "Sweetheart, it sounds like you may need some time to process all of this before you make a commitment about it. Is that true?"

When your partner confirms this, the next step is to ask how much more time he needs. Depending on what that is, schedule another time to continue the discussion. Meanwhile, leave it alone! The other person's process can be undermined (and therefore delayed longer) if we attempt to get into the conversation before that time has passed.

Trying to Fix, Change, or Control

In all of these processes, it is important to stay away from the trap of trying to fix, change, or control our partner. While it is important to ask for what we want, it is not constructive to tip the balance over into being controlling.

In essence, trying to fix, change, or control another person stems from lack of acceptance of who the person is. It means that, all evidence to the contrary, we keep hoping that the person we are with will magically become the person we want. It means that the basic patterns of behavior our partner displays do not work for us. We want something different. *We want a different person.*

If I date a person who lives, eats, and breathes sports, and I decide after marrying him that I want someone who will limit his time watching sports to one hour per week, then I am not honoring the person I chose. I am expecting an entirely new person to show up. That is not realistic and leads to controlling behavior.

On the other hand, if I date someone who enjoys sports, and after we move in together, he stops taking me out to dinner (as he did previously), gives almost no focus to me at the end of the day (whereas before, we shared about our day), and watches sports for hours at a time, then I must sit up and take notice. The person that I fell in love with is retreating. In this case, it is my job as his Soul Partner to point out the negative changes and to open a conversation for the possibility of altering that. To ignore a negative trend in a relationship is crippling to our connection and to our souls' journey together.

Though we may identify the issue as a negative trend that we want to intervene in, we must still avoid the trap of trying to fix, change, or control. How can we do this?

We intervene in a problem effectively when we:

- Look to see how our own behavior may be contributing to the problem and make appropriate changes first
- State our loving intentions up front
- Address the issue truthfully and in a straightforward manner
- Open up an emotionally safe dialogue that honors each person's point of view and needs
- Ask for partnership in creating solutions
- Keep the conversation alive until we find solutions together that take care of us both

In essence, we approach our partner with the intention to *reconnect in partnership*. Rather than taking the approach that I am unhappy and he had better fix it, I take the approach that he is my partner and our job is to fix it together.

Making Demands

There are times when it is appropriate to make certain demands in a relationship. Because doing so places tremendous stress on our connection, we must carefully weigh the consequences in advance. Before taking action in that way, consider the following questions:

- Am I clear about the difference between my real needs and the possibility of earlier, unmet needs?
- Am I taking care of myself, making sure that I have other sources of satisfaction outside of my partnership?
- Am I confident in my partner's love for me and my love for him?
- Am I being a loving partner, attending to his/her needs as well as considering my own?
- Is my partner well? What is the possibility of outside factors (stress, illness, depression, anxiety, work, etc.) influencing what is happening between us?
- Am I confident that I am making requests in an empowering way?
- Am I totally confident that my partner understands what I want and is capable of giving it?

If your final answer, after long and careful consideration, is that your partner is not meeting your needs no matter how loving your efforts, it is time to deal with that. In that case, your demand may be that your partner face a particular issue and work with you (perhaps with professional help) to resolve it. It is a demand in the sense that there is no negotiating: "Either we pull together and deal with this or I am beginning the process of leaving."

That is the nature of a demand—there is no room for negotiation and there are severe consequences if the demand is not honored. Use this very carefully. It is not appropriate to make ordinary requests for needs into demands. *It is highly appropriate to demand that your partner collaborate with you to find solutions to major relationship and life issues.* It is also appropriate to demand that your partner immediately stop any behavior that is abusive to you or to your children.

Generally, it is wise to begin with requests. Move to demands only after not getting results over a period of time. Make certain that you are prepared to follow through with consequences before you make a demand!

An Empowering Demand

As with every other aspect of communication, making a demand can be done in a way that is unlikely to get good results and it can be done in a way that is. Instead of, "Either you quit smoking around us or I'm taking the baby and

I'm leaving you!" try, "I love being with you and being a family together, but there is something standing in the way of that. When you smoke around the baby and me, my eyes water and my throat gets irritated. The smell makes me feel nauseous, and I don't want to be in the same room with you. I feel protective of the baby and do not want him to be sick from the effects of secondary smoke inhalation. I feel hurt that you do this, and I have asked repeatedly for you to go outside to smoke with no results. Therefore, I feel that I must take a stand. I cannot tolerate this anymore. If you choose to smoke in the house, you choose to lose the baby's company and mine. We will leave and go over to friends' homes or my parents for the evening. I feel sad about having to take these steps, but I feel that I must, for my sake and for the sake of the baby. Please, please think this over, sweetheart. I do not want to take these steps, but I will."

In a nutshell, we make an empowering demand when we:

- State loving intentions
- State clearly and in a non-blaming way what the issue is
- Share our feelings and how the issue affects us
- Summarize our past efforts to intervene about the issue
- Take a stand
- State the demand
- State the consequence if partner refuses to comply

Urge our partner to consider what we have said
Follow through, no matter how uncomfortable or painful it is!

With compassion, respect, and love, a demand can be a positive turning point for Soul Partners. When used very sparingly in a relationship, if ever, a demand is a powerful tool for effective intervention. It can put a relationship back on track and even prevent divorce.

Arguments

Couples argue for many reasons, including wanting to be "right," wanting to avoid the feeling of "losing," for self-protection, and because of a desire for competition.

Sometimes we argue because we do not understand the true dynamics taking place in our relationship. We argue to "let off steam" about other issues, conscious or unconscious. Arguments can also paradoxically result in greater intimacy. First we fight, then we cool off, then we make up, and then we make love.

The destructive side of arguing is that it can lead to verbal and other kinds of abuse. On the milder end of the spectrum, arguments create disconnection.

Arguing creates the dynamic of *polarization*, meaning that the longer and harder we disagree, the more intense our attachment to our position. If my partner says "green" and I say "blue," and if we throw in lots of emotion, soon I am more convinced than ever that "I am right about blue!" and "You are wrong about green!" This is exhausting, and when it is over, we still have conflicting points of view.

The more we practice listening empty and mirroring, the less we argue. However, when we feel strongly that our partner has a point of view that is standing in the way of our connection, it may be time to speak up. The following steps can help shift the discussion from an argument to a dialogue that makes a positive difference in the relationship.

When you hear your partner express something with which you fundamentally disagree, begin by repeating back the essence of what you heard—mirroring—to make certain that you heard correctly.

Gently ask, "Is that what you believe?" Ask clarifying questions if needed.

Ask, "Would you like to hear my point of view?" Express it gently.

Allow your partner to shift to a new perspective.

Often when our partner says things that strike us as absurd, we make the mistake of jumping on those statements and pointing out how wrong she is. Instead, listen compassionately and ask gentle questions. Make gentle statements of your own point of view, thereby gradually allowing a new perspective to emerge.

Sometimes, we say things that do not sound right even to our own ears. As soon as the words are out, we "hear" the absurdity of what we said. The reality is that *we often shift perspective simply by having our words repeated back to us.* Suddenly, we see it in a new light, and we see the false premise inside of the belief. With a compassionate listener, we can backtrack and say what we really mean to say.

Agree to Disagree

If your partner's point of view is something that you absolutely cannot live with, that is one thing. Rarely does a couple fail to see that they have a huge fundamental value difference until deep into the relationship, but sometimes it happens. If you feel that is the case, it may be wise to seek outside counsel with both of you to make sure that it is something that truly cannot be reconciled. Often the perspective of a third party can reveal new possibilities.

Otherwise, be willing to agree to disagree. The reality of life and relationships is that it is rare for couples to agree about absolutely everything. What works is that we are aligned on our most basic and important values. Anything outside of that can usually be lived with, and often will shift over time so that we meet one another in the middle.

Chapter Twelve
Commitment

Conscious, intentional Soul Partnership requires tremendous commitment, but not as we traditionally think of it. In the past, we understood commitment to be a promise to "stay together no matter what." Traditional marriage vows confirmed this, as we promised that only death would part us.

The reality of life is that it is unpredictable. The person we marry today, the relationship that we cherish, and the values that we hold dear, are all subject to change. There is no way of knowing today if we can live with this person for fifty or sixty years and be truly happy. Nor is there any safeguard against that person leaving at the drop of a hat. Additionally, we now place our fundamental right to be fulfilled above the duty to stay married for a lifetime. Therefore, the old model of commitment does not work. We cannot realistically promise that we will be together, no matter what, forever.

As our model of love shifts into the new paradigm of Soul Partnership, so we must also find a new model of commitment, one that supports the relationship as well as the growth of our spirits.

A New Model of Commitment

Soul Partnership commitment is a new model, one toward which we are gradually moving, in search of a path that is in our highest good as individuals and as partners. It begins with the premise that we are in this relationship by choice, not by obligation, for the purpose of our souls' growth, not solely to take care of life business or get our needs met.

Soul Partnership commitment focuses primarily on the promise to be open, honest, and communicative, in a loving way. It focuses on the commitment to be a *contributing partner*, one who gives freely with no expectations. This means taking on the job of nurturing a relationship, not merely coexisting.

Soul Partnership commitment focuses on the promise to do one's part for the *quality of the relationship itself.* It is actually a far greater and, in many ways, more challenging commitment to fulfill than the promise to stay no matter what. To agree as partners that our job is to maintain a quality connection, in the face of all that we must handle in life, is truly meaningful.

Conscious Soul Partners know that a good relationship is *created,* not found. They begin with genuine love and attraction, and they build on that with strong intentions, loving behavior, and heart and soul communication.

This kind of commitment asks a lot of us as individuals! It asks us to be conscious in our relationships, to have our eyes wide open as we date, court, and choose who to share our lives with. It asks us to be honest and open every step of the way, first with ourselves, and then with our partners, that we dedicate ourselves to doing only that which is in our highest good and in the highest good of those whose lives we touch. This leaves no room for neediness, selfishness, and pettiness.

This kind of commitment requires that we move beyond looking to relationships to fulfill us in every way. Rather, it asks that we fulfill ourselves and then contribute that bounty to a partner.

Gone are the days when we could sit back and be lazy in a marriage, knowing that our partner has promised to never leave. Instead, we must dedicate ourselves to the job of nurturing the relationship, being accountable and responsible for that every day. We must give up the question, "What have you done for me lately?" in favor of the inquiry, "What can I do for you today?"

Soul Partnership commitment is not a light one. It means that when we choose a life partner, we do so with the full intention of honoring that person and the relationship with all of our heart and soul. It means that we take on the relationship with the intention to grow, realizing that only through expanding our souls will we be able to fulfill such a powerful commitment.

When two Soul Partners make the conscious choice to live their lives together in this way, and then choose to honor that commitment each and every day, it is difficult to imagine failure. Clearly, the path to making that choice is neither the traditional nor the easy path of love.

The Path to Soul Partner Commitment

Traditionally, the path to making a marriage or lifelong commitment involves these basic steps:

1) Meet, feel attracted
2) Date, fall in love
3) Become more deeply attached, consider marriage
4) Decide on marriage based on feelings of love (sometimes based on common values and life goals as well, though not necessarily)
5) Get married

After marriage, we are confronted with the following realities:

- Partner is not perfect
- Relationship is not everything that we wanted
- Love is more than feelings, it is behavior
- Conflict happens
- Negative emotions happen

There is work to do if we are to nurture our connection!

Though we may have chosen one another in love and promised to honor one another in marriage, that does not mean that we have formed a true, conscious, intentional partnership.

The step not yet made is into Soul Partnership. Without it, we simply cannot weather the storms of life and love and grow together. We may stay together, either for the children or because of the stigma of divorce, but that is not true commitment. True, powerful Soul Partnership commitment means *being in full communication and giving the relationship all that it needs*, even when it is difficult.

The path to this kind of commitment involves searching our hearts and speaking what we feel. It entails hours of heart and soul conversation about what we truly wish to create together as a couple and what is our commitment in that process. It also means learning how to have mature, active love.

The journey to Soul Partnership is available to any couple. Whether dating and considering marriage, living together in love or married for many years, a couple may walk the path to Soul Partnership Commitment, if they choose to do so.

Commitment to Full Communication

Though this sounds like a given, it is actually a huge commitment and one that is rarely chosen consciously. Typically, after the initial "rapture stage" is over, and reality sets in, we begin storing up complaints. In a secret file labeled "what is wrong with my partner," we store away all of the judgments, negative stories, and resentments that pile up over time.

Gradually, we remove ourselves from our partner, becoming more emotionally distant and less involved in the relationship. Some couples drift along in this way for years and even decades. Sometimes, this dynamic continues until the natural end of the marriage, when someone dies.

More often, the size of the file expands to an intolerable size, and then one day we simply decide to call it quits. The reality of today's relationships is that *most people do not know their relationship is in real trouble until their partner announces that they are leaving.*

With no commitment to being in full communication, we are vulnerable to this dynamic. In fact, *the absence of full, open Soul Talk is the most common breaking point in our relationships.*

When we do not express our true thoughts and feelings, there is no opportunity to examine them. There is no opportunity to add greater wisdom to them through the feedback loop with our partner. There is no chance we may discover that many of them are simply assumptions, impressions, and reactions based on our own past history and our history together.

Stored up negativity in our thoughts and feelings is one of the primary symptoms of relationship breakdown. Most couples therapists know this, as they bear witness to the most astonishing conclusions drawn by otherwise intelligent people when they are exiting a relationship.

Often it is not so much what we say that destroys our relationships, but *what we do not say.* When we withhold our true thoughts and feelings, we cut off our partnership at the knees. We do not have a chance at real love that way.

Though we may offer convincing testimony about our partner's betrayals at the end of a relationship, the truth is that most of the time we leave for one or both of two reasons:

1) We chose our partner based on an incomplete picture and an unrealistic view of love; thus, we failed to establish a true, loving partnership in the beginning.
2) We neglected to nurture the love that we shared through actively fulfilling the commitment to be a loving partner (i.e., full and complete communication plus the behavior of love); thus, we "killed off" the love we once had for our partner.

Establishing up front the commitment to be in full, open, honest communication gives our relationship a real chance at success.

Commitment to Partnership

Clearly, we cannot fulfill the commitment to be totally open and expressed in the relationship unless we have a genuine partnership based in trust. Before we can declare this level of commitment, we must be aligned as partners, clear about our purpose and mission together.

Perhaps you have serious doubts about partnering with the person you are currently with. Those doubts may be valid, or they may be based in past experiences that act as emotional fog, obscuring the truth. How do we know the difference?

The place to begin is always the closest: oneself. Begin with a rigorous inventory of self, with the help of an objective third person (counselor, therapist, or spiritual advisor) if you find that supportive. If you find that your side of the relationship dynamic is not clean, the first step is to clean it up.

It takes courage to examine oneself first, before going to one's partner. We must be willing to be vulnerable and open, letting our deepest, darkest truths emerge. Yet, to be vulnerable and open is vital in true Soul Partnership. There is no other way.

Once you have cleaned up your side of the relationship dynamic, the next step is to make the internal conversation external. What does that mean?

It means sitting down with your partner and "coming clean" about what you want and about your doubts that you could have it together. Be honest without being brutal, straightforward without being blaming. Put the truth, the whole truth, and nothing but the truth on the table. Invite open, honest dialogue. Make it "safe" for your partner to open up.

In a nutshell, *honor the partnering process even if you do not view yourselves as lifetime Soul Partners at this point.* Vow to stay fully connected, not indulging in outside relationships or emotional distance, until the process is complete.

The partnering process is complete when we have said all there is to say, keeping our hearts open all the way, and we have forgiven one another for past transgressions. Then, we consider all possibilities for staying together, honestly addressing our needs to see if we can fulfill them for one another. If the picture emerges that we either cannot or do not wish to fulfill one another's needs, and we are in a state of true forgiveness, then we are pretty much complete as partners.

This process may take days, weeks, or months. It cannot be rushed—it is over when it is over and not one minute before that. Even though we enter the process believing that we are coming to an end, new possibilities may emerge through being open and honest. The path of completion is unpredictable, often involving spontaneous changes in course.

To honor a relationship that holds a special place in our lives in this way strengthens our ability to make a real commitment in the future. It is an act of great integrity and a fulfillment of our original commitment. In so doing, we are prepared to step away graciously and to open our hearts to the search for a new partner.

No Quick Exits

The evidence of real commitment is in staying until everything possible has been done to recreate a loving partnership. It is easy to run away; it is much more difficult to stay, be honest, look at oneself, and honor the relationship.

If we are to move to the next level and discover how to make love last, we must create our own structures for commitment from deep within our own hearts and souls. We must release the naïve belief that getting married guarantees a good outcome or keeps our partners close to us. We must embrace the truth that *only our own commitment and integrity to the work of relating gives us what we want.*

Soul Partnering means making the commitment to stay connected through difficult, seemingly impossible times. We do not give ourselves permission for "quick exits." We resolve to do the work of the relationship, especially when it is most tempting to go. In this way, *we choose separation and/or divorce together,* if that is appropriate, just as we chose to connect in the first place. Only then do we attain true completion that frees us to move on in grace and dignity, if that is our path.

The "No Exit Agreement"

When we co-create conscious, Soul Partnership commitment, we create a powerful foundation for our love. We give it strength where it counts—from the bottom up. We empower our connection by placing a loving "safety net" underneath us. When we remove the threat of abrupt abandonment from our relationship, we open the gates for a deeper and more vulnerable connection. I call this the "No Exit Agreement," and it means, basically, that we agree to honor the partnering process throughout our relationship.

We agree to *stay connected,* even through a separation and divorce, if that is what is appropriate. By agreeing to stay connected, we commit to the heart and soul of relationships—communicating, openly and honestly, and treating one another with respect and dignity.

The "No Exit Agreement" does not mean that you are guaranteed never to split up. Instead, when your relationship is stressed, you are agreeing to give it all you have *prior to indulging in plans to leave.*

No Partnership in Communication

Sometimes, we aim for completion but find that we have a partner who does not support that process. It is not unusual for this to happen. Often, the couple that does not have true partnership up front struggles to create it later.

The truth is that we cannot force another person to open up and be honest about their inner thoughts and feelings. If this happens in your relationship, keep in mind that we hold the power to respond with compassion and to communicate honestly and openly, regardless of the behavior of our partner. When we remain steadfast in our own commitment, we often open the door for the other person to feel less fearful and defensive. New possibilities may emerge and the energy in the relationship can shift to a more positive note.

A Dynamic, Creative Process

A relationship is a dynamic process that is uniquely creative in its expression. Because the individuals that make up a relationship are unique, the energy that we co-create is unique. We stimulate one another in ways that no other person can, and we bring out aspects of one another that may not show up in any other relationship in life.

The key element of any relationship is communication. Because we are so creative in the way we express ourselves, how we relate to one another is not only unique to our relationship, but it also unfolds in ever more unique ways over time.

Relationships are so unique and creative that no set of tools can possibly address every situation that may arise, nor can any set of tools be perfect for every couple. Therefore, use the tools in this book to the degree that they empower you as individuals and as a couple. Use them as a framework while you continue to interact in the unique ways that define your relationship.

The Secrets to Great Communication

At the heart of it all, there are three basic principles that, if we follow them, allow us to communicate heart and soul regardless of what structures we follow. They are to:

1) Show Up
2) Be Open
3) Trust the Process

Show up

For anything positive to happen in our relationships, we must show up. Not just in body, but in mind, heart, and soul, *fully emotionally present* for connection with our partner.

To really show up in a relationship means having no excuses, no longer procrastinating giving attention to our connection. "Not now, I'm reading the paper," or "Not this week, I have too much to do with the kids" are not acceptable reasons.

To show up does not mean that we never have time alone or "down time." Quite the contrary. In a healthy Soul Partnership, we communicate when we need "time off," giving our partner lots of notice.

Showing up means that when our partner has something to say, we do not avoid that discussion or put up barriers to connection. If it bothers one of us, it is an issue for both of us. Therefore, whatever needs to be said gets top priority in our lives. We show up, ready to listen and ready to respond.

Be Open

To be open means to be open-minded. That is a great start. *To be powerfully open means to be open-hearted.* Miracles happen when we show up and open our hearts to one another!

Being open means getting out of our heads and into our hearts, setting aside judgment, analysis, stories, defensiveness, and rebuttals. We are here to connect in the only way that serves Soul Partnership—through our hearts. When our hearts are truly open to one another, there is emotional safety, deep connection, and the opportunity to create miracles together.

Trust the Process

To trust the process means allowing communication to unfold naturally, not trying to force anything in our interactions. Rather, we allow them to flow.

To trust the process means that we recognize the power of listening and speaking, letting that process guide us to the awareness of what will best serve us individually and as Soul Partners.

Trusting the process also means giving up our desire for "instant results," exercising patience and being willing to let things unfold. On a deeper level, it means *trusting the process of life itself.*

When we trust the process of life, we say to ourselves, in essence, "I am not entirely sure what all of this is about, but I choose to surrender and let it unfold. I release my attachment to knowing in advance what it all means. I give up the desire to be in control. I trust that it will be clear in good time."

There is tremendous power in this stance, particularly in our relationships. Trusting the process of communication puts us squarely in the present, able to experience all of the richness of life and love.

Soul Lessons

When we show up, openhearted and trusting the process, we make ourselves available for the true purpose of our relationships—to learn the "soul lessons" we came here for.

Learning our soul lessons means being open to more than the obvious. It requires that we are open-minded and hearted, able to look beyond the surface and into the depths of seemingly ordinary events. Not that we do this all the time, but rather, that we do this when we find we have strong emotions about something in a way that initially appears to make no sense.

The soul lessons that arise in our relationship often come from old areas of pain that still need healing. Initially, the issue appears to be one thing, but if we listen to one another intuitively and from the heart, we find that there is something else—an old emotional wound. When we side-step the temptation to argue about the surface issue, allowing the deeper ones to come forward, and then respond with compassion, we empower one another in our healing processes.

When we allow one another's deeper issues to be expressed, we connect on a much more intimate level in the relationship. This deepens our commitment and love at the same time that it helps us grow individually.

The healing that we have to offer one another through finding our soul lessons in the relationship is powerful! The emotional blocks that might have stood between us become stepping-stones to growth.

It is in our relationship that we have the opportunity to rejoice in the connection of our souls. What a gift that is! We make that gift possible by dedicating ourselves to being more and more aware of and open to our soul lessons.

Building Future Equity

Most of us know that in order to survive later in life we must save and invest money today. To make sure that the money is put aside, we "carve it out" first, before the taxes, bills, shopping, vacations, and so on. Save first, then spend, we realize, is the only way to build financial future equity. With money, these concepts are easy to understand.

The idea of building future equity in our relationships is more difficult to grasp. *We have completely unrealistic expectations with regard to our love relationships.*

Once the courtship phase has passed, we settle into a routine. We work all day; we spend time on our homes, with friends, working out, and on the fun things that we enjoy. After marriage, and especially with children, our lives are consumed with the daily rituals of earning a living and taking care of a family. Our time together as a couple is spent grocery shopping, cleaning house, preparing meals, interacting with children, falling into bed exhausted, and occasionally having sex.

"Nurturing our relationship" is a job that is just as important as the other jobs in our lives. Rarely, if ever, do we step back, look at the "spending" we are doing with the emotional bank account of the relationship, and decide to make an investment.

Rarely, or never, do we stop, make a plan, and carve out the time to be together as a couple with no distractions. We build little or no future equity in our relationship. We live like this, as a couple, week after week, month after month, and year after year, making little or no investment in "us."

Yet, we expect the return! We expect to have a loving, nurturing, romantic, vibrant, alive connection for all of the days of our lives.

Where's the incentive to build future equity? Why not spend today and just hope it all works out later? *We must create the incentive for ourselves.* We do so when we stop, take stock of the priceless gift that our relationship is, and look far down the road.

When we look down the road ten years, twenty, thirty, and so on, what do we see? Given our current patterns and behaviors, where will we be? Where are we going?

With the tools of Soul Partnering, where might we go? What new possibilities are open for us when we behave in ways now that build relationship equity for the future?

The model of Soul Partnering demands that we stop and look ahead in this way. If we are to move to the next level in our relationships, we must have a focus that is expanded beyond today. We must decide to build future equity now, while we have the heart (full emotional bank account) to do so. This is the challenge and the opportunity of Soul Partnership.

This book is about doing precisely that. It is intended to raise consciousness about our souls' journey together, the true purpose of our love, and how we can enrich our relationship for the future through our actions today.

The possibilities that emerge out of that are endless! How exciting it is to consider what we might create together in our lives, and the infinite ways we can grow together as a couple, by applying our focused intentions and actions. With that in mind, I have some final "relationship prescriptions" that I like to give to my clients, and that I hope will help you and your partner.

Relationship Prescriptions

At first, when we adopt a new model of something, we have some old habits to overcome. Thus, you may find that, for a while, you go back and forth between the behaviors that do not work and the new ones that you are attempting to incorporate into your life and your relationship. This is normal. Expect some soreness and discomfort, just as we often have sore muscles when we go to the gym for the first time, or following long periods without exercise.

My first and primary "relationship prescription" to get through this transition is to *be gentle*. This will help you both to relax and allow the learning process to unfold. If you get stuck, stop, relax, and be gentle with one another. This helps you find new energy to work together again.

Second, *be flexible*. This is not about perfection! Expect mistakes, yours, and your partner's. Focus on yourself, on the process of learning to be a better partner. Put very little attention on how well your partner is learning, except at the times that your mate requests your help. Remember that we all learn in different ways and at different speeds. The lower your expectations for your partner and the higher for yourself, the more rewarding your experience will be.

Third, *view this as a journey of discovery and these tools as help along the way.* Release any attachment to a particular outcome in a certain period of time. Instead, lean into the journey itself, looking for treasures along the way in the learning process.

Fourth, *use these tools primarily to become a better partner, not to teach your partner how to be better.* They work best *from the inside out*, not the outside in. Going to your partner with this, or any relationship book, and saying, "See here, it says this, and therefore you should..." works against what you want. Real growth happens from a very personal choice to grow, not because someone else wants it.

Fifth, *share your progress with friends and extended family.* The more we make our growth a public conversation, the more we affirm it and deepen it, making it come alive in every part of our lives.

Sixth, if you want to be really adventurous, *start a couples relationship group.* Study these principles and practice them, then get together as couples to talk about what you are learning. One thing that couples are really missing in our culture is structures for supporting their commitment. A relationship group sometimes helps couples get through difficult times, especially when you have a mix of couples who have been together for many years as well as new relationships.

Seventh, *love your partner with all of your heart and soul.* Love your mate as if your life depends on it. Give as you have never given before. Regardless of how it all turns out in fifty years, you are guaranteed to enrich your life experience by being totally devoted to your mate today. It is my firm belief that those who love without reservation are always winners.

Soul Partnering: A Lifelong Journey

Congratulations! You have embarked on a very special, empowering journey. You and your soul mate are in for the adventure of a lifetime. My parting wish for you is that you discover all of the joy and fulfillment your hearts can contain, and that your souls dance together blissfully every step of the way.

Exercises and Inventories

Women's Self-Empowerment Inventory

The following statements are designed to raise awareness about you and your life. Reflect on them, asking yourself, "*To what degree* is this statement true for me?" Then, set new intentions as you feel they are warranted and appropriate for growth into a more self-empowered woman.

- I am aware of what my needs are emotionally, intellectually, physically, spiritually, socially, financially, creatively, and with regard to my self-expression.
- I include something in each day that addresses one or more of my needs.
- I consider my own needs before I consider the needs of others.
- I take care of my own needs before I take care of the needs of others.
- I let my partner know what my needs are and how he may contribute to me wherever possible.
- I have outlets for my creative energy and fulfillment outside of my marriage and my children.
- If my relationship ends, I am confident that I:
    - Can support myself and my children in the lifestyle that I desire.
    - Have resources to turn to for emotional support; i.e, close friends, extended family, counseling, etc.
    - Will go forward in my life, heal the emotional wounds, open my heart, and love again.
- I have zero tolerance for any abusive act from my partner, emotionally, physically, or through an active addiction.

Beliefs that support my empowerment:

- I am intrinsically worthy for who I am, aside from my roles in life: wife, mother, worker, friend.
- When I care for myself first, I have more to give to those I love.
- It is okay to have my own financial resources and to make my own choices in life.

- Making myself happy first makes me a better partner to my mate.
- It is really OK and sometimes necessary to say "no."
- It is OK to have a marriage that is different from my parents' and from what religious leaders say I should have.
- It is OK to want more in life than my mother did.
- It is OK to leave my partner if he is disrespectful, emotionally abusive, neglectful, violent in any way, unfaithful, or an addict, and he refuses to get help to change these dynamics.

Negative Communication Habits: Widening the Gap

This exercise is designed to help raise your awareness about what is happening internally when you get emotionally "triggered" by something your partner does. Then, to create solutions for managing those kinds of upsets in the future.

1. Using the "Communication Habits That Don't Work" list, put a star beside the ones that you find yourself doing most frequently in your relationship.
2. Choose one of the starred items and recall a recent incident in which you found yourself reacting to your partner in that way.
3. Then, identify the triggering event (something that happened or something that your partner did or said) and the resulting feelings that led to your reaction.
4. Now, share about that with your partner, keeping your statements in the first person and non-accusatory; i.e., "When you _____ (what partner did), I felt _____." If insights arise while sharing those feelings, talk about them with your partner, keeping it in the first person.
5. Create new intentions—positive outcomes that you want in the future at times like that, and share them.
6. Then, create a strategy together about how you can "widen the gap" in the future when these feelings are triggered so that you achieve your positive outcome together.

Individual Exercise: Taking Back the Projections

When you find that certain *traits* or *habits* in your partner continually trigger you, set aside some time for this exercise.

1. First, describe the behavior of your partner that is upsetting you.

2. Next, list the "character traits" that you may be assigning to him or her as a result of the behavior. That might look like this:

- Behavior: Every time we plan a special night out, he comes home thirty minutes late, drags his heels about getting ready, and makes us late. If I try to speed him up, he gets angry and slows down even more.
- Traits: Inconsiderate, slow, not punctual, uncaring of my needs, and stubborn.

Now, looking over those traits, ask yourself: Have I ever displayed this trait myself? Be fearlessly honest! Recall a time, place, relationship or circumstance in which you have displayed this trait. If you think you *never* have, then you are probably denying a part of yourself. Look again, this may be the very trait that you have worked hard to overcome and that you are attempting to be "perfect" about.

3. Find a place of compassion within yourself toward yourself about these traits. Set an intention to forgive yourself for being less than perfect. Now, notice how much alike you and your partner are in these ways! Find compassion for your partner as well and forgive him/her.

4. When you are ready, have a conversation with your partner about what you discovered about yourself and how you have been trying to change him/her in order to deal with your own issue.

5. Collaborate with your partner about how you can best deal with this issue in the future so that it is a win for you both.

Personal Feedback Survey

Create a feedback survey for your closest friends and family, asking questions such as the ones below. This exercise takes tons of courage but can be extremely eye opening!

Communicate to your friend, associate, or family member the following:

Thank you for agreeing to give me feedback about myself, as you see me. This is for my personal growth, so please be honest and hold nothing back. I promise to use this to evaluate how I can make positive changes in my life.

Questions:

Please rate me (overall) on the following questions on a 1 to 5 scale, 1 being "poor" and 5 being "excellent":

- How well do I listen to you and really hear what you are saying?
- After we talk about matters in our relationship, how well do I leave you with a clear understanding about what we discussed and any appropriate actions each of us will take?
- How available am I when you really need to talk?
- Have you ever felt put down or demeaned after interacting with me? (yes or no) If yes, please describe.
- In general, how open do I seem to be toward your thoughts and feelings?
- In general, how open am I when you have something to say that you feel displeases me?
- When I give you feedback, how good is it; i.e., empowering, useful, makes a difference?
- How well do I acknowledge you and express appreciation to you?
- What specific things do you think I could do to improve my ability to relate well to others in general in my life?
- What things do I currently do that you appreciate about the way I relate?

Thank you so much!

Listening Exercise for Distressed Couple

This exercise is for opening up communication in your relationship when it has been shut down and strained for a period of time. Do this together only if you both feel confident that you can handle it without adding more damage to your connection. If you do not feel that you can even begin to talk to one another without escalating into a destructive interaction, seek professional help.

1. Begin by acknowledging in your own words to one another that you are in a difficult period in your relationship.
2. State your intentions in your own words for healing in the relationship.
3. Promise one another to be completely open and honest, without being vicious.
4. Choose the first listener and speaker. Listener agrees to listen empty, but without mirroring. Just be very emotionally present, nod, or say, "I hear you," and then ask the next question.
5. Listener, ask these questions over and over of your partner, rotating to the next one when you get three "blank" responses in a row.
6. Speaker, wait for the question, listen to it, then say whatever comes to mind as a response, without thinking about it or editing it first. When you get a blank, say "blank."
7. After three "blanks" on every question, listener ask, "What else is there?" If speaker begins talking again, go back through all the questions and rotate them until you get three blanks on all, then in answer to "what else is there?" a "blank."

Now you are ready to switch roles.

After you have gone through the entire exercise for one person, take a short break, then come back and switch roles.

When you are completely done, be very gentle with one another. Reach out and thank your partner in a loving way for sharing so openly. Be extra caring of one another for the next few hours or days.

Do not try to resolve any issues at this time or make any decisions! Allow the effect of this exercise to sink in.

Later, on reflection, you can create an issues list and set intentions from that, then in a separate session, talk about each one, using the listening empty and mirroring tools.

Questions:
- What do you want to tell me?
- What do you *not* want to tell me?
- What else?

Personal Growth Intentions

Reflect on several incidents with other people in which you have experienced anger, frustration, or pain. List the qualities in other people that drive you crazy. Now, do a fearless inventory. Ask, which are mine? Which have I *ever* been/done? Put a check mark by those. Then, notice the ones that have the most negative energy (shame, loathing, denial, and pain) for you. These are the ones that need the most healing.

For each characteristic, try to imagine what that quality would be if you "turned down the volume." Selfish might be self-caring, defensive might be self-protective, and so on. In this way, create a way to view each trait so that you can gradually embrace it as a part of you.

Next, for each characteristic, create a personal growth intention. For "selfish" you might say, "My intention is to practice diligent self-care in every area of my life." For "defensive" you might say, "My intention is to be attentive to situations that may not be in my highest good, or that may be harmful to me, and to move out of those situations while creating new ones that take excellent care of me."

Real Needs Inventory

This exercise is for helping to understand the difference between real needs and those that come from unmet needs in the past. First, spend a few moments relaxing with no distractions. Take pen and paper and begin by just writing down all of the needs (emotional and otherwise) that you believe you have, real or not. Don't edit at this point, just outflow onto paper until you can't think of anymore. Your list at this point may look like this:

My needs:
Food, water, air, love, happiness, fulfillment, a safe home environment, friendships, self-expression, respect, creativity, health, sufficient money, and so on.

When you reach a stopping point, ask yourself, "What other needs do I have?" and keep writing until you get a blank. Stop, take a moment and a deep breath, and then go to the next part.

Begin at the top of the list, and for each item, ask yourself, "Which of these do I *require* for my happiness and well-being, both in my life and in my relationship?" Put a check mark by the ones that you give a definite, solid "yes" to. Now, go back to the beginning of your list and ask yourself, "Which ones do I *feel as though I cannot survive without,* even though I know that is not true, and I often *expect my partner to fulfill for me?*" Put a star beside each of those items. (Some of these may overlap with check-marked ones.)

On a clean sheet of paper, write "Real Needs" and list the check-marked items. These are the needs that must be met in order for your life and a relationship to be healthy for you.

After this list, write the words "Old, Unmet Needs" and list all of the starred items. These are your needs that need require healing so that you no longer feel "needy" about them.

Now, write the words "Wants and Desires" and list all of the remaining items. These are the things that you want for your life, perhaps want them strongly, and you recognize that it is your job to create them for yourself and then share the bounty with your partner.

Last, set intentions for healing and growth with regard to all of your needs. Look to see how you can take care of some of those old, unmet needs for yourself so that they do not contaminate your relationship.

Notes

Chapter One

1. From "'Never Marrieds' Ranks of the Singles Growing Fast," ABC News.com, January 9, 2002.

Chapter Two

2. Two that truly made a difference for me were the Landmark Forum and Radical Forgiveness (with Colin Tipping).

Chapter Three

3. A very powerful resource I have found for clarifying life goals and having a plan for accomplishing them is the book *The Game* by Sarano Kelley.

Chapter Four

4. Walker, Lou Ann, "We Can Control How We Age," *Parade Magazine*, September 16, 2001.

5. For a comprehensive overview of the brain chemistry of love, as well as a plethora of eye-opening information about the path of romance and marriage, see *The Truth About Love* by Dr. Pat Love (Simon & Schuster, 2001).

Chapter Five

6. Love, Patricia, *The Truth About Love*, 2001, Simon & Schuster.

Chapter Six

7. Gaynor, Mitchell L., M.D., *Healing Essence*, Kodansha International (1995).

Chapter Eight

8. Mitchener, Brandon. "Controlling a Computer by the Power of Thought," *The Wall Street Journal*, March 14, 2001.

Chapter 9

9. Tipping, Colin. *Radical Forgiveness: Making Room For The Miracle*, Global 13 Publications (1997).

About the Author

Nina Atwood, M.Ed., LPC, is an internationally recognized expert on romantic love and communication, and author of two enormously popular books on dating relationships. She has been featured on numerous regional television shows and hundreds of radio shows. Her expertise is regularly sought by national publications, including *The Wall Street Journal, Health Magazine, Men's Health, Cosmopolitan, Glamour,* and *Mademoiselle.* Nina has conducted hundreds of workshops that have made a positive difference in the lives of countless individuals and couples.

Nina lives in Texas where she maintains a private therapy practice, and does executive coaching and corporate training. You may contact Nina at either www.soulpartnercoach.com or www.ninaatwood.com for coaching or counseling, in person, or by telephone.